OXFORD MODERN LANGUAGES AND LITERATURE MONOGRAPHS

THE LITERARY BALLAD IN EARLY NINETEENTH-CENTURY RUSSIAN LITERATURE

MICHAEL R. KATZ

OXFORD UNIVERSITY PRESS
1976

Oxford University Press, Ely House, London W. 1

GLASGOW NEW YORK TORONTO MELBOURNE WELLINGTON
CAPE TOWN IBADAN NAIROBI DAR ES SALAAM LUSKA ADDIS ABABA
DELHI BOMBAY CALCUTTA MADRAS KARACHI LAHORE DACCA
KUALA LUMPUR SINGAPORE HONG KONG TOKYO

ISBN 0 19 815528 X

Text set in 11/12 pt Monotype Plantin, printed by letterpress, and bound in Great Britain at The Pitman Press, Bath

to Dar'ya Andreevna de Keyserlingk,
with admiration and affection

ACKNOWLEDGEMENTS

Professor J. L. I. Fennell (New College, Oxford) for his continued assistance and encouragement;

The Keasbey Memorial Foundation (Philadelphia), the International Research and Exchanges Board (New York), and the Class of 1900 Fund (Williams College) for their generous grants.

CONTENTS

ABBREVIATIONS

Am SEER	*American Slavic and East European Review.*
AN SSSR	Akademiya nauk SSSR.
IRL	*Istoriya russkoi literatury*, I–X, M.–L., 1941–56.
IRP	*Istoriya russkoi poezii*, I–II, L., 1968–9.
LGPI	Leningradskii gosudarstvennyi pedagogicheskii institut.
LGU	Leningradskii gosudarstvennyi universitet.
MAO	Moskovskoe arkheologicheskoe obshchestvo.
MGPIIYa	Moskovskii gosudarstvennyi pedagogicheskii institut inostrannykh yazykov.
Priyatnoe i poleznoe	*Priyatnoe i poleznoe preprovozhdenie vremeni.*
SEEJ	*Slavic and East European Journal.*
SEER	*Slavonic and East European Review.*
TGU	Tartuskii gosudarstvennyi universitet.
TODRL	*Trudy Otdela drevnei russkoi literatury.*
TONRL	*Trudy Otdela novoi russkoi literatury.*

NOTE ON QUOTATIONS AND TRANSLITERATION

AFTER the first full reference, the sources of quotations from collected works will be abbreviated to *PSS* (*Polnoe sobranie sochinenii*) or *SS* (*Sobranie sochinenii*), followed by the volume number and page.

The sources of quotations from unpublished manuscripts will be identified by GPB (Gosudarstvennaya Publichnaya biblioteka im. M. E. Saltykova-Shchedrina, Leningrad), PD (Institut russkoi literatury, Pushkinskii dom, AN SSSR, Leningrad), or TsGALI (Tsentral'nyi gosudarstvennyi arkhiv literatury i iskusstva, Moscow), followed by a 'code' which indicates *fond*; *opis'*; *No.*; *list.*

The system of transliteration adopted is that used in the *Oxford Slavonic Papers*, which includes the transliteration of -ий and -ый in surnames as -y.

INTRODUCTION

Читать стихотворцев, не каждого особенно, но всех одинакового рода вместе. Частный характер каждого сделается ощутительнее от сравнения.

—Жуковский[1]

THERE has been very little research into the history of the Russian literary ballad or on its principal practitioner, V. A. Zhukovsky. This work is an attempt to remedy the situation: it follows the development of the genre of the literary ballad in Russian literature from its emergence in the 1790s to its demise in the 1840s. It is hoped that this particular approach to the study of literature, recommended by Zhukovsky himself in one of his early notebooks, will produce the results he predicted: namely, that it will render more perceptible the individual characteristics of each author. It has been decided to concentrate on the style of the literary ballads as the most original feature of the genre, and in particular on the epithets in Zhukovsky's ballads, as his most important contribution to the development of Russian poetic style. Consequently, there will be no consideration of metrics, and only occasional reference to syntax.

Chapter I treats the relationship of the Russian literary ballad to the traditional folk genre, to the so-called 'ballad revival' in eighteenth-century European literature, and to late eighteenth-century 'pre-romantic' developments in Russian literature. In Chapter II the Russian literary ballads of the 1790s are analysed, including those by M. N. Murav'ev, N. M. Karamzin, A. F. Merzlyakov, and I. I. Dmitriev. Chapters III and IV are devoted to Zhukovsky's literary ballads, and include a discussion of his theory and practice of translation, analyses of eight representative ballads, and a thorough investigation of the epithets in his ballads. Chapter V treats the polemics in Russian literary criticism which surrounded the ballad genre and its creator during the early decades of the nineteenth century. In Chapter VI the ballads of Zhukovsky's imitators are examined, particularly those by his

[1] *Sochineniya V. A. Zhukovskogo*, V (SPb., 1878), 551.

'opponent' P. A. Katenin, his 'double' A. I. Meshchevsky, and his 'disciple' I. I. Kozlov. Chapters VII and VIII follow the poetic careers of Pushkin and Lermontov respectively, from their early imitation of Zhukovsky's ballads through their subsequent parody of his model, to their individual and original use of the literary ballad genre.

The terms 'classicism' and 'romanticism' are used throughout in the conventionally accepted sense to refer to historical movements in European literature during the eighteenth and early nineteenth century. 'Pre-romanticism' is used to identify certain literary developments which characterized the first stages of the romantic movement; no precise distinction between 'pre-romanticism' and 'romanticism' is intended. 'Sentimentalism' is used to describe one particular aspect of 'pre-romanticism', namely that tearful emotionalism associated with N. M. Karamzin and others.

I

THE INFLUENCE OF FOLK BALLADS AND THE BALLAD REVIVAL ON RUSSIAN LITERARY BALLADS

How do you recognize a ballad ?[1]

THE particular problems of 'recognition' and 'definition' have plagued ballad criticism since the literary world first took an interest in the traditional folk genre. The word *ballad* comes from the Old French form *balade* (dancing-song), which in turn is derived from the late Latin verb *ballāre* (to dance).[2] First used to describe medieval Provençal and Italian dancing songs, the term was then applied to a specific metrical form in Old French poetry which consisted of three stanzas of eight to twelve lines each and a concluding envoy of four to six lines, all in a strict rhyme scheme. The same word was also used to describe medieval English and Scottish short narrative popular songs, which belong to the oral tradition and which are completely unrelated to the French form. It was these popular songs which were 'revived' in the eighteenth century, and which were first collected and then imitated in England and Germany, and soon afterwards in Russia.

The most concise description of the features common to all traditional folk ballads has been provided by the critic G. H. Gerould: 'A ballad is a folk song that tells a story with stress on the crucial situation, tells it by letting the action unfold itself in event and speech, and tells it objectively with little comment or intrusion of personal bias.'[3] Gerould discusses these features at some length: the 'narrative unit', the 'narrative method', and the 'narrative attitude'.

[1] *Second Public Examination*, Honour School of English (Oxford University 1961).

[2] *Oxford English Dictionary* (Oxford, 1933), s.v. 'ballad'.

[3] *The Ballad of Tradition* (Oxford, 1932), 11. Cf. W. J. Entwistle, *European Balladry* (Oxford, 1951) and M. J. C. Hodgart, *The Ballads* (New York, 1962).

The 'narrative unit' of a ballad consists of a compressed, centralized incident, event, or conflict related in approximately 30 to 80 lines. Events preceding and following the climax are reported laconically with little comment or continuity. The emphasis is on action, not on characters or their motivation. The drama results in part from what a Soviet critic has called the *zagadochnost'* or *nedoskazannost'*[4] of the ballad: the reasons and circumstances for the events are never fully revealed.

The ballad employs a 'narrative method' characterized by its concentration, compression, and dynamism. Its structure is simple: the ballad begins abruptly, without an introduction and proceeds from one dramatic moment to the next; dialogue is used to illustrate the action without any indication of a change in speaker; there is no conclusion. Nothing superfluous can retard the action or distract attention from the central incident. Verbal and thematic repetition, parallelism, stylized diction, sequential syntax, and strong reliance on verbs are all functional and thus contribute to the total dramatic effect of the ballad.[5]

The 'narrative attitude' of the ballad is one of absolute impersonality. There are no lyrical digressions, no moralization, no emotionalism, no physical or psychological description—in short, no interference in or interpretation of the action. The anonymous ballad-writers attempted to express the experience itself and to share it with their audience.

Ballad subjects include any striking situation drawn from everyday life. The love theme is common in its many variations: faithfulness, reconciliation, insistence on the lovers' freedom of choice, family despotism, parental interference, jealousy, revenge, incest, and so forth. The characters are ordinary men and women, often nameless, and always passively resigned to their fates. These generalized types are revealed in action and dialogue, but are rarely characterized by their speech patterns.

But no description of the traditional ballad genre can be complete if it does not account for the fact that 'recognition' of a ballad is easier than 'definition'. In a series of lectures delivered at Oxford entitled *Ballads and their Influence*, C. M. Ing chose to describe this recognizable, though intangible, element as the

[4] D. M. Balashov, *Istoriya razvitiya zhanra russkoi ballady* (Petrozavodsk, 1966), 9.

[5] See below, Ch. IV, pp. 78–81 on the epithet in folk ballads.

ballad 'world' or 'code'. It consists of all those common characteristics relating to physical setting, weather, vegetation, dwellings, inhabitants, and supernature which render it almost impossible to mistake the presence of a real ballad. This ballad 'world' is that of concrete reality, at best apathetic, at worst hostile to man. Supernature is conceived in real terms, as a part of the natural order, and frequently appears in dreams, superstitions, premonitions, and omens.

The term 'illiterature' was invented by A. B. Friedman to describe the traditional ballad genre and to serve as an antonym for Herder's concept of *Kunstpoesie*.[6] One could easily multiply the differences between the folk ballad and so-called 'sophisticated poetry', but the conclusion would remain the same: the ballad requires its own special aesthetic.

Russian folk ballads are almost identical to their Western European counterparts in subject, form, and style, with two important exceptions: Russian ballads are written in tonic verse and they have no refrains.[7] In order to illustrate the narrative unit, method, and attitude of the traditional Russian folk ballads, two examples have been selected from the anthology *Narodnye ballady* (1963): *Dmitrii i Domna* and *Brat'ya razboiniki i sestra.*

The plot of *Dmitrii i Domna* is typical of Russian ballads. Dmitrii rides past the window where Domna sits and she mocks his appearance; Dmitrii's sister urges him to invite Domna to a feast; envoys come to Domna's mother and present their invitation three times; each time the mother refuses, but Domna declares that she will go anyway. The mother recounts her ominous dream, warns her daughter of the impending dangers, and gives her some farewell advice: to take three dresses with her—the first for her wedding, the second for her disgrace, and the third for her death. Domna disregards her mother's warning and goes to meet Dmitrii; first he welcomes her and then he beats her to death; when Domna's mother comes to mourn her daughter, she too is killed. Then Dmitrii turns on his own sister and accuses her of having inspired both murders, and he kills her.

[6] *The Ballad Revival* (Chicago, 1961), 2 ff.

[7] In Russian literary criticism the concept of a traditional ballad genre was only recently introduced. See *Russkaya ballada, Biblioteka poeta, Bol'shaya seriya*, ed. V. I. Chernyshev (L., 1936), Intro., and *Narodnye ballady, Biblioteka poeta, Bol'shaya seriya*, 2-oe izd., ed. D. M. Balashov (M-L., 1963), 5–41.

This ballad consists of a narrative unit of some ninety lines relating one connected episode. Emphasis is on the action, not on the characters of Dmitrii or Domna. The narrative method is apparent in the movement from one dramatic moment to the next, in the dialogues between Domna, Dmitrii's sister, the envoys, Domna's mother, and Dmitrii himself, and also in the ternary repetition. The narrative attitude is maintained: there are no digressions, no explanations, and no interpretation of the events by the author. Finally, the 'world' is that of concrete reality; the supernatural intrudes only in the mother's foreboding dream.

The other example of a traditional Russian folk ballad, *Brat'ya razboiniki i sestra*, relates the story of a widow who lives in a little hut together with her nine sons and one daughter; the sons abandon their home to become robbers; a matchmaker marries off the daughter to a rich merchant, and she goes to live with him. The daughter is so unhappy that she and her husband embark on a journey back to her home; on the way they are attacked by robbers who kill the merchant and ravish his wife. That night the youngest robber questions the wife, and, hearing her story, rouses his brothers to tell them that they have unknowingly murdered their brother-in-law and raped their own sister.

This ballad also demonstrates the constant features of the genre (narrative unit, method, attitude, and the ballad world). In addition, the retelling of the wife's story in lines 40–53 is an exact repetition of the opening lines of the ballad (1–14). Thus the exposition is cleverly repeated as recapitulation and brings about the realization of the full horror in the situation.

In contrast to the folk ballad, the literary ballad is a form of *Kunstpoesie*. It has been accurately defined as 'a ballad or ballad-like poem written with a deliberate and serious artistic purpose, that is, by a poet using the ballad as a form for the expression of his inspiration'.[8] In other words, the literary ballad represents a conscious choice by an individual poet to employ a form and to adopt the techniques of folk poetry.

When the folk ballad was 'discovered' by the literary world in the eighteenth century and 'sophisticated' poets began imitating the form, they found that not all the aesthetic principles of the

[8] J. S. Bratton, 'Studies in the Literary and Sub-Literary Ballad in the Nineteenth Century', unpublished D. Phil. Thesis (Oxford University, 1969), 2.

traditional ballad were applicable in their own poetry. These poets manifested little interest in constructing an accurate copy of the genuine article, merely to display their ingenuity. The narrative unit of the folk ballad seemed to be too compressed. Poets had become interested in the causation of events, in the physical description and psychological motivation of their characters, and in the localization of the setting. The narrative method of the traditional genre seemed awkward, the language unrefined and the metre either too irregular or too monotonous. The writers of literary ballads sought greater richness of diction, greater density of rhythms—in short, a style which, in its striking originality, would express each poet's individuality. Nor could sophisticated poets abide the uncompromising superficiality, impersonality, and distance from characters and events which distinguished the narrative attitude in the folk ballads. They wanted not merely to express the experience and share it with their readers, but to explain it and interpret its significance.

Thus the aesthetic principles of the folk ballad were completely antithetical to the canons of neo-classical, pre-romantic, and romantic taste. As one English critic has concluded: 'The [folk] ballads ignored or de-emphasized precisely those elements which sophisticated poets would savour most and develop most fully.'[9] One is left with a paradox: the literary world adopted and imitated the supreme genre of 'illiterature'.

Explanations for this phenomenon vary. The attraction of the ballad form in the eighteenth-century can be interpreted as a reaction against classical genres and aesthetics. The ballad was 'natural' rather than artificial; 'popular' rather than aristocratic; and 'national' rather than cosmopolitan.[10] These arguments are valid, but neglect the important appeal of the form for sophisticated poets, namely, enchantment with the exotic 'world' which the ballad offered. The physical setting, weather, vegetation, dwellings, inhabitants, supernature—all the components of the intangible ballad 'code'—were so totally different from the serene, rational world of classical poetry that the ballad offered to both poets and readers something really new and exciting. And it is precisely this 'code' which would be variously recognized and used,

[9] Friedman, *The Ballad Revival*, 295

[10] Hodgart, *The Ballads*, 148.

distorted and misused by each writer of literary ballads as he altered the form to accommodate his own talents and tastes.

The so-called 'ballad revival' in Western European literature developed in three interrelated stages: firstly, a change in the literary world's perception of the folk ballad; secondly, the collection of ballad texts; thirdly, the imitation of the traditional form and the subsequent creation of the literary ballad genre.

The English 'revival' developed slowly. Elizabethans had little affection for the folk ballad; the form was considered vulgar and undignified, the preserve of the common people. Sir Philip Sidney's famous declaration in his *Defence of Poesie* (1595), presumably about some version of *Chevy Chase*, is the exception to the pervading attitude: '. . . I never heard the old song of *Percy and Duglas*, that I founde not my heart mooved more than with a Trumpet; and yet it is sung but by some blinde Crowder, with no rougher voyce, than rude stile . . .'[11]

In the early eighteenth century Joseph Addison, in his criticism of *Chevy Chase*, reflects a similar attitude towards the ballad; however, he hoped to change that attitude by showing that '. . . the Sentiments in that Ballad [*Chevy Chase*] are extremely Natural and Poetical, and full of the majestic Simplicity which we admire in the greatest of the ancient Poets'.[12]. Although he was taken to task by his fellow neo-classical critics, Addison's views proved to be far-sighted.

The publication of a fifteenth-century ballad, *The Nut-browne Maid*, in the *Muses Mercury* in 1707 resulted in the first literary imitation of the traditional folk genre. Matthew Prior wrote *Henry and Emma, a Poem, Upon the Model of the Nut-browne Maid*, and published it together with the text of the original ballad.[13] The original was later included by Thomas Percy in his *Reliques* (1765), while Prior's imitation was translated into German by F. J. Bertuch in 1753, and from Bertuch's version into Russian prose by N. Markov in 1788.

Thomas Percy's *Reliques of Ancient English Poetry* can be considered the culmination of neo-classical interest in folk ballads.

[11] *The Complete Works of Sir Philip Sidney*, ed. A. Feuillerat, III (Cambridge, 1923), 24.

[12] *Spectator*, No. 74 (1711).

[13] See K. Kroeber, *Romantic Narrative Art* (Madison, Wisc., 1966), 13–19, for a comparison of the original with Prior's imitation.

This three-volume collection contained a variety of Scottish and English songs, ballads, sonnets, and romances, selected and organized haphazardly, and freely rewritten in order to make them 'readable'. Percy eliminated the bawdy bits, simplified the syntax, replaced archaic words and phrases, and made the plots more explicit. The *Reliques* had an extraordinary influence on the perception of popular poetry. Percy forced the traditional ballad into the English literary consciousness, and the excitement which was generated in England spread throughout Northern Europe.[14] Percy's practice of editing the texts to make them conform to contemporary standards of taste became the guide for later collectors and imitators.[15] Friedrich Schlegel, summarizing the influence of the *Reliques*, wrote that through Percy the 'universal passion for national ballads' had overcome all other kinds of writing and had engrossed 'the whole of English literature'.[16]

Percy's influence was felt in Russian literature only indirectly, through Bürger's imitations of English ballads and through the collections of Herder and Ursinus, both inspired by the *Reliques*. Far more important for the Russian ballad movement were other non-balladic developments in pre-romantic English literature.

James Thomson's *The Seasons* (1727–30) inaugurated a new era in nature poetry with its description of a purely national landscape and its insistence on the intimate connection between nature and man's soul. The work was translated into French and German during the 1740s and 1750s, and short excerpts began to appear in Russian journals from 1781. The first full translation into Russian was completed by D. I. Dmitrevsky in 1798.[17]

Edward Young's *Night Thoughts* (1742–5), full of pensive melancholy and reconciliation with death, enjoyed similar popularity in European literature. The work was translated into German in the 1750s by J. A. Ebert, and into French prose by Le Tourneur in 1769. Excerpts in Russian prose translated by M. V. Sushkova

[14] See Friedman, *The Ballad Revival*, 185–232.

[15] Joseph Ritson was a notable exception: in the preface to his collection of songs and romances he attacked Percy's editorial method and advocated closer adherence to the original texts.

[16] *Lectures on the History of Literature*, trans. J. G. Lockhart, II (Edinburgh, 1818), 218.

[17] Yu. D. Levin, 'Angliiskaya poeziya i literatura russkogo sentimentalizma' in *Ot klassitsizma k romantizmu*, ed. M. P. Alekseev (L., 1970), 229–32.

appeared in Kheraskov's journal *Vechera* in 1772.[18] The first full prose version was made from Ebert's translation, probably by A. M. Kutuzov, and appeared in Novikov's Masonic journal *Utrennii svet* between 1778 and 1780. The first verse translation was completed by S. N. Glinka from Le Tourneur's version and published in 1806.[19]

Perhaps the single most influential poem of the pre-romantic period was Thomas Gray's *Elegy written in a country churchyard* (1750). An excerpt from the poem appeared in Russian translation in the journal *Pokoyashchiisya trudolyubets* in 1784, and a full prose translation was included in the same journal a year later. The first verse translation was published by V. A. Zhukovsky in *Vestnik Evropy* in 1802, and marked the beginning of Zhukovsky's literary career.[20]

A phenomenon which had as much impact on Western European literature as Percy's *Reliques* was James Macpherson's creation of the Ossianic myth. His liberal editing of traditional Gaelic songs and the insertion of numerous passages of his own invention resulted in a literary imitation of popular poetry not unlike the ballads in both content and form. Full of local colour, national lore, melancholy, and supernature, and written in a strikingly original style, Macpherson's hoax swept through Europe and Russia.[21]

The earliest Russian references to Ossian occur in a translation of Goethe's *Die Leiden des jungen Werthers* (1774) made in 1781 and in Karamzin's *Poeziya* in 1787.[22] A. I. Dmitriev first translated Ossian into Russian verse in 1788. One of the poems and some of Macpherson's commentary were translated in *Moskovskii zhurnal* in 1791, and E. I. Kostrov translated Le Tourneur's French version into Russian in 1792, which he published together with a long article on the bard and his epoch. Imitations of Ossianic poems were later written by Kapnist, Derzhavin, Murav'ev, Karamzin, Gnedich, and Pushkin, and exerted considerable influence on the development of Russian poetry.

[18] Ibid. 210.

[19] Ibid. 211–25.

[20] See K. H. and W. U. Ober, 'Žukovskij's First Translation of Gray's *Elegy*, *SEEJ* X (1966), 167–72.

[21] See R. P. Fitzgerald, 'The Style of Ossian', *Studies in Romanticism*, VI (Boston, 1966), No. 1, 22–33.

[22] See V. I. Maslov, *Ossian v Rossii* (*Bibliografiya*) (L., 1928).

No account of the influence of English pre-romanticism on the Russian ballad movement can omit the rediscovery of Shakespeare in Russia through Le Tourneur's French versions. Russian translations by Karamzin, Pomerantsev, and A. I. Turgenev began to appear in the late eighteenth and early nineteenth century.[23] Some of this new interest in Shakespeare was due to the discovery that he had used ballads, folk-songs, and popular legends as one of the sources for his plays.

The two English ballad imitators who exerted the most profound influence on Russian literary ballads were Robert Southey and Sir Walter Scott. Southey was attracted to the ballad form partly as a result of his admiration for William Taylor's translation of Bürger's *Lenore*, one of six English versions published in 1796.[24] While his serious Gothic ballads are concise and suitably macabre, Southey's comic ballads range from the wryly amusing to the ridiculous.

Bürger's *Lenore* also aroused Scott's interest in the ballads. After his anonymous version of *Lenore* in 1796, he translated another Bürger ballad, *Der wilde Jäger*. In 1801 Scott collaborated with Southey and Matthew ('Monk') Lewis in a collection of Gothic poems called *Tales of Wonder* which included his own rendition of Goethe's *Erlkönig*.

Scott's major contribution to the ballad revival was his collection of texts entitled *Minstrelsy of the Scottish Border* (1802–3). His principles of editing conformed to Percy's standards of contemporary good taste. Scott made composite versions of the ballads, adapting 'the best or most poetical readings' from all extant copies. He regularized the rhythms, eliminated any vulgarisms, and made numerous insertions and alterations, not all of which are discernible even now.

Although they later proved to be the greatest literary ballads written in English, Wordsworth and Coleridge's *Lyrical Ballads* (1798), which included *The Rime of the Ancient Mariner*, and Keats's *La Belle Dame Sans Merci* (1819) had far less impact on the European ballad revival, and almost no influence in Russia.

In Germany the influence of the English ballad revival coincided

[23] See *Shekspir i russkaya kul'tura*, ed. M. P. Alekseev (M.-L., 1965).

[24] See O. F. Emerson, *The Earliest English Translations of Bürger's "Lenore"* (Cleveland, Ohio, 1915).

with increased national interest in folk poetry.[25] Bürger's *Lenore*, published in *Musenalmanach* in 1773, became the rage in European literatures from Scotland to Russia, and from Scandinavia to Italy. Some critics have claimed that *Lenore* was a reworking of Percy's *Sweet William's Ghost*.[26] Others have seen its source in German folk legends, in Herder's essay on Ossian (1773), or in Goethe's drama *Götz von Berlichingen* (1771–3).[27] Whatever its origin, the novelty, supernatural dread, popular speech, and sound effects of Bürger's ballad produced a literary sensation. At the height of *Lenore*'s popularity, Bürger wrote to his fellow poets: 'With trembling knees all of you shall prostrate yourselves before me, and acknowledge me as a Genghis Khan, that is, the greatest Khan of the ballad . . . For all who shall write ballads after me will be my unquestionable vassals and will borrow their tone from me.'[28]

In the same year in which Bürger's *Lenore* was published, Herder edited what was to become the manifesto of the *Sturm und Drang* movement, *Von deutscher Art und Kunst* (1773), to which he contributed essays on Ossian and on Shakespeare.[29] He put forward his own idealized view of Ossian as a lyric poet, and defended popular poetry as the only genuine poetry. He challenged Germany to collect her own folk-songs and to become conscious of her national traditions.

In 1777, one year before the publication of Herder's major collection of texts, A. F. Ursinus had edited a slim volume of English ballads borrowed from Percy's *Reliques*, together with their German translations.[30] Epigraphs to the collection were selected from Addison's criticism of *Chevy Chase* and from Montaigne's essay on the nature of popular poetry: 'La poésie populaire et purement naturelle a des naïvetés et des grâces par où elle se compare à la principale beauté de la poésie parfaite selon l'art.' An explanatory essay by the German critic J. J. Eschenburg preceded

[25] See W. Kayser, *Geschichte der deutschen Ballade* (Berlin, 1936), 70–88.

[26] See Entwistle, *European Balladry*, 123–4; and Kayser, *Geschichte*, 89–100.

[27] See J. G. Robertson, *A History of German Literature* (London, 1962), 259–60.

[28] *Briefe von und an Gottfried August Bürger*, ed. A. Strodtmann (Berlin, 1874), 132.

[29] Bürger remarked upon completion of his ballad: "I think that to a certain extent *Lenore* will correspond to Herder's precepts" (Kayser, *Geschichte*, 91).

[30] *Balladen und Lieder altenglischer und altschottischer Dichtart* (Berlin, 1777).

the text and translations. This obscure work was to become the principal source of ballad translations into Russian in the late eighteenth century.

In 1778–9 Herder published his *Volkslieder*, an anthology of foreign texts including selections from Percy's English and Scottish ballads, Shakespeare's songs, Spanish romances, and Scandinavian songs. He argued that his collection should be regarded more as a foundation for future poetry than as poetry itself. German poets were to recover their authentic voice by attuning themselves to the sources of inspiration of the *Volkslied*.

Goethe accepted Herder's challenge and wrote a number of literary ballads during his Weimar period, including *Der Fischer* (1778) and *Erlkönig* (1782), and another series in 1797 which was published in *Musenalmanach*. He also persuaded Schiller to contribute some ballads to the same journal. These included *Der Taucher* and *Der Handschuh*. Both Goethe and Schiller were to play a major role in the development of the Russian literary ballad. However, it was J. L. Uhland's *Balladen und Romanzen* (1805–15) which proved to be the major source of Russian translations from German in the early nineteenth century.

The ballad revival in France occurred much later than in England or Germany. The collections by Percy and Herder aroused little excitement among French readers. Only Fauriel's *Chants populaires de la Grèce moderne* (1824–5) began to awaken some interest in folk literature.[31] While this resulted in many translations and imitations of the folk poetry of other countries, there was little enthusiasm shown for the investigation of French sources. Later developments in the French literary ballad, particularly the works of Hugo and Musset, had only a limited effect on the Russian ballad movement.[32]

Sir Walter Scott, in his *Essay on Imitations of the Ancient Ballad* (1830), summarized one of the results of the Western European ballad revival:

> . . . a new species of poetry seems to have arisen, which in some cases endeavoured to pass itself as the production of genuine antiquity, and in others honestly avowed an attempt to emulate the merits and avoid the errors with which the old ballad was encumbered; and in the effort

[31] N. H. Clement, *Romanticism in France* (New York, 1939), 103.

[32] See below, Ch. VIII, for Hugo's influence on Lermontov's ballads.

to accomplish this a species of composition was discovered which is capable of being subjected to peculiar rules of criticism and of exhibiting excellences of its own.[33]

This 'new species of poetry' had established itself as an original genre in English and German poetry. The aesthetic principles of the literary ballad, so unlike those of the traditional folk ballad, inevitably required that it be 'subjected to peculiar rules of criticism'. The ballads of Scott himself, Southey, Wordsworth, Coleridge, and Keats, and those of Bürger, Goethe, Schiller, and Uhland demonstrated that the form was indeed capable of 'exhibiting excellences of its own'. The Russian literary ballad owes its origin and early development to the Western European ballad revival.

The influence of the European ballad revival on the Russian ballad movement has been underestimated or flatly denied by Soviet scholars. In a recent article one critic declares: 'The reasons for the conception [of the literary ballad genre] were of a social-historical nature, and not narrowly literary, and in any case were not rooted in the aspiration of Russian poets to imitate European models, as it has been thought previously'.[34] However, the interest aroused in Russia by French translations of English and German works and the proliferation of Russian translations of these same works suggest that Western European pre-romantic literature, and particularly the ballad revival, had much greater significance for the development of the Russian ballad than Soviet critics would care to admit.

It must, however, be admitted that, with the general development of national consciousness in Europe during the eighteenth century, the popular literary tradition was also discovered in Russia. Collections of folk literature and subsequent literary imitations, especially of the folk-song, played an important role in the history of the Russian literary ballad.

Although the aesthetic theory of both French and Russian classicism rejected folklore as a valid component of style, eighteenth-century Russian poets were far more interested in collecting and imitating folk poetry than were their French

[33] *Minstrelsy*, ed. T. Henderson (London, 1931), 539.

[34] E. A. Tudorovskaya, 'Stanovlenie zhanra narodroi ballady v tvorchestve A. S. Pushkina', *Russkii fol'klor*, VII (M.-L., 1962), 67.

counterparts. Trediakovsky claimed that his tonic verse was strongly influenced by popular poetry.[35] Sumarokov wrote several imitations of folk-songs, including *Negde v malen'kom lesu* (1755), *Gde ni gulyayu, ni khozhu* (1765), and *Ne grusti, moi svet, mne grustno i samoi* (1770), all of which were later included in Chulkov's collection of popular songs. Even the Empress Catherine began collecting and reworking motifs from popular poetry. Her comic opera *Novgorodskii bogatyr' Boeslavich* (1786) was, in the author's own words, 'composed of *skazki*, Russian songs and other works'.[36]

This interest in folklore found expression in the various collections and anthologies of M. D. Chulkov and M. I. Popov. Chulkov's *Kratkii mifologicheskii slovar'* (1767) included explanations of Slavonic, as well as classical, mythology. Popov's *Opisanie drevnego slavyanskogo yazycheskogo basnosloviya . . .* (1768) pointed out parallels between Slavonic and Western European myths. Chulkov's four-volume *Sobranie raznykh pesen* (1770–4), frequently reprinted during the 1780s, contained approximately 800 songs, including genuine folk-songs and Sumarokov's imitations. Chulkov also published a *Slovar' russkikh sueverii* (1782); the title of the second edition (1786) enumerated its contents: *ABC of Russian superstitions, idol-worshipping sacrifices, nuptial and popular rites, sorcery, shamanism, etc., etc.* V. A. Levshin issued a collection of tales in ten parts entitled *Russkie skazki* (1780–3), which contained 'ancient narratives of renowned *bogatyri* and popular *skazki*'.[37]

In 1765 Popov published thirteen of his own songs, the first such collection by a single poet in Russian literature. He added three more songs to the second edition in 1768, and another five to his *Dosugi* in 1772, including *Ty, besschastnyi dobryi molodets*, a variation on a folk-song taken from Chulkov's collection, and *Ne golubushka v chistom pole vorkuet*, an original experiment in the style of a folk-song with the rhythm, epithets, negative comparisons, and reliance on verbs characteristic of traditional folk-songs.[38]

[35] G. A. Gukovsky, *Russkaya literatura XVIII veka* (M., 1939), 223.

[36] I. I. Zamotin, *Romantizm dvadtsatykh godov XIX stoletiya v russkoi literature*, II (SPb.-M., 1911–13), 353.

[37] See V. B. Shklovsky, *Chulkov i Levshin* (L., 1933) for an analysis of their work and their influence on nineteenth-century Russian literature.

[38] For texts, see *Poety XVIII veka*, *Biblioteka poeta*, *Malaya seriya*, 3-e izd. I (L., 1958), 510–12.

During the last few decades of the eighteenth century several works were published which foreshadowed the emergence of the literary ballad genre. One of these is a narrative poem entitled *Nakazannaya nevernost'* (*Romans*) (1778) by Ya. B. Knyazhnin, who was known primarily as a classical dramatist and as a translator of French sentimental literature. The romance is a story of a mysterious love which wreaks a terrible vengeance: the beautiful heroine Liza loves the handsome Flor, but he spurns her to marry someone richer; Liza, overcome by grief, dies of a broken heart; her body is placed in the church where Flor is about to be married; but Flor sees Liza's corpse, is smitten with remorse, and expires. The lovers are buried together in one grave.

The characters in Knyazhnin's poem possess no individuality: on the one hand, there is the beautiful, faithful heroine, on the other, the fortune-seeking, faithless hero. The setting is nominally Moscow, but, in fact, is completely generalized. The author intrudes in the narrative with an admonition to Flor ('Ty klyalsya . . . trepeshchi, nevernyi . . .'), to Liza ('Ne ver' l'stetsu, o Liza nezhna!'), and a moral lesson for us all: ('Da budet vam primer uzhasnyi,/ Goryashchim v strasti, —ne mechta'). The language of the romance is highly literary and employs none of the devices of folk poetry. The intonation, which alternates between exclamatory and interrogative, and the descriptive epithets, including *gor'kii ston*, *bledna liliya*, *tomnyi zrak*, *temnyi grob*, and *smutny vzory*, foreshadow the language of the literary ballads. In fact, the subject, characters, authorial attitude, and language of Knyazhnin's romance are all closely related to the Russian ballads of the 1790s.

The translation into Russian of a French history of Scandinavia resulted in an attempt to create a new genre close to the literary ballad, the so-called *rytsarskaya pesn'*.[39] In 1755 one P. H. Mallet published *L'Introduction à l'histoire de Dannemarc*, which contained materials on the origin, beliefs, and customs of the people of Scandinavia, as well as several examples of their poetry. Excerpts from Mallet's book were translated into Russian and published in the *Sankt-Peterburgskii Vestnik* in 1778, and the complete work

[39] See R. V. Iezuitova, 'Iz istorii russkoi ballady 1790-kh-pervoi poloviny 1820-kh godov', unpublished Candidate's Thesis (Institut russkoi literatury, L., 1966), 98 ff.

was translated by F. Moiseenko in 1785.[40] Two songs were included in prose translation: *Pesnya korolya Regnera Lodbroga*, based on a twelfth-century original, translated into German in the 1760s and much praised by Herder; and *Pesnya Garal'da khrabrogo.*

A translation of the latter song, called *Pesn' norvezhskogo vityazya Garal'da khrabrogo* (1793), was written by N. A. L'vov, also known as the editor of a collection of Russian folk-songs (1790) and as the author of an unfinished *bogatyrskaya pesnya, Dobrynya* (1794). The same song was translated during the 1790s as *Pesn' khrabrogo shvedskogo rytsarya Garal'da* by I. F. Bogdanovich, whose long poem *Dushen'ka* (1778–83) also contained numerous folkloric elements.[41] Anonymous translations of both songs from Mallet's book appeared in the journal *Ippokrena* in 1801.[42] As in the versions by L'vov and Bogdanovich, the language of these translations was a stylized imitation of Russian folk poetry. The songs were preceded by a brief introduction on Scandinavian chivalry, borrowed from the Russian translation of Mallet's text. Since the genre of the *rytsarskaya pesn'* lacks the narrative unit characteristic of the ballad, it can only be considered as a related form. Each stanza in these *pesni* relates a separate episode, rather than contributing to the dramatic development of a single ballad subject.

Another genre related to the literary ballad is the heroic *poema* which became popular during the late 1790s and early 1800s. These stylized imitations of folklore in the epic tradition, with their conventional settings and artificial historical colour, included Karamzin's *Il'ya Muromets* (1795), A. I. Radishchev's *Bova* (1797–1800), Kheraskov's *Bakhariana* (1803), and Derzhavin's *Dobrynya* (1804) and *Tsar'-devitsa* (1806).[43]

The emergence of the Russian literary ballad as a genre of *Kunstpoesie* could not have resulted from the imitation of traditional Russian folk ballads because neither the concept of a folk ballad

[40] *Vvedenie v istoriyu datskuyu g. Malleta, perev. s. frants. F. Moiseenko* (SPb., 1785). The work was translated into English by Percy and published as *Northern antiquities* (London, 1770).

[41] When Bogdanovich's version was published in 1810 it inspired Batyushkov to retranslate the song as *Pesn' Garal'da smelogo.*

[42] VIII (1801), 355–68.

[43] See A. N. Sokolov, *Ocherki po istorii russkoi poemy XVIII i pervoi poloviny XIX veka* (M., 1955).

genre nor any collections of texts existed until fairly recently. Anthologies of Russian traditions, superstitions, and myths, as well as imitations of related genres of folk literature, including the folk-song, *rytsarskaya pesn'*, and *poema*, indicate a growing interest in popular sources among eighteenth-century poets and their readers. But the impetus for the Russian literary ballad was undoubtedly provided by the Western European ballad revival, a conclusion which has been accepted, albeit grudgingly, by at least one Soviet critic, although a national bias remains obvious: 'The use of the tradition of Western European ballads in the creation of the Russian ballad in no way signifies thoughtless, blind copying of individual foreign models, but proceeded along a complicated path on the foundation of national literary development'.[44]

[44] Iezuitova, 'Iz istorii', 47.

II

RUSSIAN LITERARY BALLADS OF THE 1790s

One of the universal characteristics of the Romantic temperament, whatever its incarnation, seems to be a fascination for the ballad.[1]

THE first Russian literary ballads began to appear in various periodicals during the 1790s. Some were published anonymously, although specific authors or translators for certain of these have since been identified. Other ballads were written or translated by well-known poets.

One of the earliest published ballads is a prose translation from German entitled *Edvin i Malli*, which appeared in *Priyatnoe i poleznoe preprovozhdenie vremeni* in 1795.[2] It has been ascribed to one of the editors of that journal, V. S. Podshivalov.[3] The source of the translation was established by V. I. Rezanov as F. Kind's ballad *Edwin und Mally*, published in *Lenardo's Schwarmereyen* (1793), which in turn was Kind's prose version of Bürger's ballad *Lenardo und Blandine*.[4]

The ballad opens with an extensive description of the setting which closely conforms to its German source. This is followed by the hero's elegiac lament which employs rhetorical questions and exclamations to praise the heroine and to express the hero's grief. The background is then related by the narrator: Edvin, an orphan, and Malli, a nobleman's daughter, were brought up together and fell in love. At a dinner given by Malli's father, she is encouraged to reveal her heart's favourite. When she indicates the lowly Edvin, he is banished and Malli is confined. Malli frustrates her father's plan to marry her off to a knight when, at the wedding

[1] K. H. and W. U. Ober, 'Žukovskij's Early Translations of the Ballads of Robert Southey', *SEEJ* IX (1965), 182.

[2] VII (1795), 23–31, 303–11.

[3] A. N. Neustroev, *Istoricheskie rozyskaniya o russkikh povremennykh izdaniyakh* (SPb., 1874), 766.

[4] *Iz razyskanii o sochineniyakh V. A. Zhukovskogo*, I (SPb., 1906), 205.

feast, she hurls herself from her tower window. Edvin discovers her corpse and takes his own life so that the two lovers can be united.

Throughout there is an explicit parallel between external nature and the human soul. Edvin's lament concludes with invocations to the elements urging them to echo his own misery: 'Zavyvai, svirepaya burya!' The narrator intervenes to silence nature in order that he can proceed with the story: 'Razbivaites' tishe, yarye volny!/ Dui nezhnee, zavyvayushchii vetr!' The ballad ends with a brief description of the natural serenity which surrounds the lovers' graves. This parallelism between nature and the soul was to become a typical characteristic of the Russian ballads.

Another important example of the early literary ballads is the work *Alvin i Rena*, published anonymously in Podshivalov's journal in 1797.[5] Neither an author nor a definite source has yet been identified. The story is presented in the form of a dialogue between two characters. Alvin is setting off to war; Rena is caught between love and duty, but finally bids him farewell. After a long time only Alvin's corpse returns; the distraught Rena attempts suicide, but is restrained by her 'holy faith'. She dies a natural death soon afterwards, and is buried alongside her Alvin.

The symbolic intertwining of laurel and myrtle on the graves of the lovers, mentioned in the first and last stanzas, is a common folkloric device which functions as a frame for the action. But *Alvin i Rena* is by no means an impersonal folk ballad; rather, it is a literary creation designed to elicit the maximum possible emotional response. It begins and ends with a direct apostrophe to the reader: 'Akh! prolei slezu na grob!' The motif of tears accompanies the narrative at every stage: Rena's farewell promise to Alvin ('Slez sikh bole ne uvidish'); Alvin's immediate observation ('No sleza uzhe skatilas'/ Na rumyanuyu shcheku'); Rena's actual farewell ('I—skvoz' slezy ulybayas'); and her subsequent loneliness and death:

Но из томных, нежных глаз
Токи слез лились, доколе—
Сердце высохло совсем. (21: 2–4)

[5] *Priyatnoe i poleznoe*, XV (1797), 285–8.

The heavy influence of Karamzin's sentimentalism, in particular of his tearful tale *Bednaya Liza* (1792), is here clearly manifested.[6]

The action of the ballad is not located in any particular setting until Rena attempts suicide; then comes a dynamic description of an exotic ballad seascape:

Волны ярые крутятся,
С пеной плещутся, ревут,
Вся дрожит громада страшна,
Как бы рухнуть хочет вдруг. (18)

The storm in nature is compared implicitly to the *burya grusti* in Rena's soul, and earlier in the ballad this parallel is stated explicitly: 'Luch [luny] pechal'nyi, tomnyi/ Reny grust' usugublyal'. The author's apostrophe to his readers, the tearful sentimentalism, as well as the parallelism between the natural setting and the psychological state of the heroine are among the distinguishing characteristics of the literary ballads of the 1790s.

In 1799–1800 two ballads by the obscure poetess Anna Turchaninova were published in *Ippokrena*, P. A. Sokhatsky's journal which superseded *Priyatnoe i poleznoe*. The first, *Leonard i Blondina*, sub-titled *pesenka*, was inserted in the middle of the prose tale *Nochekhodets, ili lunatik*.[7] Although no specific source has been identified, F. W. Neumann suggested that the ballad may be a translation of a Spanish romance.[8] Iezuitova observed that, although the title is the same as that of one of Bürger's ballads, the two works are in no way related.[9] Thus, until a source is discovered, *Leonard i Blondina* can be considered an original Russian literary ballad.

The plot is the conventional tale of two young lovers. The hero's father urges his son Leonard to take part in the bullfights in order to win the admiration of the heroine Blondina. Although she is afraid, Leonard insists on obeying his father. Not surprisingly he perishes in the ring. The ghosts of the two lovers are united after Blondina's death. The pretence of local colour—the bullfight in Granada—is soon abandoned. The language of the ballad combines conventional eighteenth-century epithets in the narration

[6] The narrator in *Bednaya Liza* confesses to his readers: "Oh, how I love those things which touch my heart and force me to shed tears of tender grief."

[7] *Ippokrena*, IV (1799), 274–9.

[8] *Geschichte der russischen Ballade* (Königsberg and Berlin, 1937), 36.

[9] 'Iz istorii', 68.

(*prelestnyi*, *prekrasnyi*, *priyatnyi*, *nezhnyi*, *lyutyi*) and 'pre-romantic' epithets in the description of the lovers' ghosts and of the setting which frames the narration (*zybkie tsvety*, *tonkaya ten'*, *savan belyi*, *bledna ten'*). Blondina's reaction to Leonard's departure lacks the sentimentality of *Alvin i Rena*: 'Bezmolvna, smyatenna, pechal'na, bledna,/ Podobna fialke uvyadshei stoit.' Both the choice of epithets and their inclusion in a series reflect the changes in style at the end of the eighteenth century and foreshadow future developments in Zhukovsky's style.

Turchaninova's second ballad, *Vill'yam i Margarita*, published in 1800, is a prose translation of David Mallet's *William and Margaret* (1723), which is alleged to be a literary imitation of two traditional ballads included in Percy's *Reliques*. In 1772 the ballad was translated into German by J. J. Eschenburg and published as *Lykas und Myrta* in *Musenalmanach*. Eschenburg's version was corrected and included, together with Mallet's original, in Ursinus's collection in 1777. It was this text which was translated into Russian.[10] A comparison of the three versions shows that Turchaninova, by means of a literal translation of the German, came very close to the English original.

The narrative element in this ballad is almost insignificant: one night Margarita's ghost appears to Vill'yam in a dream to reproach him for his infidelity. In the morning Vill'yam awakes, staggers to Margarita's grave, and, weeping, expires. The setting is vague; the time is established by the conventional phrase—'Kogda vse pokryto bylo polunochnym mrakom';[11] and the atmosphere is created by the frequent use of 'pre-romantic' epithets, such as *polunochnaya grobnitsa*, *mrachnyi i uzhasnyi chas*, *strashnye mogily*, *rokovoe mesto*.[12] Margarita's elegiac monologue, describing her own previous beauty, Vill'yam's infidelity, and her death, consists of a series of parallel rhetorical questions, reproaching poor Vill'yam on each one of his broken promises:

> Как ты мог говорить, что лице мое прекрасное,
> а после пренеберечь оное? . . .
> Как ты мог уверять, что мои губы приятны, а довел
> до того, что багрец их зделался бледен?

[10] Ibid. 44–5.

[11] Cf. the beginning of *Edvin i Malli*: 'Cheren, kak krylie vrana, krov polunochi'.

[12] All these combinations are literal translations of the German and come close to the original English, except for *strashnye mogily*, which replaces Mallet's 'yawning graves'.

The heroine concludes with the words 'No chu! petukh otzyvaet menya otsele'—both the emotional interjection (*chu*!) and the motif (*petukh*) were to become clichés of the ballad genre. The author intervenes after the monologue to castigate the faithless hero:

> Ступай, вероломец! посмотри, как лежит она уничиженна; она которая скончалась от любви к тебе.

Turchaninova's two literary ballads lack the tearful sentimentality and the parallelism between nature and the soul characteristic of the anonymous ballads. On the other hand, the style of both *Leonard i Blondina* and *Vill'yam i Margarita* reflects the evolution of the genre. The frequency of authorial interventions and the increase of 'pre-romantic' epithets and syntactical constructions exerted a considerable influence on the literary ballads of the nineteenth century.

The earliest *original* Russian literary ballad predates all the anonymous ballads and Turchaninova's work by a decade. It is called *Nevernost'* and was written by M. N. Murav'ev in 1781. The text of the ballad, without any genre-defining sub-title, was supposed to be included in the edition of Murav'ev's work which was being prepared by Batyushkov and Zhukovsky in 1819–20. However, for some unknown reason, in the manuscript of this edition[13] the entire poem, uncorrected, was simply crossed out, presumably by one of the editors; the work remained unpublished until the 1967 edition of Murav'ev's collected poetry.[14]

The subject of the ballad is as follows: a maiden weeps, waiting for her beloved to return from battle; at midnight, when she no longer has strength even to cry, a merciful spirit appears to deliver her from her suffering and her ghost is received in heaven. In the meantime her lover has lost his way home and is being hounded by natural and supernatural omens. He too weeps in despair, wanders about for nine days, and finally returns only to find his beloved dead. He builds her a funeral mound and expires.

The most striking innovation in Murav'ev's *Nevernost'* is his introduction of the ballad 'world' or 'code'. Knyazhnin's romance

[13] GPB-499/54; (called earlier GPB-8).

[14] M. N. Murav'ev, *Stikhotvoreniya*, *Biblioteka poeta*, *Bol'shaya seriya*, 2-oe izd. (L., 1967), 210–11.

Nakazannaya nevernost' (1778) was cited earlier as a story of infidelity, grief, and the union of lovers after death.[15] To a very similar narrative Murav'ev adds a barren landscape, moonlight, midnight, hostile nature (*sovy* and *filiny*), and supernature (*leshie*) —all of which heighten the dramatic tension and help to create an atmosphere of mystery and fear. Murav'ev's attempt to produce a sense of local colour is barely noticeable: the lovers swear by Polel', the Slavonic god of love and marriage; the heroine is a native of Tver'; and her lover has gone off to defend Rus' against the Muslims.

Although the language of the ballad is composed of various elements, the use of folk epithets predominates: *temna noch'*, *chuzhu dal'nu storonku*, *zlye busurmany*, *syra zemlya*, *goryuchie slezy*. But both the corpse and the omens are described in literary language ('Telo . . ./ Bezdykhanno, pokoino/ I nestrashno, khot' bledno').

A narrative attitude of impersonality and non-interference is maintained throughout; only the title *Nevernost'* provides the moral framework within which the reader is to interpret the events of the ballad. Where Knyazhnin's hero consciously betrays the heroine and chooses wealth, Murav'ev's is unintentionally unfaithful, and helpless in the face of natural and supernatural obstacles. One can only speculate as to why Zhukovsky and Batyushkov excluded the ballad from their edition of Murav'ev's poetry. Somehow both of them failed to recognize a genuine literary ballad when confronted with one.

The history of Murav'ev's other ballad is equally unusual. *Boleslav, Korol' pol'skii* is a balladic work with a historical theme which was written in the 1790s but not published until 1810 when it was included in Zhukovsky's *Sobranie russkikh stikhotvorenii* under the sub-title *Ballada*[16] and in *Vestnik Evropy* without any sub-title.[17] The poem was also included in the 1819–20 edition of Murav'ev's works without a sub-title. All these versions had been corrected by Zhukovsky and other editors.

Boleslav is not strictly a literary ballad; rather it is a narrative based on actual events which consists of a series of dramatic incidents, not one compressed episode. The historical Boleslav III

[15] See above, Ch. I, p. 16.
[16] II (M., 1810–11), 277.
[17] No. 9 (1810), 45–7.

was king of Poland from 1102 to 1138. His bastard half-brother Zbigniev, supported by the German emperor and the Czechs, attempted to seize power. But Zbigniev was captured and blinded, and Poland was reunited.

The poem is a romanticized version of these facts, narrated as four distinct episodes: Zbigniev's attempted *coup*; Boleslav's unsuccessful wooing of Zbigniev's fiancée; Zbigniev's second assault, defeat, and death; and Boleslav's remorse, renunciation of the throne, and self-imposed exile. As in *Nevernost'* there is a slight attempt to create local colour (Poland). Allusions to the values of service, battle, love, and friendship establish the work in the traditional context of Western European chivalry.

Boleslav, the hero, is, relatively speaking, a psychologically complex character ('Sokhranyal on sil'ny strasti/ V voskipayushchei krovi'): he manifests a generous love for the covetous Zbigniev, but conceives a passion for his betrothed; he suffers from *lyubovnaya toska* when his suit is rejected, and from *glubokaya gorest'* after Zbigniev's death; he attempts suicide, but, when restrained by his courtiers, he resorts to a life of eternal wandering in search of salvation. Like that of Coleridge's Ancient Mariner, Boleslav's penance consists in the continual recitation of his tale.

The author intrudes freely in the ballad to comment on the action, addressing rhetorical questions to the betrothed ('Akh! Zbigneeva nevesta!/ Dlya chego on zrel tebya?'), commenting on her great beauty, supporting her faithfulness to Zbigniev, and concluding with a sentimental moral:

Должно думать, что спокойство
Наконец сошло с небес.
Ах! ни чести, ни геройства
Не спасают нас от слез. (18)

The folk epithets which predominate in Murav'ev's *Nevernost'* have here been replaced by an abundance of 'pre-romantic' epithets: *sil'ny strasti*, *nezhnaya vesna*, *lyubovnaya toska*, *zlobnyi dukh*. The frequency of epithets in some passages has been considerably increased, as in this description of Boleslav's renunciation and remorse:

Свой оставив трон высокий
И во рубищах простых,
Ходит в горести глубокой
По обителям святых. (16)

The introduction of the ballad 'world' or 'code' in *Nevernost'* and the portrayal of a psychologically complex hero in *Boleslav* were features overlooked by Murav'ev's contemporaries, by Zhukovsky and successive editors, and by Russian critics of the literary ballad. These innovations, as well as Murav'ev's attempts at local colour, his authorial intrusions, and his 'pre-romantic' epithets demonstrate his importance in the history of the ballad genre.

Since Murav'ev's *Nevernost'* remained unpublished for so long, Karamzin's *Raisa* (1791), sub-titled *drevnyaya ballada*, can be considered the earliest published literary ballad, and its sub-title the first accurate use of the genre name.[18] Rezanov traced its source to Mallet's ballad *William and Margaret*,[19] which was cited above as the source of Turchaninova's translation *Vill'yam i Margarita*. H. M. Nebel, in a study of Karamzin, suggests the influence of Bürger's ballad *Des Pfarrers Tochter von Taubenhain* (1781) on *Raisa*.[20] The plot of Karamzin's ballad bears a distinct resemblance to the action in the ballads of Mallet and Bürger; most likely *Raisa* is Karamzin's independent reworking of motifs common to both sources.

The story is as follows: on a stormy night Raisa climbs a steep cliff and bemoans her fate; she had left home to join her lover Kronid, but he soon deserted her. In desperation Raisa hurls herself into the sea; nature echoes with thunder, foretelling destruction for her faithless lover.

The ballad is set in a completely abstract time and place, with not even a conventional attempt at local colour. Characteristically, the disturbance in nature corresponds to the turmoil in the heroine's soul; however, Raisa is so blinded by her suffering, that she herself is unaware of the surroundings:

Она не чувствует грозы,
И бури страшный вой не может
Ее стенаний заглушить. (3: 2–4)

The heroine's monologue reveals the basic psychological contradiction in her character, namely her love/hate for Kronid. He is

[18] *Moskovskii zhurnal*, No. 2 (1791), 118.
[19] *Iz razyskanii*, 199–200.
[20] *N. M. Karamzin. A Russian Sentimentalist* (The Hague, 1967), 106.

not only Raisa's *angel* and *bozhestvo*, but also her seducer and deserter. Both emotions are in constant conflict within the heroine. The hero is presented in a more schematic, conventional way, as a wicked tempter and merciless betrayer, with no psychological development.

The structure of the ballad is simple. It begins abruptly, with no introduction; the exposition is not provided until the heroine's extended monologue. A brief conclusion presents the author's moral interpretation—that vice is to be punished—a condemnation far more explicit than that in Murav'ev's *Nevernost'*. Fate is depicted as the real villain, being the force which destroys Raisa's happiness. Love and faithfulness are mere illusions to be swept away by the impersonal, irrevocable will of Fate. The author addresses Kronid with the words 'No rok sudil, chtob ty druguyu/ Raise vernoi predpochel'.

It is in the style of the ballad that Karamzin reveals his greatest originality and makes his most important contribution to the development of the genre. Emotionalism pervades all the elements of his language. Karamzin frequently employs hyperbole in the emotive descriptions of nature, the characters, and the action itself. The syntax is distinguished by frequent emotional interruptions in the form of interjections (*Uvy!*) and three dots. Epithets assume an overwhelming importance. The description of the setting in the first stanza contains one 'pre-romantic' epithet per line:

Во тьме ночной ярилась буря;
Сверкал на небе грозный луч:
Гремели громы в черных тучах,
И сильный дождь в лесу шумел. (1)

Additional details are added to the setting in subsequent stanzas: *vlazhnaya zemlya*, *granitnye gory*, *kamni ostrye*, *ognennye luchi*. The ballad atmosphere is created in part by the use of the epithets *strashnyi* and *uzhasnyi* (*strashnyi voi*, *uzhasnaya t'ma*) which help to make the 'horror' explicit. The reader is repeatedly 'told' that everything is horrible or terrible; he is not left to infer it from the details of the description.

The portrait of the heroine in the fourth stanza also contains a considerable number of epithets (*ona bledna; mertvyi tsvet*, *tomnyi mrak*); she refers to herself as *bednaya* ('No ty neidesh' k Raise bednoi!'), as does the narrator in his exclamation 'Raisa, bednaya

Raisa!'; she describes herself as *vernaya*, *neschastnaya*, and *zloschastnaya*; her love for Kronid, as depicted by the narrator, is accompanied by *nezhnyi vzdokh*, *serdechnyi trepet*, and *plamennaya sleza*. The epithets in Raisa's apostrophe to her lover summarize the fundamental contradiction in her character: 'Kronid, Kronid, zhestokii, milyi!'

In his emphasis on the psychology of the heroine, rather than on the situation, and in the frequency and choice of epithets, Karamzin established the pattern for the Russian literary ballad which was to be followed and developed by his contemporaries and successors, particularly by Zhukovsky.

In 1792, one year after the publication of *Raisa*, Karamzin published two translations in *Moskovskii zhurnal*, one of a historical song, the other a prose rendition of a Scottish ballad. *Graf Gvarinos*, sub-titled *Drevnyaya gishpanskaya istoricheskaya pesnya*,[21] has been traced by M. P. Alekseev to an old Spanish source, *Romance del Conde Guarinos Almirante de la Mar*, referred to by Cervantes in *Don Quixote*, and included in Spanish song books from the mid-sixteenth century. This romance was translated into German and published by F. J. Bertuch in his *Magazin der Spanischen und Portugiesischen Literatur* (1780). Bertuch's work was mentioned by Karamzin in his *Pis'ma russkogo puteshestvennika* (1797–1801).[22] Nebel juxtaposed the Spanish original and Karamzin's version, concluding that 'the German translation must have followed the Spanish version closely, for Karamzin's work, when compared with the Spanish, differs only in minor details from the original.'[23]

The other balladic work which has been ascribed to Karamzin is *Shotlandskaya ballada*.[24] It is said to have originated in a French source, *Étrennes sentimentales*, about which no information has been discovered.[25] This sad tale is related by the heroine Jenny: her young lover Jimmy became a sailor in order to earn some money before their wedding. In his absence, Jenny's father breaks his arm, her mother becomes ill, and her cow is stolen. An old friend Robin Gray assists the family, falls in love with Jenny, and

[21] *Moskovskii zhurnal*, No. 3 (1792), 219–26.

[22] M. P. Alekseev, "K literaturnoi istorii odnogo iz romansov v *Don Kikhote*" in *Servantes, Stat'i i materialy* (L., 1948), 113–20.

[23] *N. M.Karamzin*, 104–5.

[24] *Moskovskii zhurnal*, No. 1 (1792), 99–101.

[25] Neustroev, *Istoricheskie rozyskaniya*, 707.

marries her. When Jimmy returns, Jenny's life becomes miserable: she dares not think about Jimmy; instead, she tries only to please her husband. The Russian prose version is little more than an unemotional recitation of the events. The only trace of emotion occurs in the lovers' bittersweet reunion:

> Ах! Свидание наше было и сладко и горестно! . . .
> Ах! Как досадна мне моя молодость!

Karamzin's only other balladic work was *Alina*, published in *Pis'ma russkogo puteshestvennika*, where it was included in a letter dated June 1790 (Paris). This long narrative poem combines some of the features characteristic of the ballad genre and the verse tale. It purports to be based on a factual episode of which Karamzin heard from an acquaintance, and which he agreed to include in his *Pis'ma* only if he was permitted to 'adorn it'.[26]

The plot is the conventional one: the angelic Alina loves and is loved by the tender Milon; they marry, but Milon soon grows bored and goes off with another woman. Alina languishes, and then takes her own life. Milon repents, attempts suicide, but is restrained by his friends; instead, he must live out his life in torment.

The narrative is interrupted by discursive observations by the author on sentimentality, on the wisdom of the lovers' choices, and on the nature of love, despondency, and disaffection. The setting of the work is that of the eighteenth-century idylls: *svetlye vody*, *zelenye brega*, *sady*, and *luga*. However, when the heroine wanders off into the forest, she comes upon a setting strikingly similar to that in the ballads:

> Алина в мрачный лес приходит
> (Несчастным тень лесов мила!)
> И видит храм уединенный,
> Остаток древности священный;
> Там ветр в развалинах свистит
> И мрамор желтым мхом покрыт . . . (111–16)

This curious contrast of settings within a single work was to be further developed by Merzlyakov.

Karamzin's heroine is *milaya* and *nezhnaya*, the epitome of

[26] N. M. Karamzin, *Polnoe sobranie stikhotvorenii*, *Biblioteka poeta*, *Bol'shaya seriya*, 2-oe izd. (M.-L., 1966), 381–2.

physical and spiritual beauty. She generously refuses to blame or condemn her faithless Milon. The hero is presented as worthy of the heroine (*nezhnyi, umnyi, lyubeznyi*), but he falls out of love with her, and becomes *zadumchivyi* and *unylyi*. Nor is Milon condemned by the narrator; the most severe epithets applied to him are *vetrenyi* and *nevernyi*. The real villain is once again Fate. Both the characters and the narrator frequently allude to its power to destroy all love and happiness.

If *Raisa* can be considered Karamzin's 'pre-romantic' ballad, then *Alina* is typical of his sentimental work and has close affinities with the genre of the idyll in setting, characters, and language.[27] Only the passages which describe Milon's disenchantment and Alina's excursion into the forest anticipate the changes in the psychology of characters and in the perception of the natural setting which were to become characteristic features of the literary ballad in the nineteenth century.

The contrast between idyllic and balladic settings assumes thematic significance in a literary ballad by Merzlyakov entitled *Milon* (1797) which later appeared in Podshivalov's journal[28]. The plot is similar to that of *Alvin i Rena*, which appeared in the following issue of the journal in which Merzlyakov's work was published. The hero, Milon, has led a sheltered life, rejoicing in the beauties of nature. Once, while walking through a forest, he discovers a grotto in which he finds a row of graves and a collection of weapons. A document addressed to him summons him to take up the armour, follow in the path of his forebears, and seek after glory. He accepts the challenge, bids farewell to the lovely Temira, and goes off to battle. Victory is achieved, but Milon perishes. Temira is plunged into grief and lies near death.

Merzlyakov's ballad is neither a love story nor a deep psychological analysis of the characters. Rather, it is a vivid contrast between two sets of values, two ways of life. On the one hand, Milon's sheltered existence is characterized by serenity ('Blazhennyi, tikhii vek'), by a sensitive appreciation of nature, and by modest aspirations ('Chto v svete zlato, pyshnost', slava ?/ Dlya

[27] Karamzin's prose works *Bednaya Liza* (1792) and *Ostrov Borngol'm* (1794) have affinities with his ballads; the former with *Alina*, and the latter with *Raisa*. See A. G. Cross, *N. M. Karamzin* (Carbondale, Ill., 1971), 102.

[28] *Priyatnoe i poleznoe*, XIV (1797), 219–23.

dobrykh chistykh dush otrava!'). The guiding principle of this life is reason, which resists the force of man's passions: 'Rassudka strasti ne plenyali/ Blistan'em lozhnoi krasoty.' On the other hand, the temptation of the grotto offers Milon happiness and fame through bold military exploits. An acceptance of this alternative results in a victory of passion over reason: 'K nemu vse strasti vdrug tolpoyu/ Predstali, l'stili, krov' vozzhgli.'

The psychologically uncomplicated Milon does not hesitate in choosing between the alternatives: in fact, the narrator states that, after his experience in the grotto, Milon could no longer enjoy his former pursuits ('S tekh por Milon ne naslazhdalsya/ Spokoistvom krotkikh, mirnykh dnei'). The equally uncomplicated Temira is unable to prevent Milon's departure. She sinks into despondency to await his return, tacitly accepting his new values: 'S soboyu razdelit' zhelala/ Priobretenny lavry im.'

Only the narrator's psychology is complicated. In presenting the two alternatives, he obviously prefers the tranquil to the heroic, the rational to the passionate. It is Milon's lack of self-knowledge which is the narrator's explanation for his rejection of the 'true values'. Temira is warned by the narrator, and she wins his sympathy when Milon does not return: 'Kto mozhet, tomnaya Temira,/ Tebya v to vremya opisat'?' The narrator also tries to imply some ambiguity: although Milon stumbles into the grotto by chance, he finds that the document is addressed to him personally. The coincidence is, of course, only superficial; all events are predetermined and man's only choice is to submit to Fate.

This contrast in values is expressed through a corresponding contrast of styles. The hero's tranquil life and the false allure of the heroic alternative are described in language characteristic of eighteenth-century idylls: *blazhennyi vek*, *blazhennye mesta*, *lozhnaya krasota*, *svet prostrannyi*. In contrast, Milon's experience in the grotto is described in 'pre-romantic' language which, in its emphasis on gloom and horror, establishes a typical balladic atmosphere: *trepet svyashchennyi*, *mrachnyi grot*, *khladnye ruki*:

Через ущелины пустые
Ужасный с воем ветр шумит;
Трясутся доски гробовые,
И хладный мрамор там гремит. (11)

The modern critic is tempted to interpret Merzlyakov's *Milon* as an allegory; the classical hero foresakes his rationality, his serenity, and his enjoyment of nature for the romantic experience —a heroic search for happiness and fame, and a life governed entirely by passions. The theme is reflected in the language: classical diction for the former and 'pre-romantic' epithets for the latter. Merzlyakov clearly prefers classicism, but chooses the 'pre-romantic' genre of the literary ballad to demonstrate his preferences and to reassert his values.

Merzlyakov's only other ballad, *Laura i Sel'mar*, was published in 1798.[29] Rezanov traced its source to a work entitled *Song* in Ramsay's *Tea-Table Miscellany* (1775), which was reprinted by Ursinus with a German translation under the double title *The damsel deploring/Das klagende Mädchen* (1777).[30] This source is rejected by Iezuitova, who regards the ballad as an original reworking by Merzlyakov of a general motif, under the strong influence of Karamzin.[31] A comparison of *Laura i Sel'mar* with the English text, however, demonstrates unmistakable similarities.

The heroine Laura sits weeping on a cliff, scanning the waves for some sign of her beloved. She utters a long lament, at the end of which she discovers that a corpse has been washed ashore. She runs down to it, embraces her Sel'mar, and dies. A parallel between the natural setting (*bezdna*, *mgla*, *skaly*, *vetr*) and the heroine's emotions (*gorest'*, *grust'*, *slezy*) is implied through the juxtaposition of descriptive details; this parallel is made explicit in the beginning of Laura's monologue as she asks God to quell the storm in nature and the agitation in her soul. The lament which follows is written in the classical style, similar to that of an eighteenth-century ode; in it, Laura protests against man's avarice (*strast' k bogatstvu*) which results in misery for all concerned.

Epithets in the ballad are restricted to the description of the setting before and after the heroine's monologue (*surova bezdna*, *luna unylaya*, *burnye vody*, *groznye volny*, *volny strashnye*) and to the narrator's description of Laura's psychology (*Laura blednaya*, *zhelan'e plamennoe i nezhnoe*, *gorestnaya lyubov'*). The actual lament and the account of the discovery of the corpse are written in elevated diction employing relatively few epithets.

[29] *Priyatnoe i poleznoe*, XVIII (1798), 141–2.
[30] *Iz razyskanii*, 208–9.
[31] 'Iz istorii', 80.

As in *Milon*, so too in *Laura i Sel'mar*, Merzlyakov combines classical and 'pre-romantic' themes and styles. Here a classical lament is put into the mouth of a romantic heroine and placed in a typical balladic setting. Merzlyakov remains a classical poet, desperately trying to employ the new, fashionable genre of the literary ballad, but still clinging to his conventional eighteenth-century values.

During the early 1790s Karamzin's *Moskovskii zhurnal* published two ballads by I. I. Dmitriev. The first, *Byl'*,[32] shares with Merzlyakov's *Milon* the contrast of two ways of life, and with the anonymous ballad *Alvin i Rena* its over-abundance of tears. Cheston, the hero of Dmitriev's *Byl'*, inspired by patriotism, decides to seek after military glory. His father approves his decision, and presents him with a rifle. Suddenly, a shot is heard: Cheston's sister has been slain. The hero swears to take revenge: 'No prezhde, akh, sestre ustroil/ Edinokrovnoi smertnyi rov.'

The narrative is accompanied by tears at every stage, and the father's farewell advice explains their relevance:

Будь верный сын, будь храбрый воин,
Но будь чувствителен притом:
Сугубо лавров тот достоин,
Кто слезы льет и над врагом. (8)

The contrast of values in *Byl'* is between Cheston's early life of wealth and amusement and a life of heroic exploits. Unlike Merzlyakov, Dmitriev approves the heroic alternative. The theme of individual heroism is combined with that of national patriotism, as expressed by the narrator in the words: *Ross imenem i delom bud'* and *No Rossy vse userdny chada*. But blind, senseless Fate interferes with Cheston's heroic and patriotic ambitions, and causes him to postpone temporarily his search for glory.

Dmitriev's second ballad can be read as an ironic sequel to *Byl'*. It was published in 1792 under the title *Otstavnoi vakhmistr (ballada)*,[33] included with revisions in Dmitriev's *I moi bezdelki* (1795), under the title *Karikatura*, republished with large omissions in *Sochineniya i Perevody* (1803–5), and excluded altogether

[32] *Moskovskii zhurnal*, No. 1 (1791), 6.
[33] Ibid. No. 3 (1792), 295.

from the sixth edition of Dmitriev's collected works in 1823. The second title, *Karikatura*, is probably a pun on Carric-thura, Cathulla's palace which Ossian's Fingal delivers from siege on his way home from an expedition.

In Dmitriev's ballad a cavalry sergeant-major returns home after a long period of service and finds his house deserted except for a scraggy cat. An old servant supplies him with the sordid details: the hero's wife had been running a haven for ruffians, one of whom was captured and subsequently informed on her. The wife disappeared without trace. Upon hearing the news, the hero sheds a few tears; soon he remarries and now he serves as a *zemskii sud'ya*. M. A. Dmitriev, a Russian critic and memoirist, recorded in his reminiscences the episode on which the ballad is allegedly based, and claimed to have in his possession a drawing by the poet showing the hero's return to his native village.[34]

The stanzas which were omitted from the 1803–5 edition must be read *in situ* in order to understand the intention of Dmitriev's original work, namely, the debunking of the sentimental literary ballad. It is as if the hero of *Byl'* had returned from his glorious exploits, or as if the Russian Fingal had come home from his expeditions to discover, instead of a beautiful wife and a peaceful retirement, only a deserted house.

The ballad, written in blank verse, begins with a stylized apostrophe to *sedaya starina*, which at once establishes an ironic tone of false historicism. Thereafter every attempt at moderately serious description or narration is immediately followed by an ironic passage which undercuts the solemnity. Almost all of these passages were excluded from the 1803–5 edition.[35] For example, the hero is identified in the following manner: after the narrator poses the rhetorical question, 'Who is this tattered figure returning home?', one possible answer follows:

Не древний ли крыжатик?
Вот сунуло куда!
Изрядный я историк.
Простите—заврался.

[34] *Melochi iz zapasa moei pamyati* (M., 1869), 124–5.

[35] See Karamzin–Dmitriev, *Izbrannye stikhotvoreniya*, *Biblioteka poeta*, *Bol'shaya seriya* (L., 1953), 492–3.

Then the real answer is provided: it is a former cavalry sergeant-major. As the hero draws closer to home, his emotional reaction to familiar sights is described. This is immediately undercut:

Завидя ж дым в деревне,
Растаял пуще он;
Тогдашний день субботу
И баню вспомянул.

Finally, the hero's reaction to the servant's story is ironically presented:

Несчастный муж поплакал;
Потом, вздохнув, пошел
К Терентьичу в избушку
И с горести лег спать.

Thus at every stage in the description and in the narration, Dmitriev's original intention was to deride the hero and the situation. *Karikatura* is indeed a 'caricature' of the serious episode recorded by M. A. Dmitriev, of the drawing made by the poet himself, of the exploits of Ossian's Fingal, and, finally, of the sentimental ballad. It is the first attempt at a parody of the new genre, so ahead of its time that Dmitriev revised it and eventually omitted it from later editions of his collected works.[36]

Dmitriev's last ballad, *Starinnaya lyubov'*, was written in 1804[37] and is a conscious stylization of a folk ballad, lacking the irony of *Karikatura*. Rezanov suggests a possible source in Bürger's *Lenardo und Blandine*.[38] Dmitriev's work may indeed be based on Bürger's ballad, but it also shows the influence of Karamzin, as well as a superficial attempt at Russification of setting and characters.

The plot of the ballad is conventional: a captain and his lovely daughter live in Moscow; boyars and princes woo her, but she only loves a poor young poet. Her father learns of their secret love and confines his daughter. The poet wastes away and dies. The heroine is freed, sees her lover's corpse, and expires.

[36] Perhaps Pushkin recognized this element of parody when in *Stantsionnyi smotritel'* the narrator states: 'Such was the tale of my friend, the station master, a tale interrupted by tears several times, which he picturesquely wiped away with his shirt flap, as did the zealous Terent'ich in the wonderful ballad by Dmitriev.'

[37] *Sochineniya i perevody*, III (M. 1803–5), 64.

[38] *Iz razyskanii*, 203.

Irony has been replaced by a slightly condescending romanticized view of the Russian past (*Kak milo zhili v starinu!*), and by a conclusion which indicates that the tragic story is not meant to be taken seriously (*Pesn' eta—byl'*). The setting is stylized (*vysokie teremy, belokamennaya Moskva, staraya lipa*), as is the narrative itself (*Zhil-byl kogda-to . . .*). The heroine is a *chernookaya krasavitsa* called Milolika, who democratically rejects all social distinctions: 'Chto znatnost'! serdtsu vse ravny!' The hero serenades his maiden *skvoz' slezy* to the accompaniment of his *tomnaya lira*.[39] And the father, a *vozhd' velikii* with a prejudice against indigent poets, finally relents. While Dmitriev's *Karikatura* was ahead of its time in being the first parody of the new genre, his *Starinnaya lyubov'* was behind its time, being a typical ballad of the 1790s, written when the literary ballad genre was about to be totally transformed.

The Russian literary ballad of the 1790s developed as a genre independent of folk poetry. The imitative folk-songs of the eighteenth-century, although related in content and language to the genuine folk-songs, had almost no influence on the ballad genre. The sources of the Russian literary ballad, as has been demonstrated, were basically foreign; they consisted of direct translations from English and German ballads, or reworkings of motifs which were common in Western European pre-romantic literature. Zhukovsky's *Lyudmila*, the first of his forty literary ballads, was published in 1808; with it the genre was transformed and the literary ballad became the most influential and controversial form in Russian poetry for almost two decades.

[39] The early version (*Pel o lyubvi svoei skvoz' slezy*) was altered to a less tearful one in the 1823 edition (*Pel prelesti svoei tsaritsy*).

III

ZHUKOVSKY'S LITERARY BALLADS

Je crois qu'il [Zhukovsky] a ajouté quelque chose á la langue poétique en exprimant dans ses vers un genre d'idées et de sentiment qui étaient nouveaux.

—Zhukovsky[1]

THE name of Zhukovsky and the genre of the literary ballad are inseparable. It was Zhukovsky who made the first theoretical statements about the genre and who influenced all subsequent attempts at definition. Zhukovsky considered himself, and was considered by his contemporaries, primarily as a writer of ballads. Moreover, the content and the style of Zhukovsky's forty ballads established the model for all future Russian literary ballads.

The first written description of the genre is contained in an unpublished translation of J. J. Eschenburg's *Entwurf einer Theorie und Literatur der schönen Wissenschaften* (Berlin, 1783). In 1804 Zhukovsky completed his free rendition of this treatise, to which he added copious notes referring to other French and German literary theories. In the section on lyrical poetry, the 'romance' and the 'ballad' are defined as 'light, lyrical narratives of important or unimportant, touching or uplifting, tragic or comic occurrences'. The source of such works could be mythology, history, chivalry, monasticism, everyday social life, or poetic fantasy. The plot should be 'simple, natural, light, pleasant, and should correspond to the material'. For example, the narrative was to be *zhivopisen* whenever the poet describes something *chudesnoe, mrachnoe, uzhasnoe ili neobychainoe*.[2]

The earliest published description of the ballad genre also belongs to Zhukovsky and was included in the preface to his

[1] L. B. Modzalevsky (ed.), 'Neizdannyi konspekt [Zhukovskogo] po istorii russkoi literatury (1827)', *TONRL* I (M.-L., 1948), 301.

[2] GPB-286; 1; 83. Excerpts are also included in Rezanov, *Iz razyskanii*, II. It is interesting that the epithets in the definition correspond to the most frequent epithets in the ballads themselves; see below, Ch. IV.

Sobranie russkikh stikhotvorenii (1810–11). He wrote that the ballad belongs simultaneously to two sorts of poetry since it is 'narrative' in content but 'lyrical' in form. Therefore in his anthology Zhukovsky includes short ballads in the section of lyrical poetry (Karamzin's *Raisa*, Murav'ev's *Boleslav*, Dmitriev's *Starinnaya lyubov'*), and long ballads in the section of narrative poetry (Kamenev's *Gromval*).

By 1816 Eschenburg's entire book had been translated and published anonymously.[3] In the appropriate section the ballad is defined as a genre of 'lyric-epic' poetry, the content of which is *pechal'noe, chudesnoe, romanicheskoe, inogda zabavnoe.* Zhukovsky is mentioned as the Russian poet who had demonstrated the 'outstanding attractions of this genre'.

One year earlier excerpts from N. F. Ostolopov's *Slovar' drevnei i novoi poezii*, including one on the characteristics of the ballad, had been published in *Vestnik Evropy*. In 1821 the entire *Slovar'* was published; it contains a long article on the genre which begins with the derivation of the word 'ballad' and is followed by a discussion of the French *ballade* and by a definition of the German *Ballade* as a narrative about 'amorous or unfortunate adventures', always based on the *chudesnoe.* In the section on the Russiao *ballada*, Ostolopov needed to mention only one name, Zhukovsky. He quotes the entire text of *Svetlana*, and then lists the first stanzas of nine other ballads to demonstrate the variety of Zhukovsky's skills as a ballad-writer.

In 1822 N. I. Grech, in one of the first attempts at writing a history of Russian literature, referred to the ballad as a 'new genre', 'created by Zhukovsky'.[4] When in 1832 N. I. Nadezhdin surveyed the state of Russian poetry for the previous year and wrote that 'ballads . . . have replaced the ode as reigning genre', he was of course referring almost exclusively to Zhukovsky's achievement.[5] During the first few decades of the nineteenth century the ballad genre attained the popularity and the literary status which the ode had enjoyed during the mid-eighteenth century.

Belinsky's articles written during the 1840s show the most perceptive understanding of Zhukovsky's transformation of the ballad. In his series on Pushkin (1843) Belinsky describes the genre as it

[3] *Pravila stikhotvorstva, pocherpnutye iz teorii Eshenburga* (M., 1816).
[4] *Opyt kratkoi istorii russkoi literatury* (SPb., 1822), 304.
[5] *Teleskop*, VII (1832).

existed before Zhukovsky: 'a short story about love, usually unhappy; graves, crosses, ghosts, night-time, moonlight, and sometimes *domovye* and witches.'[6] Then he alludes to the 'deeper meaning' with which Zhukovsky had endowed his literary ballads, but does not elaborate. However, in an earlier article on poetic genres (1841) Belinsky's definition of the ballad clearly indicates his view of the transformation which Zhukovsky had effected: 'In the ballad the poet takes some sort of fantastic and popular legend, or he himself invents an episode of this kind. But the main feature in it is not the episode, but the experience (*oshchushchenie*), which it awakens, the thoughts which it suggests to the reader.'[7] Thus Belinsky implies that the 'deeper meaning' of Zhukovsky's ballads is contained in their total subjectivity: they all express private emotional experience shared by the poet with the reader.

Zhukovsky's own words demonstrate that he considered himself primarily as a ballad-writer. As early as 1813 he admitted in a letter to A. I. Turgenev: 'My chosen genre of poetry is the ballad.'[8] And in 1849, almost at the end of his literary career, he referred to himself in a letter to A. S. Sturdza as 'the father of German romanticism in Russia and the poetic uncle (*dyad'ka*) of German and English demons and witches'.[9]

The most famous portrait of Zhukovsky as a young poet painted by O. Kiprensky in 1815 and engraved by F. Vendramina two years later undoubtedly portrays him as a *balladnik*.[10] The background of stormy sky, steep cliffs, rough sea, wind-blown trees, and medieval castle is the typical setting of his literary ballads. The poet himself is pictured as a youthful, melancholy visionary with tousled hair, gazing into the distance.

Zhukovsky was virtually identified with his ballads by most of his contemporaries, poets and critics alike. Batyushov begins his *poslanie*, *K Zhukovskomu* (1812) with the lines: 'Prosti, balladnik moi,/ Beleva mirnyi zhitel'.' An anonymous review published in

[6] *PSS* VII (M., 1953–9), 167.

[7] *PSS* V. 51.

[8] *Russkii arkhiv* (M., 1895), 104.

[9] *Sochineniya V. A. Zhukovskogo*, VI (SPb., 1878), 541. In a similar vein, A. I. Turgenev, in his *Khronika russkogo* (1835), referring to Salvatore Vigano's ballet *Il noce di Benevento*, wrote: 'The ballet was an unbearable farce! There were more witches on stage than in Zhukovsky's ballads.'

[10] See Ts. S. Vol'pe, *V. A. Zhukovsky v portretakh i illyustratsiyakh* (L., 1935).

1821 of an anthology of verse contains a portrait of Zhukovsky with the inscription 'Germaniya! tvoya s toboyu chest':/ Na beregakh Nevy—Balladnik est' . . .' Belinsky, in the same article on Pushkin (1843), also states that it was Zhukovsky who created and established the genre of the ballad, and that contemporary readers thought of him almost exclusively as a *balladnik*.[12] In 1855 N. G. Chernyshevsky, referring to Zhukovsky's translations from Schiller, wrote that 'Zhukovsky interested his readers as a *balladnik*, and not as a translator of Schiller'.[13] Finally, an unintentionally amusing tribute to Zhukovsky was penned by Ieronim Trofimovsky, a pupil at the No. 2 Gymnasium in Kiev in 1883, Zhukovsky's jubilee year:

> Ты, кроткий Светланы прекрасной певец,
> Пел песни те с лирой унылой;
> Для нас незабвенный баллады творец,
> Давно уже скрытый могилой.[14]

What was it that attracted Zhukovsky to the genre of the ballad? The question is ultimately unanswerable, but several theories have been advanced. One postulates that the ballad offered the poet an escape from the subjectivity of his lyrics, since it enabled him to objectify lyrical situations and characters. This explanation was implied as early as 1825 by A. I. Galich, whose definition of the ballad is based on Zhukovsky's poetic practice: 'a romantic elegy in which the internal condition of the soul is expressed indirectly, namely by means of some story or adventure'.[15] All but the most superficial reading of the ballads eliminates this theory. Zhukovsky was not really interested in objective characters or events, in time or place, or even in the psychology of his heroes. Zhukovsky's ballads are an extension of his lyrical poetry: a lyrical effusion of the poet's soul.

It has also been suggested that Zhukovsky's choice of the ballad genre was related to a larger trend in Russian literature towards

[11] *Syn otechestva*, No. 13 (1821), 282–4. The anthology reviewed is *Karmannaya biblioteka Aonid* (SPb., 1821).

[12] *PSS* VII, 167.

[13] *PSS* II (M., 1949), 474.

[14] *Pamyati V. A. Zhukovskogo* (Kiev, 1883).

[15] *Opyt nauki izyashchnago* (SPb., 1825), section 189. See also N. Kovarsky, 'Poeziya Zhukovskogo', *Stikhotvoreniya i poemy*, *Biblioteka poeta*, *Malaya seriya* (L., 1958), intro.

narodnost'. According to this explanation, the ballad provided the poet with a means for expressing his interest in popular legends, beliefs, customs, and so forth. This theory, propounded by Yu. M. Lotman[16] and R. I. Iezuitova,[17] ignores several facts. Only three of Zhukovsky's forty ballads contain so-called 'Russian motifs'; the vast majority are translations from Western European sources; and 'Russification' in these translations is conventional and artificial. Lotman has also suggested that the length of the ballad could have provided Zhukovsky with the potential for more significant thematic statements than could either the lyric or the elegy.[18] However, some of the ballads are shorter than some of the lyrical poems, and both the *poslanie* and *povest'* also offered the possibility of writing a larger work.

Finally, N. V. Izmailov has suggested that Zhukovsky chose the ballad for thematic reasons: his sympathy for human suffering and man's compulsory submission to Fate caused him to reject the external world and create an ideal dream world of inner experience.[19] Izmailov has erroneously transformed Zhukovsky into a social critic who deliberately created the ballad genre in order to escape the horrors of nineteenth-century Russian reality. Zhukovsky was neither a Decembrist nor even a social critic; he spent a large part of his life at court, as tutor to the imperial family, and particularly to the future Alexander II.

There is reason to believe that the real explanation for Zhukovsky's choice of the ballad genre lies elsewhere. Firstly, the ballad was undergoing a revival throughout Western Europe, and was, for a time, the most popular genre in English and German poetry. Secondly, the ballad form was new, exciting, and exotic. It opened up a whole new world to the imagination: a world of nature and supernature; of strong passions, secret affairs, and extraordinary characters. The Russian memoirist F. F. Vigel' captures the novelty of the genre in his reminiscences:

Nourished on the classics and on French literature, and on submissive imitations of the same, . . . we saw something monstrous in his

[16] 'Problema narodnosti i puti razvitiya literatury preddekabristskogo perioda', in *O russkom realizme XIX veka i voprosy narodnosti literatury* (M.-L., 1960), 8–51.

[17] 'Iz istorii', 98 ff.

[18] 'Problema narodnosti', 40.

[19] *IRP* I, 246.

[Zhukovsky's] choices. Corpses, visions, demons, murders by moonlight; all this belongs to the *skazki* and even to English novels; instead of Hero awaiting his drowning Leander, he presented us a madly passionate Lenora with her galloping corpse of a lover! His [Zhukovsky's] miraculous talent was needed to force us not only to read the ballads without repugnance, but also, finally, to fall in love with them. I do not know if he spoiled our taste; but at least he created new sensations, new enjoyments for us. That was the beginning of our romanticism.[20]

An important component of the 'new sensations' was the Gothic element of fear and the pure emotional excitement of being frightened. Zhukovsky was not unaware of this new delight in fear; as an inscription in an album reveals:

Во вторник ввечеру
Я буду, если не умру
Иль не поссорюсь с Аполлоном,
Читать вам погребальным тоном,
Как ведьму черт унес,
И напугаю вас до слез.[21]

Belinsky describes the appeal of the ballads as 'some sort of sweetly-horrible pleasure, and the more they horrified us, the more passionately we read them'.[22]

In all probability it was the ballad's popularity in Western Europe, the novelty of its exotic world, and the delight in the emotional experience of fear which attracted Zhukovsky to the genre. The nature of his transformation of the literary ballad will emerge in the analysis of representative texts; but first let us look at Zhukovsky's theory of translation and an example of that theory put into practice.

Zhukovsky expressed his views on the principles of translation[23]

[20] *Zapiski*, III (M., 1891–3), 137.

[21] G. A. Gukovsky, *Pushkin i russkie romantiki* (M., 1965), 79.

[22] *PSS* V. 168. Compare Chapter VI in Jane Austin's *Northanger Abbey*: Isabella offers some new Gothic novels to Catherine, who asks excitedly: 'but are they all horrid, are you sure they are all horrid?'

[23] Zhukovsky as a translator has been the subject of considerable research. M. H. Volm in *W. A. Zhukowski als Übersetzer* (Ann Arbor, Mich., 1945–50) presents a detailed analysis of Zhukovsky's translations from Goethe. H. Eichstädt in *Žukovskij als Übersetzer* (Munich, 1970) studies his prose translations (1807–11), his Dorpat cycle of lyrics (1815–17), and his translation of Fouqué's *Undine* (1831–6).

at the beginning of his literary career in two critical articles and in a translation of a French work, all published in *Vestnik Evropy* (1809–10); close to the end of his life, in 1848 he once again set forth his ideas on the subject. Zhukovsky's basic aesthetic principles remained the same throughout his career. The only difference between his earlier and later statements is the more philosophical, almost mystical, language of the 1848 pronouncements.

One of Zhukovsky's first articles (1809) was devoted to the genre of the fable, and in particular to Krylov.[24] He begins with a brief discussion of Krylov's debt to La Fontaine, and then defines Krylov's originality as his ability to adapt the original author's thoughts, feelings, and genius, and to express all this in his own style. Then Zhukovsky develops his general views on translation, beginning with a motto which could well serve as a justification for his own poetic career: 'A translator of prose is a slave; a translator of verse is a rival.' Zhukovsky contrasts the 'poet-imitator', who is inspired by the actual model, with the 'original poet', who is inspired by 'an ideal contained within his own imagination'. Therefore the translator must have the same imagination, style, intelligence, and emotions as the creator of the original work. He must find in his own imagination the corresponding beauty to serve as a replacement for the original beauty, and it should be equal or even superior to it. Thus, according to Zhukovsky, the translator is a creator, and must possess talent equal in all respects to that of the original author.

This theory was further developed in Zhukovsky's review of S. Viskovatov's translation of P. J. de Crébillon's tragedy *Rhadamiste et Zénobie*.[25] The article begins with the bold assertion 'Only a poet can translate a poet' and goes on to condemn Viskovatov's poor attempt. Zhukovsky explains that to translate poetry, in addition to understanding rhyme, caesuras, grammar, and so forth, the translator must possess 'poetic talent', which is defined as 'the ability to imagine and feel vividly, combined with the ability to find in one's own language those expressions which would correspond to that which one feels and imagines'.[26] Zhukovsky once again emphasizes the originality of the translator as a 'creator of expressions'; he can create only if he is filled with the ideal of the

[24] *SS* IV (M.-L., 1959–60), 402–18.
[25] *PSS* IX (SPb., 1902), 122–8.
[26] Ibid. 122.

original work, which he then transforms into a creation of his own imagination. The final goal of the translator, then, is not a literal equivalent; rather it is to translate 'so that the translated verse produces the same total impression on the soul of the reader as does the original verse'.[27]

In 1810 Zhukovsky published a translation of an anonymous French article on the same subject.[28] The author of this article states categorically: 'I consider excessive fidelity [of a translation to its source] as excessive infidelity'; then he specifies some of the cases in which alterations are necessary to achieve the same effects in the translation as in the original. An example relevant to Zhukovsky's own work concerns the issue of local colour. If the original contains geographical details or references to the customs of a particular nation, this information is of interest only to that nation; such details would seem strange in a translation and must be avoided. The main responsibility of the translator is to 'produce that effect which the original produces'. The article concludes with some curious advice to aspiring translators—in order to partake of the sources of the original poet's inspiration, they should observe the natural landscape of that poet's native land. Thus the skilful translator must be well-travelled!

Such were Zhukovsky's views on the theory of translation in 1810, at the beginning of his literary career: the translator as creator, possessing talents equal to those of the original author; the translator as inspired by the ideal of the original, contained within his own imagination; and the translator trying to achieve the equivalent effect on the soul of the reader, rather than striving after a literal rendition.

In letters written to A. I. Turgenev in 1814 and 1816 Zhukovsky, by the same turn of phrase, as it were summarizes these views. In one letter, referring to his *Ballada o starushke* (1814), a translation of Southey's *Old Woman of Berkeley*, he wrote:

> Вчера родилась у меня еще баллада-приемыш, т.е. перевод с английского.[29]

[27] Ibid. 127.
[28] *Vestnik Evropy*, No. 3 (1810), 190–8.
[29] *Russkii arkhiv* (M., 1895), 128. (My underlining.)

In the other letter Zhukovsky refers to his lyric poem *Ovsyanyi kisel'* (1816), a translation of J. P. Hebel's *Das Habermuss:*

> Между тем написал, т.е. перевел с немецкого
> пиесу под титулом Овсяный кисель . . .[30]

After a life's work of writing, *i.e. translating*, poetry, Zhukovsky returned to his theory of translation in order to provide it with a philosophical foundation. In an article on *Faust* (1848)[31] he analyses the scene preceding the appearance of Mephistopheles, in which Faust attempts to rewrite the *Logos* passage from the Gospel of St. John, substituting for *Logos* the German words *Sinn*, *Kraft*, and *Tat*. Zhukovsky soundly disapproves of Faust's alternatives, asserting that no human mind could possibly conceive of anything more sublime or more encompassing than *Logos*. He defines the Russian *Slovo* as both a 'spiritual embodiment of thought', conceived at the same time as the thought, and as the 'material clothing of this spiritual embodiment', or the sound which expresses it. Then Zhukovsky lapses into 'proto-symbolist' mysticism: 'All our thoughts, unexpressed and expressed, separate and unified, are only fragments of something whole (*otryvki chego-to tselogo*) . . .'[32]

Zhukovsky's article entitled *On the Poet and his Contemporary Significance* (1848)[33] was intended as a reply to Gogol''s treatment of the 'word' in his *Correspondence with Friends* (1847). Zhukovsky borrows Pushkin's aphorism 'Slova poeta sut' uzhe dela ego' and elaborates on it. He starts with Rousseau's statement that 'Il n'y a de beau que ce qui n'est pas', which Zhukovsky interprets as implying that, although beauty exists, man can neither seize it nor understand it. Art is defined as the 'experience and expression of the beautiful', and the artist as a creator; the means of creation are the forms of art (poetry, music, painting), while the materials of creation are words, sounds, colours, and so forth. The poet's materials are words; Pushkin's aphorism, therefore, is substantiated.

These two articles, although concerned with the 'word' in general, really provide the foundation of Zhukovsky's theory of

30 Ibid. 164. (My underlining.)
31 *PSS* X, 124–8.
32 Ibid. 125.
33 Ibid. 80–8.

translation. The crucial importance of the 'word' for the poet-creator and the relationship between the 'word', the thought, and the 'something whole' underlie his earlier, more practical, pronouncements on the translation of verse.

Another of Zhukovsky's letters clearly summarizes the views expressed in these later articles. In February 1848 he wrote to Gogol':

> I have often noticed that I have my most lucid thoughts when I have to improvise them to express or to supplement others' thoughts. My intellect is like steel which must be struck against flint in order that a spark might leap out. In general that is the nature of my authorial work; almost everything of mine is either someone else's or apropos of someone else's; but it is still all mine.[34]

Additional evidence to substantiate the claim for the 'originality' of Zhukovsky's translations is provided by his method of publication and by the reactions of contemporary readers to his works. In preparing his poetry for publication, Zhukovsky rarely specified whether a given work was a translation from a foreign source, or whether it was an original composition. Furthermore his contemporaries received his translations as if they were original works, and in their reviews usually emphasized Zhukovsky's independence from his source.

In an article on Zhukovsky's translation of Byron's *Prisoner of Chillon*, Pletnov wrote: 'We even dare to state emphatically that to translate as Zhukovsky translates, is the same as creating.'[35] Bestuzhev, in his survey of Russian literature for 1823, noted: 'Many of Zhukovsky's translations are better than their originals, since euphony and versatility of language adorn the accuracy of his expression.'[36] In articles written in the early 1840s, Belinsky developed the same theme:

> They say that Zhukovsky has little of his own, that it is almost all translation: a mistaken opinion! Zhukovsky is a poet, and not a translator.[37]

[34] *Otchet imperatorskoi Publichnoi biblioteki za 1887 god* (SPb., 1890), 54.
[35] *Sorevnovatel' prosveshcheniya i blagotvoreniya*, No. 2 (1822), 220–1.
[36] *Polyarnaya zvezda* (1824), 23.
[37] *PSS* III. 508.

As children, having no clear idea as yet of what was a translation and what an original, we learned his renditions by heart as the *works of Zhukovsky*.[38]

Pletnev had the final say in his sketch of Zhukovsky's life and works:

Zhukovsky imparted to his translations the life and inspiration of their originals. Therefore each of his translations was accorded the value and force of an original composition. This original talent afforded him the means for transforming our literature.[39]

An example of Zhukovsky's theory of translation put into practice is his ballad *Rybak* (1818),[40] a translation of Goethe's *Der Fischer* (1778). The theme of Goethe's ballad is the irrational attraction of the natural elements and their power over rational beings. Although Goethe disparaged any attempts to analyse his work, *Der Fischer* is much plainer in rhythm and more complex in meaning than a simple folk ballad.[41] The fisherman can be seen as a symbol of rational self-sufficiency, of non-resistance to the fatal attraction of the elements, and perhaps of a narcissistic attraction to his own reflection. The mermaid's colloquial speech, the narrator's sophistication, the sensual imagery, and the hypnotic repetitions all contribute to the ballad's charm.

Zhukovsky's translation transforms Goethe's original into a very different work. In the first stanza Goethe's unemotional *ruhevoll* (peacefully, tranquilly) becomes *zadumchiv* (plunged in thought, reflection), one of Zhukovsky's most important emotional epithets. *Kühl bis ans Herz hinan* (implying spiritual serenity and rationality) is rendered as *dusha polna/ Prokhladnoi tishinoi*, in which the phrase *prokhladnaya tishina* attempts to combine the two German epithets *kühl* and *ruhevoll*. Goethe's *Und wie . . . er lauscht* (with its temporal conjunction and standard punctuation) is replaced by *Vdrug . . . pritikh . . .*: *vdrug* is Zhukovsky's favourite temporal adverb, most often used to interrupt the narrative, and usually

[38] *PSS* V. 548.

[39] *O zhizni i sochineniyakh V. A. Zhukovskogo* (SPb., 1853), 5. Blok, in a diary entry for 1920, indicates that his contemporaries still considered Zhukovsky as the "standard translator". Referring to M. Lozinsky's translations from Delille, he wrote: "Gumilev considers him a better translator than Zhukovsky." See Blok, *SS* VII (M.-L., 1963), 371.

[40] *Für Wenige—Dlya nemnogikh*, No. 1 (1818), 50.

[41] See R. Gray, *The Poems of Goethe* (Cambridge, 1966), 106.

followed by three dots to indicate expectation; *pritikh* returns to the motif of silence introduced in line 4 (*tishina*). Goethe's stanza ends with the words *rauscht/ Ein feuchtes Weib hervor* (the verb expresses the sound "rushing", and is repeated from line 1; *feuchtes Weib* is a poetic expression for mermaid). Zhukovsky's rendition, *I vlazhnaya vsplyla glavoi/Krasavitsa . . .*, employs a less forceful, more poetic verb, translates Goethe's *feuchtes* literally as *vlazhnaya*, and supplies the more literary *krasavitsa* to identify the mermaid.

In the second stanza *Sie sang zu ihm, sie sprach zu ihm* is rendered as *Glyadit ona, poet ona*: instead of 'speaking', Zhukovsky's mermaid will 'sing' her fifteen lines. Her monologue contains numerous epithets which are introduced by Zhukovsky and which have no equivalents in Goethe's original. Zhukovsky translates *Todesglut* as *kipuchii zhar*, and then combines *rodnoe* + *dno* to form its opposite, probably by analogy with *rodnaya strana* or *zemlya*. The colloquial speech of Goethe's mermaid (*wie's Fischlein ist/ So wohlig*) is replaced by the neutral expression *Kak rybkoi zhit'/ Privol'no*. The second stanza ends with another of Zhukovsky's unusual combinations, *znoinaya vyshina*, a synonym for *kipuchii zhar*, both of which are in contrast to the fish's *rodnoe dno* and to the fisherman's *prokhlada*.

The syntax of Goethe's third stanza is varied (*nicht* occurs in initial, medial, and final positions) and the word order is reasonably logical. Zhukovsky's syntax is monotonous: the negative particle is fixed in the initial position; the word order, however, leads to some confusion. Goethe's epithet *feuchverklärte Blau* is rendered as *prokhladno-goluboi*: Zhukovsky avoids the idea of moisture, returns to the motif of *prokhlada*, and invents a compound epithet combining temperature and colour, but with vague spiritual overtones. He ignores Goethe's other, more difficult epithet *wellenatmend*.

The final stanza of the German original begins with a vivid sensual image: *Netzt' ihm den nackten Fuss*; Zhukovsky's modesty was probably responsible for his abstract, poetic replacement: *Na bereg val plesnul!* The exclamatory intonation not only of this line, but of the entire fourth stanza, and the use of three dots in lines 1 and 7, replace Goethe's declarative intonation and standard punctuation. The order of the clauses in line 5 is the reverse of that in the second stanza (*Sie sprach zu ihm, sie sang zu ihm*); Goethe's mermaid 'sings' to lure the fishermen into the sea. Zhukovsky's mermaid is still 'singing' (*Ona poet, ona manit*), and the second verb demonstrates his propensity to make the meaning more explicit, to explain rather than to depict. Line 7 in the original is another vivid physical image (*Halb zog sie ihn, halb sank er hin*), which contains the complex resolution of Goethe's theme, namely, the fisherman enters the sea, partly dragged by the mermaid and partly of his own free will. Zhukovsky's abstract version (*K nemu ona, on k nei bezhit*) lacks the force of the German and resembles a conventional meeting of two lovers.

This juxtaposition of one of Zhukovsky's translations with its original source indicates that his poetic practice conforms in full to his own theory of translation. Inspired by some ideal of the original in his own imagination, Zhukovsky creates an equivalent work rather than a literal rendition. But the original is not replaced by some objectively equivalent imagination, style, intelligence, and emotion, but rather by Zhukovsky's own individual interpretation of the original, influenced by his criteria of good taste, and expressed in his own subjective language. For example, he freely alters the epithets of his source, combining, eliminating, or inventing others as he pleases. He introduces elaborate verbal leitmotivs (*tishina, prokhlada*). His syntax is characterized by parallelism, exclamatory and interrogative intonation, and inverted word order; the action is frequently interrupted by dots, dashes, and temporal adverbs (*vdrug*). Concrete images of the original ballad become generalized in translation; physical, sensual ones become abstract and poetical. The colloquial tone of certain passages is transmuted into one that is neutral or elevated; themes are made more explicit in some cases, and in others the sense is sacrificed for the total emotional effect.

One can only speculate on the impression which Zhukovsky's translations made on his readers; what is clear both from this comparison of source with translation and from the testimony of his contemporaries is that Zhukovsky was not a 'translator' in the ordinary sense of the word. He created original works, equivalents of foreign sources, and his contemporaries were justified in perceiving those works as original creations.

Throughout his literary career, Zhukovsky's principles and practice of translation never altered. His techniques evolved as he gained more experience and greater linguistic facility. His later translations and revisions of earlier ones tend to be more accurate with respect to the source, although this is not always the case. In 1831, for example, Zhukovsky retranslated Bürger's *Lenore*, which he had rendered in 1808 as *Lyudmila*. The manuscript of the second translation demonstrates how difficult it was for the poet to get any closer to the German original. Compare the following versions of the heroine's rhetorical question in the first stanza:

Lenore	(1773):	Bist untreu, Wilhelm, oder tot? Wie lange whilst du säumen?
Lyudmila	(1808):	Где ты, милый? Что с тобой? С чужеземною красою, Знать, в далекой стороне Изменил, неверный, мне; Иль безвременно могила Светлый взор твой угасила.
Lenora—MS.	(1831):	О милый! Где ты? Что с тобой? Придет ли весть о друге?[42]
Lenora—pub.	(1831):	Где милый? Что с ним? Жив ли он? И верен ли подруге?

Both the manuscript and the final published version of the new translation bear a stronger resemblance to Zhukovsky's own *Lyudmila* than to Bürger's *Lenore*. Any 'translation' by Zhukovsky must indeed be considered as the creation of an original poet.

Zhukovsky wrote forty literary ballads between 1808 and 1833. Of these, twenty-two were translated from German sources: two each from Bürger and Goethe, and nine each from Schiller and Uhland. Eleven ballads were translated from English sources: one each from Goldsmith, Mallet, and Campbell; two from Scott, and six from Southey. One ballad was translated from a French source: F. A. de Moncriff. Of the remaining six so-called 'original' ballads: *Svetlana* is a reworking of Bürger's *Lenore*; *Akhill* is strongly influenced by Schiller's Trojan cycle; *Eolova arfa* may have originated as a translation from another of Bürger's ballads; *Gromoboi* and *Vadim* are based on a novel by the German author C. H. Speiss; and *Uznik* has its source in an elegy by Chénier.

In addition to the forty ballads, Zhukovsky also translated from balladic sources and employed balladic techniques in other genres. Among his lyrics, *Teon i Eskhin* (1814) is an original balladic

[42] GPB-286; 1; 30; 61.

elegy; *Tri putnika* (1820) is a translation of Uhland's balladic *Der Wirtin Töchterlein*; and *Nochnoi smotr* (1836) is a translation of J. C. F. von Zedlitz's *Die nächtliche Heerschau.* Among Zhukovsky's *povesti, Perchatka* (1831) is a translation of Schiller's ballad *Der Handschuh,*[43] and *Dve byli i eshche odna* (1831) includes translations of two Southey ballads, *Mary, the Maid of the Inn* and *Jaspar*. Zhukovsky's early prose tale *Mar'ina roshcha* (1809) also employs balladic techniques and language.

Eight representative literary ballads from Zhukovsky's corpus will be examined with reference to their subject, characters, setting, theme, and style. The choice has been made on the following basis: firstly, in order to illustrate Zhukovsky's treatment of different foreign sources, ballads based on original works by Bürger, Schiller, Southey, and Scott were selected; secondly, ballads have been chosen from the most prolific and influential period of Zhukovsky's career (1808–22); and thirdly, the selection is intended to display the variety of Zhukovsky's innovations in the content and style of the Russian literary ballad.

Zhukovsky's first ballad *Lyudmila* (1808) created something of the same excitement in Russia that Bürger's *Lenore* (1773) had caused in Germany and later in England.[44] Zhukovsky's version was finished in April 1808 and published in *Vestnik Evropy*[45] with the sub-title *Russkaya ballada* and with the note: *Podrazhanie Birgerovoi Leonore* [*sic*]. The sub-title and the note demonstrate the twofold importance of *Lyudmila*: the former established the genre of the Russian literary ballad as an original form of poetry; and the latter indicated that the content of this first ballad was derivative, being an 'imitation' of a Western European work adapted for Russian readers.

The ballad begins with a description of the heroine's anxiety at her lover's long absence in the war. When the men return, Lyudmila's *milyi* is not among them. She laments her fate and

[43] Schiller's poem was also translated by Lermontov as *Perchatka* (1829); see below, Ch. VIII, p. 167.

[44] Gogol''s *Mertvye dushi* (Ch. VIII) contains the following passage: 'Many [of the townspeople] were not without education: the chairman of the chamber knew Zhukovsky's *Lyudmila* by heart, which was then still a great novelty, and he brilliantly recited many places, especially: *Bor zasnul, dolina spit*, and the word *chu!* so that it actually looked as if the valley was asleep; for greater verisimilitude he even shut his eyes.'

[45] No. 9 (1808), 41.

rejects her mother's religious consolation. Late that night her lover returns to claim his sweetheart and to carry her off to their bridal bed. They ride through the night and arrive in the morning at their destination: the lover turns out to be a corpse, and his home a grave. The ballad ends with Lyudmila's death, presented as proof of God's justice.

Although the subject of *Lyudmila* and *Lenore* is basically the same, Zhukovsky's 'imitation' contains numerous deviations from the original which both illuminate his method of adapting foreign sources and demonstrate the most typical characteristics of his literary ballads. Bürger's *Lenore* begins with a reference to a particular historical setting: the hero had gone off to fight with the Prussian army against the Austrians at the Battle of Prague (1757). The armistice and the victorious homecomings of both armies are treated satirically. In contrast, Zhukovsky's *Lyudmila* has no definite period or location. The situation is abstract and generalized, in spite of a vague hint at Old Russian local colour (*rat'*, *druzhina*).

Bürger's characters are called Lenore and Wilhelm: the heroine demonstrates genuine courage; her dramatic lament begins and ends with violent physical gestures (tearing her hair, throwing herself to the ground, and beating her breast). The hero is presented as a real man of action whose few utterances are terse and rapid. In contrast, Zhukovsky's heroine is given the Slavonic name Lyudmila and is transformed into a sentimental, melancholy character. The narrator describes her in the first stanza with verbs which express emotion, not action: *priunyv*, *vzdykhala*, *mechtala*. Her physical gestures differ considerably from those of Bürger's heroine: *K persyam ochi prekloniv* (1: 7) and *Tikho v terem svoi idet,/ Tomnu golovu sklonila* (3: 8–9).[46] Whereas Lenore rants and raves against her cruel fate, Lyudmila accepts hers and submits to its decrees. Unlike Bürger, Zhukovsky intervenes directly in the narrative to express his emotional sympathy for the heroine:

Где ж, Людмила, твой герой?
Где твоя, Людмила, радость?
Ах! прости, надежда-сладость!
Все погибло: друга нет. (3: 4–7)

[46] Cf. the phrases *golovu tomno sklonyaet* and *tomno idet* from Turchaninova's ballad *Leonard i Blondina*.

The alternation of interrogative and exclamatory intonation in this passage is repeated in Lyudmila's extended lament. Zhukovsky's hero is transformed into an anonymous melancholy character, referred to only as *milyi*, whose speech, even to his horse, is saturated with sentimentality:

Конь, мой конь, бежит песок;
Чую ранний ветерок;
Конь, мой конь, быстрее мчися;
Звезды утренни зажглися,
Месяц в облаке потух.
Конь, мой конь, кричит петух. (17: 7–12)

The lament in Bürger's ballad is based on a series of symmetrical alternations between mother and daughter, gradually increasing in length as the statements become more serious.[47] Zhukovsky dispenses with both the symmetry and the gradual expansion, and greatly reduces the number of lines spoken by the mother.[48] While she expresses herself almost entirely in aphorisms, Lyudmila echoes elegiac motifs from Zhukovsky's lyrics. The syntax of the lament also recalls that of the lyrics in its alternation of interrogative and exclamatory intonation, its use of rhetorical questions, negative constructions, repetition, and parallelism.

The lament is followed by the dramatic midnight appearance of the lover. Bürger has only three lines of transition in which he describes the sunset and nightfall. Zhukovsky expands the transition to nineteen lines (7: 9–9: 3); the passage contains no fewer than thirteen epithets.[49] These epithets, characterized by their emotional overtones, inundate the reader's senses with a multitude of vague visual and aural impressions in order to create a mood of uncanny mystery.

Bürger's midnight ride is famous for its dramatic sound effects: *trapp trapp trapp; klinglingling; hurre hurre hop hop hop*; and so on. Zhukovsky's ride, reduced from 104 to 83 lines, has no equivalent onomatopoeic expressions. Furthermore, the dynamic description

[47] Schematically, let M = mother, L = Lenore, number = lines spoken: M-2, L-4, M-4, L-4, M-4, L-4, M-8, L-8, M-8, L-8. Totals: M 26; L 28.

[48] Schematically, let M = mother, L = Lyudmila, number = lines spoken: M-3, L-9, M-4, L-14, M-6, L-8. Totals: M 13; L 31.

[49] *Spokoinyi, mrachnyi (bis), velichavyi, tikhii, dlinnyi, dremuchii, zybkii, dalekii, svetlyi, otdalennyi, polunochnyi, pereletnyi.*

in stanzas 14–15, which contains no epithets but numerous verbs, is not original but a literal translation of Bürger's stanzas 19–20.

Bürger introduces his refrain in stanza 17: 6, 'Wir und die Toten reiten schnell', which is repeated with increasing frequency to heighten the dramatic tension.[50] Zhukovsky introduces his refrain in stanza 15: 2, 'Mertvyi s devitseyu mchitsya', and it is repeated only once, in 17: 2. Its meaning anticipates the climax of the ballad and consequently lessens the dramatic tension. Neither Bürger's weird funeral procession (stanza 21) nor the haunting dirge (stanza 22) has any equivalent in Zhukovsky's version. Whereas the grotesque transformation of Wilhelm into a skeleton is graphically depicted in *Lenore*, Zhukovsky's description is expressed in his favourite epithets:

Видит труп оцепенелый;
Прям, недвижим, посинелый
Длинным саваном обвит. (20: 1–3)

The moral of Bürger's ballad is fairly straightforward: 'Mit Gott im Himmel hadre nicht!' (32: 6), which refers back to Lenore's transgression as defined earlier by her mother: 'Sie fuhr mit Gottes Vorsehung/ Vermessen fort zu hadern' (12: 3–4). Bürger implies that whether God is just or unjust one must accept his will with forbearance ('Geduld! Geduld!'). Lenore would not; therefore she was punished.

Zhukovsky's conclusion is more difficult to interpret:

Смертных ропот безрассуден;
Царь всевышний правосуден;
Твой услышал стон Творец;
Час твой бил, настал конец. (21: 9–12)

The poet implies that protest is imprudent because God is unquestionably just; therefore his will must be accepted. Rather than a punishment, Lyudmila's death seems to be a release from her sufferings, granted by a merciful Creator.

Thus while Zhukovsky's *Lyudmila* is in fact an 'imitation' of Bürger's *Lenore*, the differences are far more important than the superficial similarity of the subject. Zhukovsky's generalization of time and place, his sentimental heroine and her melancholy *milyi*, the modifications in the lament, the descriptive transition, the ride,

[50] See lines 20: 6, 24: 6, 27: 6, 28: 7.

the refrain, and the concluding moral lesson demonstrate the degree to which Zhukovsky deviated from his original source. The greatest contrast between the two works lies in the style of each. Bürger's colloquialisms, conversational expressions, vivid physical descriptions, and dynamic verbs are replaced by Zhukovsky's literary syntax and vocabulary, particularly by an increase in the use of emotional epithets. There are few traces of popular language in either dialogue or description.[51]

An entry in one of Zhukovsky's early notebooks provides an interesting perspective on his attitude towards Bürger. First he praises both the tone and the simple narrative in his ballads; then he continues with a list of Bürger's other virtues, including 'his successful use of popular expressions both in descriptions and in the expression of feelings; brevity and vividness; simplicity and variety in his rhythms'.[52] He also approves of Bürger's depiction of the *uzhasnoe*, which results from his successful description of *mrachnye* subjects and themes. Zhukovsky contrasts Bürger's style with that of Schiller; he finds Schiller's style less 'picturesque' than Bürger's, less 'colloquial', and far more 'poetic'. He concludes: 'Schiller is more the philosopher, and Bürger—the simple narrator, who, occupied with his own subject, does not concern himself with anything peripheral.'[53]

There is a significant disparity between these theoretical views on Bürger and Zhukovsky's poetic practice. The qualities which he praises in Bürger's style are precisely those which he so radically altered or eliminated in his ballad *Lyudmila*. Furthermore, in spite of his professed admiration for Bürger and his disdain for Schiller, during his lifetime Zhukovsky translated only one ballad from Bürger and nine from Schiller.[54] In spite of these critical views, the poet in Zhukovsky recognized that the subjects and style of Schiller's ballads were more suited to his own taste.

[51] Examples are rare; the colloquial forms *skokom*, *znat'*, and *krasa* occur, as do the conversational *bryaknulo kol'tso* and *bukh v nee i s sedokom*. In one copy of the ballad written in Masha Protasova's hand, the original *bukh* is crossed out and replaced by the more literary *pryg* in Zhukovsky's own hand (GPB-286; 1; 20; 1).

[52] K. K. Zeidlits, *Zhizn' i poeziya V. A. Zhukovskogo, 1783–1852* (SPb., 1883), 39.

[53] Ibid. 40.

[54] In 1805–6 Zhukovsky translated a short excerpt from Bürger's ballad *Lenardo und Blandine*. See below, on *Eolova arfa*, pp. 64–6.

Schiller became one of Zhukovsky's most important models in the creation of the Russian ballad genre.

Bürger's *Lenore* also provided the impetus for Zhukovsky's *Svetlana* (1808–12).[55] This ballad, a very free reworking of its original source, was one of Zhukovsky's most popular and most influential works. During the 1810s the poet was continually referred to by his contemporaries as 'the creator of *Svetlana*'; during the 1820s, as criticism of his poetry and his politics increased, even the most ardent Decembrists approved of *Svetlana*, considering it Zhukovsky's most *narodnyi* ballad. And it was *Svetlana* which exerted the strongest influence on Pushkin, particularly apparent in *Evgenii Onegin* and *Metel'*.[56]

The ballad has been the subject of considerable research by Soviet scholars. The most detailed analysis is that of Iezuitova, who considers it proof of Zhukovsky's 'profound interest' in Russian folklore, namely rituals, superstitions, and legends. As evidence of this new interest she quotes Zhukovsky's letter to A. P. Zontag, written in 1816 (i.e. three years after the publication of *Svetlana*), in which he asked that he be sent Russian *skazki* and legends.[57] But when Iezuitova investigates the immediate sources of Zhukovsky's folkloric material, she rejects I. P. Lupanova's suggestion that the *skazka* is the basis of *Svetlana*,[58] since it is not clear how Zhukovsky had access to *skazki* until 1816. Similarly, Iezuitova rejects the influence of traditional Russian folk ballads, since Zhukovsky could not have had any models to imitate. Her theory is that the manuscript plans for *Svetlana* show definite borrowings of detail and diction from the works of M. Chulkov; she admits, however, that it has never been established that Zhukovsky actually knew Chulkov's collections.

The earliest manuscript plan of the ballad, first called *Svyatki*, is a simple enumeration of the main scenes.[59] It deviates from Bürger's original in its inclusion of the heroine's dream; but, unlike the final version, the dream here turns out to be true and the ballad was to end tragically. The happy ending was introduced in a later manuscript plan called *Gadan'e*, which is a detailed, stanza-

[55] *Vestnik Evropy*, No. 1–2 (1813), 67.

[56] See below, Ch. VII, pp. 145–8.

[57] 'Iz istorii', 318.

[58] *Russkaya narodnaya skazka v tvorchestve pisatelei pervoi poloviny XIX veka* (Petrozavodsk, 1959), 285–336.

[59] GPB-286; 1; 78; 10.

by-stanza, summary of the action.[60] Iezuitova, who ignores the earlier plan, compares the later plan to Chulkov's chapter on fortune-telling in his *ABC of Russian superstitions* (1786),[61] and finds close similarities in the description of the mirror divination; she also discovered that the *podblyudnaya pesenka* in *Svetlana* (1:9–14) was borrowed from Chulkov's *Sobranie raznykh pesen* (1770–4).

Other critics emphasize different aspects of the ballad. N. V. Izmailov pays particular attention to Zhukovsky's philosophical optimism as reflected in *Svetlana*, citing the intervention of beneficent forces which supply a happy solution to the tragic subject.[62] On the other hand, Gukovsky emphasizes the playfulness of the work, arguing that it has no real theme, and is nothing more than an invented fairy-tale.[63] Ts. S. Vol'pe suggests the most interesting interpretation.[64] He maintains that in *Svetlana* Zhukovsky applied the principles of parody to the poetics of the Gothic ballad, and that by setting the frightening tale within the framework of a dream he created a parody of his own *Lyudmila*, and thus a parody of the whole literary ballad genre.

It must be admitted that the *narodnost'* of *Svetlana* has been overemphasized; in fact, it is limited to a very few stylistic elements and folk motifs. Zhukovsky uses diminutive forms (*podruzhen'ka*, *slovechko*, *legokhon'ko*), colloquial expressions (*vraz*, *krasa*), and folk epithets in a conscious attempt at stylization of folklore. The epithets occur primarily in the first stanza, relating specifically to the fortune-telling (*yaryi vosk*, *chistaya voda*, *zolotoi persten'*, *belyi plat*), and again in the hero's speech in the seventh stanza (*shirokii dvor*, *tesovye vorota*, *shelkovy povoda*). *Belyi* is employed most frequently as a folk epithet with such substantives as *plat*, *pelena*, *zapona*, *polotno*, and *golubochek*, and in the compound form *belosnezhnyi golubok*. The popular motifs which appear in *Svetlana* include the fortune-telling, the song (stanza 2), the description of the church (stanza 9), the *chernyi vran* (stanza 10), and the dove (stanza 13).

Certainly there are more *narodnyi* elements in *Svetlana* than in *Lyudmila*, or, for that matter, than in any of Zhukovsky's other

[60] GPB-286; 1; 78; 10.
[61] See above, Ch. I. p. 15.
[62] *IRP* I. 248.
[63] *Pushkin i russkie romantiki*, 71.
[64] Zhukovsky, *Stikhotvoreniya*, I (L., 1936), xvii.

literary ballads. But the *narodnost'*, which may conceivably be derived from Chulkov, is stylized and conventional. Folkloric language is restricted to the expression of the few folkloric motifs. Most of *Svetlana* is written in Zhukovsky's individual literary style at its most original because there was no foreign model in immediate proximity to restrain him.

Zhukovsky's heroine is described as 'molchaliva i grustna/ Milaya Svetlana', epithets which characterize a sentimental heroine, certainly not a folk heroine.[65] Svetlana's timidity (*robost'*) is her most emphasized 'spiritual' trait.[66] This characteristic is demonstrated in her acceptance of Fate and in her gentle apostrophes to her guardian angel: 'Mne sud'bina umeret'/ V grusti odinokoi' (3: 3–4) and 'Utoli pechal' moyu,/ Angel uteshitel'' (3: 13–14), both of which replace Lenore's *Hader* and Lyudmila's milder *ropot* against God's providence. The hero's remark to Svetlana, 'Tvoi uslyshan ropot' (6: 14), is illogical since there has been no *ropot*. Zhukovsky himself was right when he admitted in the nineteenth stanza that his ballad contains *ochen' malo skladu*. The poet's sympathy for the heroine is obvious from the very beginning of the ballad (*milaya Svetlana*, 2: 4), and in the various apostrophes to her: 'Akh! Svetlana, chto s toboi!/ V ch'yu zashla obitel'?' (12: 5–6), and 'Chto zhe tvoi, Svetlana, son,/ Proritsatel' muki?' (18: 1–2).

The hero of *Svetlana* is characterized by the epithets *blednyi* and *unylyi* (8: 14, 9: 14). He is the perfect sentimental hero, whose summons to his Svetlana ('Radost', svet moikh ochei/ Net dlya nas razluki', 7: 3–4) provides a striking contrast to Wilhelm's first words to his Lenore ('Holla, holla! Tu auf, mein kind!', 14: 1). Zhukovsky's thoughtful hero also describes to his bride-to-be the elaborate arrangements made for their formal church wedding (stanza 7).

The atmosphere in *Svetlana* is created in part by the frequent repetition of the word *strakh* in its various forms: *strashno* (5: 10,

[65] This line is, of course, the source of Lensky's description of Tat'yana to Onegin in III: 5:

'Скажи: которая Татьяна?'
'Да та, которая грустна,
И молчалива, как Светлана,
Вошла и села у окна.'

[66] See lines 5: 3, 5: 9, 6: 5, 8: 10, and 12: 14.

15: 6), *strakh* (5: 11, 6: 9), *strashnyi* (11: 7, 12: 6–7, 13: 6, 20: 1); this makes the horror of the story explicit, rather than demonstrating it implicitly. The dramatic tension which reaches its climax in stanza 15 is suddenly released in the final verb:

Снова бледность на устах;
В закатившихся глазах
    Смерть изобразилась . . .
Глядь, Светлана . . . о Творец!
Милый друг ее—мертвец!
    Ах! . . . и пробудилась.

With this verb the *strakh*, *uzhas*, and *mrak* dissipate momentarily; light and the sounds of morning flood the senses (*Vse blestit*). Just as one of Svetlana's friends predicted (stanza 4), her *milyi* returns to her. The amorous delights which await her are described in conventional eighteenth-century language: *priyatny vzory*, *sladostnye usta*, *mily razgovory*, and *vernye obety*.

Zhukovsky's epilogue places the whole subject in its proper perspective. The ballad is indeed frightening, but it is only a bad dream, the creation of poetic fantasy, full of *bol'shie chudesa* (19: 3). *Svetlana* is Bürger's *Lenore* and Zhukovsky's *Lyudmila* turned upside down, mocked, or parodied. Zhukovsky concludes with his usual moral, 'Vera v providen'e' (19: 11), but it is of little importance. The meaningful experience has been in the contrast between two moods: between the loneliness, anticipation, and terror of the dream world, and the 'clarity', 'pleasures', and 'brightness' (stanza 20) of the real world which promises love and happiness for all.

Svetlana is one of Zhukovsky's most original works. In spite of its conventional *narodnyi* language and stylized motifs, the poet succeeds in producing a balladic atmosphere of fear and mystery within the dream framework. Zhukovsky demonstrated that he was the undisputed master of the Russian literary ballad, who could both create its *strakh* and write a brilliant parody of it.[67]

[67] In *Lyubovnaya karusel'* (1814), originally sub-titled *Tul'skaya ballada*, Zhukovsky, in a poem for and about his nieces, wrote another playful parody of the ballad form not unlike *Svetlana:*

—О милый! милый! что с тобой?—
  Катоша закричала.
—Так, ничего, дружочек мой,
  Мне в горло кость попала!

Lyudmila and *Svetlana*, both originating in Bürger's *Lenore*, are among Zhukovsky's most successful ballads. Less successful are two translations from other sources, both written in 1813: *Adel'stan* and *Ivikovy zhuravli*. A critical analysis of these ballads must consider Zhukovsky's transformation of the original themes, his character description, and his creation of atmosphere.

Adel'stan[68] is a translation of the English ballad *Rudiger* (1796), in which Robert Southey employed a subject discovered earlier by Thomas Heywood and recorded in the latter's notes to *Hierarchies of the Blessed Angels* (1635); this, in turn, probably represents an English version of the German Lohengrin theme. Zhukovsky replaced the original title with an archaic Anglo-Saxon name, possibly because a certain Russian General Fedor Vasil'evich Rudiger was participating in campaigns in Germany and France at about the same time as the ballad was published.[69]

The action takes place near a castle on the Rhine. A swan tows a small boat up the river, carrying the Knight Adel'stan to a castle. He soon wins the love of the beautiful Lora. They marry and she gives birth to a child, but Adel'stan mysteriously postpones the baptism. He takes his wife and child on to the river, and attempts to sacrifice the child to the evil powers: but Lora appeals for divine intervention: Adel'stan is suddenly swept away into the abyss and the child is saved.

In their article on Zhukovsky's early translations from Southey, K. H. and W. U. Ober argue that Zhukovsky turns Southey's abstractions into sharply defined images. As examples they cite Southey's descriptions of the twilight, which becomes Zhukovsky's *Den' bagryanil*, his 'castle walls' which become *zubchaty steny*, and his 'damp mist' which becomes *sedeet/ Mgla syraya*.[70] They also point to the 'delicious bathos' in Zhukovsky's version of Lora's announcement that she is with child. Southey's original is: 'And Margaret her Rudiger/ Hail'd with a father's name' (15: 3–4), which Zhukovsky translates as 'Ulybayas', vozveshchaet/ Drugu Lora: "Ty otets!" ' (16: 3–4).

In fact, Zhukovsky's images are no more concrete than those in Southey's original; furthermore, the Obers overlooked a much more important difference between the source and the translation.

68 *Vestnik Evropy*, No. 3–4 (1813), 212.
69 K. H. and W. U. Ober, 'Žukovskij's Early Translations', 183.
70 Ibid. 184–5.

In Zhukovsky's manuscript and in the first published version in *Vestnik Evropy* (1813) Adel'stan succeeds in hurling his child into the waiting arms of the evil spirit:

Нет спасения! губитель
В бездну бросил уж дитя.

И дитя, виясь, стенало,
В грозных сжатое когтях . . .[71]

This conclusion, the invention of Zhukovsky's fantasy, was later reworked to bring it into closer agreement with Southey's original:

The mother holds her precious babe;
But the black arms clasp'd him round,
And dragg'd the wretched Rudiger
Adown the dark profound. (45)

И воскликнула: Спаситель!
Глас достигнул к небесам:
Жив младенец, а губитель
Ниспровергнут в бездну сам. (44)

Zhukovsky's 'translation' also emphasizes the strong supernatural element: the *ocharovannaya lad'ya* which appears with its folkloric *belyi lebed'* and *alyi parus* to bring the knight to the castle, then reappears to carry off Adel'stan, Lora, and the child. The hero of the ballad is also described as *ocharovannyi*. Although he appears to be the embodiment of physical and spiritual perfection, his soul is troubled: he seems *odinok i molchaliv*, *bezmolvno i unylo*, *sumrachen dushoyu*, *pechal'nyi*, and so on. The explanation for his spiritual discontent is provided only in the climax, when Adel'stan confesses that he had previously concluded a Faustian pact with the devil: 'Ya uzhasnoyu tsenoyu/ Za blazhenstvo zaplatil' (36: 3–4).[72] The heroine Lora is hardly described at all: she is *nezhnaya* and *robkaya*—nothing more.

The description of the setting for the last journey in the 'charmed boat' contains all the necessary components of balladic atmosphere: it is late (*Vot uzh pozdno*, 24: 1; *Pozdno milyi*, 26: 1, 28: 1); dark (*Cheren bereg opustelyi*, 24: 3; *temnyi luch*, 32: 4); moonlit (*Mesyats bleden*, 28: 3); cold (*Kholodeet veterok*, 24: 4; *S vod kholodnyi veter veet*, 26: 3); damp (*Mgla syraya*, 26: 2; *syro v*

[71] GPB-286; 1; 14; 119.
[72] Zhukovsky treated this same theme in *Gromoboi* (1810); see below, p. 67.

pole, 28: 3); and quiet (*oni*, *bezmolvny*, 33: 1; *Tikho pleshchut*, 33: 3; *I na berege molchanie*, 34: 1). The balladic mood is summarized in one stanza, which includes a series of Zhukovsky's favourite epithets to emphasize the *strakh*:

Страшен берег обнаженный;
Нет ни жила, ни древес;
Черен, дик, уединенный,
В стороне стоит утес. (39)

Zhukovsky's *Adel'stan*, as generalized and as abstract as *Rudiger*, is, nevertheless, noteworthy for the first version of the conclusion (which totally altered the meaning of the original), for the style of the descriptions of the hero, and for the atmosphere of the night journey, the latter two expressed primarily in epithets. *Adel'stan* can be considered a typical representative of Zhukovsky's translations from Southey.

The other ballad written in 1813, *Ivikovy zhuravli*,[73] is a translation of Schiller's *Die Kraniche des Ibykus* (1797). It was Goethe who first discovered the subject and who then offered it to Schiller as the basis for a friendly competition in ballad composition.[74] It is based on a Greek legend: Ibycus, while making his way to Athens, is attacked by robbers. He calls upon a passing flock of cranes to avenge his untimely death. Later, at an open assembly in Athens, the cranes appear overhead, and one of the murderers involuntarily cries out, 'Behold the avengers of Ibycus!' thus giving away their crime. Schiller reworked the Greek myth into a philosophical statement about the influence of aesthetic experience on the human soul. His murderers are spectators at a performance of Aeschylus's *Eumenides*, and it is the catharsis engendered by the tragedy which causes them to blurt out their confession. In the sixth and seventh stanzas Schiller paraphrases the chorus in the tragedy which precedes the entrance of Athena.[75] Thus the idea of revenge is relegated to a position of secondary importance; of primary importance is the power of art over the soul.

Zhukovsky's *Ivikovy zhuravli* is a good example of his complete transformation of a classical theme. He failed to take into con-

[73] *Vestnik Evropy*, No. 3 (1814).

[74] Unfortunately, Goethe never used the subject for a ballad.

[75] C. E. Passage, 'The Influence of Schiller in Russia, 1800–1840', *Am SEER* V, No. 12–13 (1946), 123.

sideration the complex philosophical implications of Schiller's ballad, and substituted instead a simple story of revenge, accompanied by his usual moral: God sees the truth, and vice is punished. Zhukovsky neither recognized the passage modelled on Aeschylus nor employed the classical concept of catharsis and its role in the theory of tragedy.

The hero is transformed from a classical poet into a romantic bard, from Schiller's *Götterfreund* and *des Gottes voll*, to Zhukovsky's *skromnyi drug bogov* and *vdokhnovennyi*. Ibycus possesses both a *prekrasnoe litso* and a *krylataya mechta*, neither of which has any equivalent in the original German. His apostrophe to the cranes:

Сказав: прости! родной стране,
Чужого брега посетитель,
Ищу приюта, как и вы; (3: 4–6)

and his dying words ('I tak pogibnu v tsvete let', 5: 4–8) are typical of the language of Zhukovsky's elegies. The narrator's reference to Fate (4: 6), never mentioned in Schiller's original, introduces another of Zhukovsky's standard themes. The atmosphere of the ballad is created by the use of characteristic verbal motifs: *strakh* (13: 3, 15: 6) and *tishina* (12: 7, 12: 8, 18: 4, 18: 5, 20: 4).

The climax of the ballad occurs in stanza 22. Schiller wrote:

Das ist der Eumeniden Macht!
Der fromme Dichter wird gerochen.

Zhukovsky first translated these lines as:

. . . то мщенья час!
То Эвменид сокрытых глас!
Певцу возмездие готово![76]

But in the published version this passage was altered to:

. . . "убийца тут;
То Эвменид ужасных суд;
Отмщенье за певца готово; (22: 3–5)

Although the exclamatory intonation of the first version has been replaced by declarative intonation, and the motif of revenge is mentioned only once, instead of twice, Zhukovsky still insists on

[76] GPB-286; 1; 14; 129.

introducing the evaluative epithet *uzhasnyi* and on replacing Schiller's philosophical *Macht* with his own moral *sud*. All these changes further emphasize Zhukovsky's individual interpretation of the subject: revenge, moral condemnation, and punishment for the wicked. In the manuscript version of the last stanza, Zhukovsky translated Schiller's original conclusion fairly literally. But the rewritten version contains no fewer than seven epithets,[77] compared to Schiller's single epithet: *schreckenbleich*.

Ivikovy zhuravli demonstrates Zhukovsky's transformation of a classical theme, received via Schiller's philosophical version, into a romantic literary ballad. The bardic concept of the poet-hero, the atmosphere established in part by leitmotivs, and the abundance of emotional epithets both in the climax and in the conclusion make the ballad typical of Zhukovsky's translations from Schiller.

The most original of Zhukovsky's forty literary ballads, one for which no specific source has yet been identified, and one in which no particular foreign influence predominates is *Eolova arfa* (1814).[78] Its subject is as follows: the aristocratic heroine Minvana is in love with a poor poet. Recognizing that their marriage would be opposed, the lovers meet to bid farewell. The poet places his harp on a branch of a tree to serve as a reminder of his love. When their romance is discovered by Minvana's father, the poet is exiled and dies; Minvana pines away until springtime when the poet's spirit returns to play his harp. Minvana dies soon afterwards.

Iezuitova investigated the history of *Eolova arfa* and suggests that its composition began in 1805-6 with Zhukovsky's unfinished translation of Bürger's *Lenardo und Blandine* (1776).[79] Zhukovsky translated only five stanzas, but the theme of Bürger's ballad, the separation and demise of two lovers, was to become the basic theme of *Eolova arfa*. The next stage, according to Iezuitova, is Zhukovsky's unfinished ballad *Nina*, various drafts of which were written between 1808 and 1810.[80] This work begins with the lovers' farewell and then describes the two characters in abstract, idealized terms. When their secret love is discovered and separation

[77] *Bleden, trepeten, smyatennyi, nezapnyi, smushchennyi, sklonennyi,* and *tshchetnyi.*

[78] *Amfion*, III (1815), 61.

[79] 'Iz istorii', 170–81. MS. GPB-286; 1; 12; 49.

[80] GPB-286; 1; 78; 7.

is enforced, one lover dies and the other soon follows. Iezuitova compares *Nina* to *Plach Lyudmily*, a lyric of the same period, and to *Eolova arfa*; she discovers similarities in theme, descriptions of the heroine, and in some specific expressions. She notes that Zhukovsky's translations from Goldsmith, Moncrif, and Mallet (1812–14) also concern the theme of terminated love and spiritual union, and include identical heroines in similar settings. Finally, she cites common Ossianic motifs such as the bardic hero, the harp, the hunt, and the northern landscape, all of which are mentioned in *Eolova arfa*.

The ballad is set in a Western European medieval castle, adorned with all the exotic accoutrements of the chivalric tradition: feasts, tournaments, armour, tales of the hunt and of heroic deeds. But this setting is purely external, serving only as an introductory visual background and as a source of minor details (*zubchatye steny*, 1: 4; *zubchatye mechi*, 4: 7). It is described once, and then ignored.

The heroine Minvana is young, beautiful, and conventionally democratic: 'Chto v slave i sane?/ Lyubov'—moi vysokii, moi tsarskii venets' (14: 1–2). Her eyes, framed by *temny resnitsy*, contain *zadumchivyi plamen'*. Her head is full of *sladkoe smyaten'e*, while her soul is *prekrasnaya* and *prelestnaya*. The hero, Arminii, is a young, handsome impoverished *sladkoglasnyi pevets*. Together they share a spiritual love which they express to each other in elevated language at secret rendezvous.

Despite the possible source in Bürger's ballad, the Ossianic influence, the Western European setting, and the heroine's democratic clichés, *Eolova arfa* is an original work—a rich verbal collage, the components of which are Zhukovsky's favourite romantic motifs, repeated and interwoven until all logical meaning dissolves. The ballad represents Zhukovsky's greatest success in creating the purely emotional experience of spiritual love and lyrical dreams; the absence of a definite source meant that no immediate model could hinder his imagination by restricting him to an external subject.

The three most important verbal motifs are 'youth', 'silence', and 'despondency'. The heroine is described as *mladaya* (5: 1, 10: 5), as are her various parts (*S glavy molodoi/ Na persi mladye*, 5: 6–7). The hero is called the *mladoi pevets* (8: 1, 24: 8). The word is also used to convey the general mood of the ballad: *mladoe vesel'e* (12: 8) and *svezhaya mladost'* (26: 7). The epithet *yunyi* is similarly applied to the characters' hearts (11: 4) and to the bloom of love (20: 1, 32: 4). *Tishina,* together with its related grammatical forms, serves as a background for the whole narrative,[81] and is supported by the synonyms *bezmolvnyi* (12: 1) and *molchan'e* (27: 3). Iezuitova observed that the concept of *tishina* alters during the narrative. At the lovers' first meeting it expresses their spiritual tranquility; later, Minvana's expectation during the brief silence before the harp is played; and finally, the silence of death in the last scene.[82] *Unynie* is the most frequent emotion experienced by the two characters. The epithet *unylyi* is applied to *dusha* (12: 2, 24: 4), *serdtse* (13: 1), *pevets* (19: 1), Minvana (31: 2), and *strannik* (32: 5); it is also used impersonally (14: 5, 25: 3, 28: 1).

In addition to these three verbal themes, Zhukovsky employs several secondary motifs. The word *kholm* as the location for various scenes occurs ten times in the relatively short space of the ballad. Epithets for 'gold' are applied to Minvana's thick curls (*struya zolotaya,* 1: 8) and to the waves ('volny/ Zlatimye tikho blestyashchei lunoi', 12: 4). The heroine is associated with the epithet *tsarskii* (*san, venets, ubor*), in contrast to the hero who is described as *bednyi* (13: 6, 15: 8) and *smirennyi* (14: 4). The strings of the harp (*arfa stroinaya,* 11: 1) are characterized as *vernye* (20: 3), *smyatennye* (30: 4), and *milye* (32: 1).

Eolova arfa is not 'about' Minvana or Arminii or 'about' an Aeolian harp. Zhukovsky merely employs setting, characters, and events to express his own profound emotional experience of youth, silence, and despondency. These themes, together with the secondary ones, are combined in an intricate pattern of verbal motifs. There are no stylized folk epithets and few traces of conventional eighteenth-century language. *Eolova arfa* is written in pure early nineteenth-century 'romantic Russian', which is Zhukovsky's original and genuine contribution to Russian style.[83]

During the three years which followed the writing of *Eolova arfa,* Zhukovsky was at work on his ballad *Vadim.* In 1817 he published this ballad together with an earlier work *Gromoboi* (written in 1810, published in *Vestnik Evropy* in 1811). Both were

[81] See lines 12: 4, 17: 8, 23: 7, 28: 3, 29: 3, and 30: 8.
[82] 'Iz istorii', 208.
[83] See below, Ch. IV.

dedicated to D. N. Blyudov and were included under the general title *Dvenadtsat' spyashchikh dev.*[84] The epigraph to *Gromoboi* was borrowed from Schiller's *Die Jungfrau von Orleans* (1801), which Zhukovsky later translated in its entirety. The epigraph to *Vadim* was taken from Schiller's poem *Sehnsucht*, previously translated by Zhukovsky as *Zhelanie* (1811). A quotation from Goethe's *Faust*, Part I, was chosen as an epigraph for the whole work: 'Das Wunder ist des Glaubens liebstes Kind'.

The immediate source for Zhukovsky's ballad *Dvenadtsat' spyashchikh dev* was a novel by C. H. Spiess entitled *Die zwölf schlafenden Jungfrauen, eine Geister Geschichte* (1797). The novel is based on medieval Catholic legends about sinners who sold their souls to the devil and about their repetance in expiation of theirn guilt. The novel contains adventures of a mildly erotic nature, all of which were eliminated by the modest Zhukovsky.[85] Other influences on Zhukovsky's ballad include Ossian, Karamzin, Slavonic mythology, and Florian's *William Tell*, which Zhukovsky later translated.

A. L. Yashchenko convincingly argues that *Gromoboi* is nothing less than Zhukovsky's own reworking of Goethe's *Faust.*[86] He cites as evidence the epigraph and dedication of the 1817 edition, the similarity of subject between the two works, Zhukovsky's treatment of the main character, and finally Zhukovsky's review of *Faust* in 1848 in which he set forth his own critical interpretation of that work.

Iezuitova makes no reference to Yashchenko's theory and abruptly dismisses the importance of the Spiess novel as a source. Instead, she analyses the subject, treatment, and imagery of the ballad in order to discover what she calls Zhukovsky's religious-philosophic ideas, genuine Russian medieval colour, and, of course, *narodnost'*. She concludes that *Dvenadtsat' spyashchikh dev* is a totally original work and speculates that there might be a connection between it and *Vladimir*, Zhukovsky's unfinished historical epic. She considers that the ballad represents the poet's unfulfilled aspirations and that it demonstrates what *Vladimir* would have

[84] *Dvenadtsat' spyashchikh dev, starinnaya povest'* (SPb., 1817).

[85] P. Zagarin in his biography of Zhukovsky (1883) juxtaposes *Vadim* and the corresponding chapter of the Spiess novel, noting the deviations from the original source.

[86] '*Faust* Gete. Rannie otkliki v Rossii', *Uchenye zapiski Gor'kovskogo universiteta*, LXV (1964), 189–204.

been like had it been completed. However, the evidence contained in Zhukovsky's letters and *poslaniya*, and the various plans for *Vladimir* contradict Iezuitova's theory. While the plans entail a concrete narrative poem with particular emphasis on the Russian location, details, and motifs, the finished work *Vadim* is an abstract literary ballad with generalized setting, characters, and themes.[87]

The genre of *Dvenadtsat' spyashchikh dev* is problematical. In an early manuscript Zhukovsky sub-titled the work *dlinnaya ballada*,[88] which reflects his distinction between short, lyrical ballads and long, epic ballads in his *Sobranie russkikh stikhotvorenii* (1810–11). In the published version the work is sub-titled *starinnaya povest' v dvukh balladakh*: that is, a *povest'* which consists of two separate ballads but which is intended to be read as a single composition.

The first ballad, *Gromoboi*, takes its title from the heroic tale by G. P. Kamenev. It concerns a Faustian hero who sells his soul to the devil in exchange for wealth and happiness. When the devil comes to collect his soul, Gromoboi offers him the souls of his innocent children in order to gain more time. He soon repents, and expresses his remorse in pasages which are reminiscent of Zhukovsky's elegies. The narrator frequently evaluates the hero's words and deeds, and advises him on the best course of action. When the devil returns, the forces of good defend Gromoboi's soul. His children sink into a deep sleep in which they will remain until someone pure in heart comes to rescue them.

Although the ballad's immediate source is the Spiess novel, Yashchenko's theory is compelling. Zhukovsky's *Gromoboi* seems to be a vague imitation of Goethe's *Faust*. However, the thematic differences between the works are significant: Zhukovsky's hero seeks 'honour and gold', not knowledge and experience; the stern moralist in Zhukovsky emphasizes the theme of repentance before an almighty deity; and the twelve maidens represent a vague ideal of beauty, goodness, or purity that is common to all Zhukovsky's poetry.

The second ballad, *Vadim*, takes its name from the sixteenth-century Nikon chronicle, and relates the story of the hero's quest

[87] Of greater importance is the possible influence of Zhukovsky's plans for *Vladimir* on Pushkin's *Ruslan i Lyudmila*. See L. N. Nazarova, 'K istorii sozdaniya poemy Pushkina *Ruslan i Lyudmila*', in *Pushkin. Issledovaniya i materialy*, I (M.-L., 1956), 216–21.

[88] GPB-286; 1; 14; 67.

for ideal beauty. Vadim sets out to discover spiritual fulfilment, overcoming various obstacles and temptations along the way. He finally releases the twelve sleeping maidens of *Gromoboi*, thereby achieving the object of his holy pilgrimage.

Dvenadtsat' spyashchikh dev is Zhukovsky's great spiritual parable: the theme of the first ballad is suffering and remorse; that of the second, aspiration and fulfilment. Its length (over 150 stanzas) precludes the detailed analysis to which the other ballads have been subjected; however, both the content and the style of the work, in particular the frequency and usage of epithets, corroborate the conclusions reached through an examination of Zhukovsky's other ballads.

The last ballad to be considered is Zhukovsky's translation of Walter Scott's *The Eve of St. John* (1801), included in the section 'Imitations of the Ancient Ballad' in his *Minstrelsy of the Scottish Border* (1802). Zhukovsky's version was written in July 1822, but not published until two years later owing to problems with the censor.[89] Because the ballad combined a love story with an ecclesiastical holiday, it was thought to be 'atheistic and immoral'. After numerous demands were made to alter the ballad, Zhukovsky agreed to change the title from *Zamok Smal'gol'm, ili Ivanov vecher* to *Dunkanov vecher* and to add notes of historical explanation and moral interpretation.

The ballad relates the tale of a baron who, on returning to his castle, summons a page to report on his wife's activity during his absence. The page tells how on each of the three successive evenings she went to meet a strange knight, whom she had invited to her chamber that very evening, the Eve of St. John. The baron enters his bedchamber, reports to his wife on his most recent battle, and sinks into a deep slumber. The knight then 'appears' before the baron's wife and tells her that the baron lied about the battle; he also reveals that her husband is his murderer. The knight then leaves a mysterious imprint on the table and on her hand. The next day the baron retires to a monastery, his wife to a convent.

Scott's ballad is a faithful literary imitation of a traditional folk ballad. He preserves the stanza form, the folk epithets (*bold*, *bright*, *fair*, *gay*, *true*), the archaic vocabulary, and the interrupted

[89] *Sorevnovanie prosveshcheniya i blagotvoreniya*, XXXV (1824), 11, as *Zamok Smal'gol'm: Shotlandskaya skazka;* and *Novosti literatury*, VII (1824), 7, as *Dunkanov vecher: Shotlandskaya skazka.*

narration of the popular genre. The narrator describes the action without intervention, while the motivations of the characters are left unexplained. However, unlike the traditional ballad, the characters' speech both contributes to their characterization and is distinct from that of the narrator. Furthermore, Scott suggests a subtle contrast between past and present *mores* and employs frequent internal rhymes. Neither of these devices is characteristic of popular poetry.

Zhukovsky's version is very different. Almost all the details of historical colour have been eliminated, either because Zhukovsky wanted to make the subject comprehensible to Russian readers or because he did not understand the details himself.[90] An example of the 'translation' of local colour can be seen from a comparison of the following passage from Scott with Zhukovsky's version:

His arms shone full bright, in the beacon's red light;
His plume it was scarlet and blue;
On his shield was a hound, in a silver leash bound,
And his crest was a branch of the yew. (26)

Показалось мне при блестящем огне:
Был шелом с соколиным пером,
И палаш боевой на цепи золотой,
Три звезды на щите голубом. (26)

The colours and details of Scott's description, derived from traditional folk ballads, are replaced by vague, emotional colours and conventional details in Zhukovsky's rendition.

The characters in *Zamok Smal'gol'm* are transformed into typical romantic heroes and heroines. The baron is characterized by unwieldy, and later parodied, epithets: *znamenityi Smal'gol'mskii baron* (1: 2).[91] While Scott's baron is 'sad and sour', Zhukovsky's is *otumanen i bleden litsom* (4: 2). On two occasions Zhukovsky resorts to a technique borrowed from Schiller, description by verbs,[92] in order to 'translate' Scott's refrain:

Then changed, I trow, was that bold Baron's brow,
From the dark to the blood-red high.

[90] See B. G. Reizov, 'V. A. Zhukovsky, perevodchik Val'tera Skotta: *Ivanov vecher*', in *Russko-evropeiskie literaturnye svyazi*, ed. P. N. Berkov *et al.* (M.-L., 1966), 439–46.

[91] Cf. the equally unwieldy and as often parodied *topor dvadtsatifuntovoi* (3: 4). See below, Ch. VIII, p. 173.

[92] Cf. *Kubok* (stanzas 6, 12), Zhukovsky's translation of Schiller's *Der Taucher*.

. . . поражен, раздражен,
И кипел, и горел, и сверкал. (25: 1–2)
. . . изумлен, поражен,
И хладел, и бледнел, и дрожал. (29: 1–2)

The baron's wife is described as *odinoko-unylaya* (32: 4) and *molodaya* (33: 1, 34: 1, 38: 4); she is summed up in the lines:

Молодая жена—и тиха, и бледна,
И в мечтании грустном глядит . . . (33: 1–2)

The page is *molodoi* (7: 3, 8: 1, 9: 1); the knight is first presented as a frightening apparition (*On uzhasen stoyal pri ogne*, 23: 2), and then as a mysterious night visitor (*mrachnyi prishlets*, 27: 2). All the characters—the baron, his wife, the page, and the knight—speak exactly the same language, identical to that of the narrator.

Zhukovsky reworks the setting of Scott's ballad in order to emphasize his favourite motifs: night-time (the epithet *nochnoi* occurs eight times, the noun *noch'* twice, and the epithet *polunochnoi* twice); silence (*taikom*, *tikhomolkom*); and desolation (*pustynnaya vershina*, *skala; pustaya vysota*).

A comparison of the concluding stanzas in Scott's original with Zhukovsky's translation provides striking evidence of the gulf which separates the two works:

There is a nun in Dryburgh bower,
Ne'er looks upon the sun;
There is a monk in Melrose tower,
He speaketh word to none. (48)

That nun, who ne'er beholds the day,
That monk who speaks to none—
That nun was Smaylho'me's lady gay,
That monk the bold Baron. (49)

Scott's first stanza contains no epithets. It presents the two anonymous figures in parallel verses. In the second stanza, each line fulfils a different function: line 1 rephrases line 48: 2; line 2 rephrases 48: 4; both lines contain no epithets and serve to repeat the description of the characters in parallel phrases and in declarative intonation; line 3 identifies the nun, and concludes with her 'tag', the folk epithet *gay*; line 4 identifies the monk, and concludes with his 'tag', the folk epithet *bold.* Scott's conclusion is laconic, enigmatic, and unemotional.

Есть монахиня в древних Драйбургскнх стенах:
И грустна и на свет не глядит;
Есть в Мельрозской обители мрачный монах:
И дичится людей и молчит. (48)

Сей монах молчаливый и мрачный—кто он?
Та монахиня—кто же она?
То убийца, суровый Смальгольмский барон;
То его молодая жена. (49)

In Zhukovsky's version of the first stanza, the parallel structure is flawed and two descriptive epithets are introduced: *grustna* for the nun,[93] and *mrachnyi* for the monk. As in Scott's original, each line of the second stanza fulfils a different function: line 1 converts the verb of 48: 4 (*molchit*) into another emotional epithet (*molchalivyi*) and repeats the first epithet *mrachnyi* from 48: 3; line 2 in no way rephrases 48: 1–2; both lines are given an intonation foreign to popular ballads, the rhetorical question; in line 3 the words *To ubiitsa* provide the narrator's interpretation of the events and his moral judgement on the characters;[94] then Zhukovsky tries to assign a 'tag' to the monk by attaching the epithet *surovyi* to his unwieldy title. But the epithet had been applied to the baron only once before (36: 4), and has little effect in this concluding stanza. Finally, line 4 identifies the nun and gives her the 'tag' *molodaya*, which had been associated with her earlier; however, the same epithet had also been used as the page's 'tag', and thus lacks originality in identifying the heroine. Zhukovsky's conclusion is verbose (particularly in his use of epithets), interpretative (in the moral judgements), and emotional (in its interrogative intonation and connotative vocabulary).

The replacement or elimination of Scott's historical colour, the depiction of characters as romantic heroes and heroines, the emphasis on favourite motifs in the description of the setting, and the 'translation' of the concluding stanzas clearly demonstrate Zhukovsky's transformation of Scott's imitation of a traditional popular ballad into a romantic literary ballad. The difference between the works is not one of quality; it lies in two conceptions of

[93] Cf. *grustnyi* in 33: 2, quoted above.
[94] Cf. *ubiitsa* in *Ivikovy zhuravli*, 22: 3, quoted above.

the ballad genre. Scott and Zhukovsky were simply writing different sorts of poetry.

Zhukovsky's theoretical statements and his forty literary ballads determined the pattern for the genre and established its importance in the first decades of the nineteenth century. His own conception of himself as a *balladnik* coincided with the views held by his contemporaries. Russian scholars have expended considerable energy trying to demonstrate the influence of folk literature on Zhukovsky's ballads, or at least trying to document his interest in folksongs and *skazki*.[95] All the arguments presented are contrived and they are prejudiced by ideological considerations concerning the value of *narodnost'*. The texts of Zhukovsky's literary ballads provide no evidence to suggest that he had any models of Russian folk poetry to imitate.

A comparison of the narrative unit, method, and attitude of the traditional Russian folk ballad with those of Zhukovsky's literary ballads is most instructive. The compressed, centralized episode of the folk genre became, in Zhukovsky's imitation, a greatly expanded narrative, often of epic proportions, with more emphasis on the setting and characters than on the action. The dramatic, dynamic functional style of the anonymous popular ballads was replaced by Zhukovsky's individual diction and syntax. Impersonality and non-interference in the action were superseded by Zhukovsky's moralizing interpretation and frequent interruptions. Finally, the combination of natural and supernatural elements in the 'world' of the traditional ballad was transformed in Zhukovsky's literary ballads to conventional local colour, where supernature was consciously employed both to frighten and to delight the reader. Zhukovsky's poetry takes place in a 'world' far distant from that of traditional folk poetry.

The impetus for Zhukovsky's literary ballads undoubtedly came from Western European literature, although he was strongly influenced by developments in Russian pre-romantic poetry. The characters, setting, structure, and style of the Russian ballads of the 1790s, themselves largely based on foreign sources, had a direct impact on Zhukovsky's work. But Zhukovsky went directly

[95] See N. N. Trubitsyn, *O narodnoi poezii v obshchestvennom i literaturnom obikhode pervoi treti XIX v.* (SPb., 1912); Lupanova, *Russkaya narodnaya skazka;* and Iezuitova, 'Iz istorii'.

to the foreign sources: to Bürger's sensational *Lenore*, to Schiller's philosophical ballads, and to Goethe's combinations of folk and literary elements; to Southey's half-serious, half-comic verse, and to Scott's literary imitations of popular ballads. Zhukovsky discovered that each author had adapted the new genre to accommodate his own particular talents and tastes. He would do likewise.

From his first ballad in 1808 to his last in 1833 Zhukovsky never altered his choice of sources, his method of 'translating' Western European themes, or his individual Russian style. While the 'events' of the original ballad plot were usually retained in outline form, the characters were metamorphosed into romantic heroes and heroines, whose speech was identical to that of the narrator. The settings were generalized, while details of historical colour were eliminated or 'Russianized'. The atmosphere of the ballads combined the elements of night-time, silence, desolation, and fear in varying proportions. Zhukovsky's real theme always remained the same: his own personal experience of melancholy, anxiety, despair, love, fear, or resignation. The style which expressed this constant theme was always 'literary': its originality resided in alternating intonations, negative constructions, parallel syntax, and, more significantly, in the frequency, choice, and meaning of his epithets.[96]

Zhukovsky has been called a romantic by Pushkin,[97] Belinsky,[98] and Trotsky[99] among others. He has also been considered a sentimentalist, a 'pre-romantic', and a realist; a reactionary, a progressive, and a mystic.[100]

Isaiah Berlin, in a preface to a recent study of European romanticism, presents some general observations on the nature of that movement.[101] He argues that, whereas classicism conceived of truth as objective, something which had to be discovered, romanticism conceived of truth as subjective, invented or created

[96] See below, Ch. IV.

[97] See Pushkin's letter to L. S. Pushkin, May 1825: 'He [Zhukovsky] is holy, although he was born a romantic, and not a Greek, and a human being, but what a human being.' *Polnoe sobranie sochinenii*, XIII (M.-L., 1937), 175.

[98] See Belinsky's articles on Zhukovsky cited above.

[99] 'Ot dvoryanina k raznochintsu: V. A. Zhukovsky', *Sochineniya*, XX (1926), 3–9; for example: 'Zhukovsky adapted German and English demons to the Russian climate—and in so doing, propagated Romanticism in Russia.'

[100] See Gukovsky, *Pushkin i russkie romantiki*, 13–23.

[101] H. G. Schenk, *The Mind of the European Romantics* (London, 1966), xv–xvi.

by its seekers. The emphasis in romanticism is on the ideal, not on the real; on the process of creation, not on its effects; on the motives, not on the consequences; and on the quality of the individual vision, not on the accurate correspondence to a stated premise.

Zhukovsky was nourished on the aesthetic theories of French and German classicism: on the laws of Boileau, the principles of Batteaux, the norms of La Harpe, and the translations of Florian; on the theories of Baumgarten and the philosophical ideas of Engel, Eschenburg, and Friedrich Bouterwek.

The irony is apparent: this same Zhukovsky, in his creation and establishment of the Russian literary ballad, the archetypal romantic genre in which subjective truth is created by its seeker, became the undisputed founder of the Russian romantic movement.

IV

THE EPITHET IN ZHUKOVSKY'S LITERARY BALLADS

История эпитета есть история поэтического стиля в сокращенном издании, и не только стиля, но и поэтического сознания.[1]

IN AN essay entitled *O literaturnoi evolyutsii* (1927) Yu. N. Tynyanov describes the concept of the *dominanta*: 'A [stylistic] system does not mean coexistence of components on the basis of equality; it presupposes the pre-eminence of one group of elements and the resulting deformation of other elements.'[2] In Zhukovsky's poetry the role of the *dominanta* is fulfilled by the epithet. The over-all frequency of epithets in his literary ballads, the repetition of a limited range, the 'obsession' with specific words in his manuscripts, and the evidence provided by the criticism, imitation, and parody of these epithets by Zhukovsky's contemporaries—all support this view of his stylistic system.

The history of the epithet as a poetic device has been fraught with controversy since the Roman rhetorician Quintilian drew a distinction between ornamental epithets in poetry (*ad ornandam non augendam orationem*)[3] and meaningful epithets in oratory. The debate has centred on the question of whether an epithet defines the typical, ideal trait or whether it limits and individualizes a concept.[4] The dilemma finally led the Russian formalist critic

[1] A. N. Veselovsky, *SS* I (SPb., 1913), 58.

[2] *Arkhaisty i novatory* (L., 1929), 41. The concept had been employed by B. Eikhenbaum in his study *Anna Akhmatova* (P., 1923). V. Erlich claims it was originally borrowed from the German aesthetician Christiansen; see *Russian Formalism* (The Hague, 1965), 199.

[3] *Institutio Oratoria*, ed. M. Winterbottom, VIII. vi. 40–3 (Oxford, 1970).

[4] See A. Zelenetsky, *Epitety literaturnoi russkoi rechi*, I (M., 1913), for a bibliography on epithets (1850–1913), and V. A. Pautynskaya, 'Ob ispol' zovanii termina "epitet"', *Uchenye zapiski l-go MGPIIYa*, X (1956), 107–24.

V. M. Zhirmunsky to restrict the term 'epithet' to the former, and to introduce the term 'attributive' (*opredelenie*) for the latter.[5] But this new stylistic terminology (epithet/attributive) coincides with previous grammatical terminology and could result in even greater confusion. Linguists define the 'epithet' as a word or expression which qualifies a substantive without an intermediary copulative verb, and the 'attributive' as a word or expression which qualifies a substantive and is related to it by means of a copulative verb.[6]

The following definition of the epithet avoids this confusion: 'L'épithète est un mot, une locution, ou une proposition conjonctive attachée à un substantif ou à son équivalent, sans l'intermédiare d'aucun verbe copule, pour donner du relief à une qualité particulière, à l'être ou à la chose représentée, soit comme individu, soit comme espèce.'[7] This definition accepts the term 'epithet' in the same sense as it is used by linguists as the opposite of the term 'attributive' (i.e. as regards the copulative verb). It does not distinguish between 'epithet' and 'attributive' in the stylistic sense as suggested by Zhirmunsky. Instead it includes all purely descriptive words under the term 'epithet' and allows for a distinction in usage or function: 'soit comme individu, soit comme espèce', that is, whether the epithet defines some individual trait, adding new and original meaning, or whether it is used for adornment, to emphasize the typical or ideal trait.

From the grammatical point of view, the epithet can be expressed by any part of speech: adjectives (either in short or long form; preposed, postposed, or in apposition); nouns (usually in apposition); adverbs; verbal forms (usually participles); and phrases (prepositional, complements, and appositives). This study of the epithet will be limited to the adjective for several reasons: it is the simplest form of the epithet, the one most frequently employed, and that most significantly stylistically.

In order to categorize these adjectival epithets the grammatical

[5] 'K voprosu ob epitete', in *Pamyati P. N. Sakulina. Sbornik statei* (M., 1931), 75–82.

[6] M. E. I. Robertson, *L'Épithète dans les oeuvres lyriques de Victor Hugo publiées avant l'exil* (Paris, 1927), 14. The definitions originate in F. Brunot, *La Pensée et la langue* (Paris, 1922). See also: E. Reiner, 'La Place de l'adjectif épithète en français: théories traditionelles et essai de solution', *Wiener romanistische Arbeiten* (Vienna, 1968), 12.

[7] Robertson, *L'Épithète*, 28.

classification of A. V. Isačenko has been adopted. He has defined the adjective as that part of speech which designates the quality of an object and has divided them into the following groups.[8]

(1) Qualitative adjectives: the quality is indicated directly by a non-derivative adjective.

(a) Qualitative-absolute adjectives: the quality indicated is absolute, and implies no evaluation by the speaker. This group includes colours, tastes, physical defects, etc. (*belyi, sladkii, glukhoi*).

(b) Qualitative-relative adjectives: the quality indicated is relative and implies some evaluation by the speaker. This group includes expressions of spatial, temporal, and sensual perception (*vysokii, kholodnyi, rannii, legkii, milyi*).

(2) Relative adjectives: the quality is defined by comparison to some other object or phenomenon; usually a derivative adjective (*grobovoi, zolotoi, nebesnyi*).

Most nineteenth-century definitions of the epithet emerged from the study of the language of folklore. The genre of the 'folk ballad' was not employed in the classification of Russian popular poetry until Chernyshev's anthology (1936).[9] Although individual texts had been included in studies of other genres, the ballad itself never before served as an object of research. Attention was directed to the language of folk literature in general, and to the language of the *byliny* in particular.

Admiral A. S. Shishkov, in one of his *Razgovory o slovesnosti* (1811), noted among the features of folk language both fixed epithets (*krasnoe solnyshko, svetlyi mesyats, sinee more*) and double epithets (*temnyi dremuchii les, belaya kudryavaya bereza*). He advocated the study of popular poetry, arguing that its language could serve as a source for the enrichment of Russian literature, and as a more salutary influence on it than foreign literatures.[10]

[8] *Grammaticheskii stroi russkogo yazyka v sopostavlenii s slovatskim*, I (Bratislava, 1965), 173–242. Group (3) Possessive adjectives (*mamin, Natalin*) and Group (4) Relative-Possessive adjectives (*sobachii, okhotnichii*) have been excluded because they are employed infrequently and conventionally in Zhukovsky's poetry.

[9] See above, Ch. I, p. 5 n. 7.

[10] See N. I. Mordovchenko, *Russkaya kritika pervoi chetverti XIX v.* (M.-L., 1959), 88–9.

The first comprehensive study of the epithet in folk literature was undertaken by P. D. Pervov in 1901–2.[11] His scope was limited to the *byliny*, and his choice of epithets to those 'which accompany . . . names of objects, particularly names of tangible objects'. Pervov maintained that the epithet is the most common stylistic device in all forms of popular poetry, and that it is precisely in its 'changelessness' that the language of folk literature differs from that of 'sophisticated' literature.

Pervov divided epithets in the *byliny* into the following categories: (1) ancient or organic epithets, mostly tautological (*belyi svet*); (2) colour (*zelena trava*); (3) material (*bulatnaya sablya*); (4) emotional relation of man to object (*milyi*, *dorogoi*); (5) size (*shirokii*, *glubokii*); and (6) 'common' epithets (*chastyi dozhd'*, *sladkii napitok*). He studied individual epithets within these categories by compiling lists of their various uses in the *byliny*, comparing the nouns modified, and deducing from the contexts the basic meanings of each epithet. By tracing the gradual development of the epithet, he hoped to determine the oldest, primary meaning. Pervov also listed several nouns with the epithets most commonly used to modify them.

Although his method was original, Pervov's conclusions are open to serious question. Firstly, he attempted to generalize about the language of folk literature on the basis of his study of only one genre. Secondly, his selection of epithets within that genre was limited to those which relate concepts to the external world. Evaluative epithets are hardly treated, and figurative epithets are completely ignored. Thirdly, Pervov's semantic analysis did not consider the stylistic function of the epithet in the context of its phrase or line or in the work as a whole.

Pervov's findings have been criticized by A. P. Evgen'eva, who also attacked the conventional views of other nineteenth-century critics concerning the 'fixedness' of fixed epithets and the concept of 'adornment'.[12] She stated that since Pervov's article there had been no study of the language of specific genres of folk poetry during the different periods of oral composition. Evgen'eva considers various theories concerning tautological epithets and concludes that the function of such epithets is not the 'renewal'

[11] 'Epitety v russkikh bylinakh', *Filologicheskie zapiski*, I–VI (1901); I (1902).

[12] *Ocherki po yazyku russkoi ustnoi poezii v zapiskakh XVII–XXvv.* (M.-L. 1963), 229–43, 298–338.

(*podnovlenie*) of the meaning of the substantive but rather the 'indication of the essential, typical characteristic of the object'. As a result of her study of laments (*prichitaniya*) Evgen'eva concludes that there is great variety and complexity in folk epithets, which she divides into four categories: (1) fixed epithets, which are constant regardless of theme (*krasna devitsa, bely ruki, chisto pole*); (2) 'relatively fixed' epithets, which are determined by the theme (*tonki bely savany, umershaya mogilushka*); (3) 'adorning' epithets (*golovushka bednaya* or *obidnaya* or *bestalannaya*); and (4) individual attributives (*suetlivaya strapnya, gor'kaya molodost'*.[13]

Finally, Evgen'eva relates the number and variety of epithets in folk literature to the date of transcription. Thus *byliny* recorded in the seventeenth century contain all the generally acknowledged 'fixed epithets', as well as numerous others which have been overlooked. Kirsha Danilov's collection (1804) contains almost exclusively fixed epithets and 'adorning' epithets, while the later collections of P. N. Rybnikov (1861–7) and A. F. Gil'ferding (1873) contain a larger number of epithets in general, a more varied selection, and some examples of new individual poetic attributives.[14]

Evgen'eva's study of tautological and fixed epithets is extremely valuable for all future research on the language of folk poetry. However, while relating the number and variety of epithets in collections of folk poetry to the date of transcription, she never attempts to explain the variations. It is likely that the literary tradition had a strong influence on popular literature and its transcription; this would explain the increase in fixed epithets in Danilov's collection and the appearance of individual poetic attributives in the later collections.

Furthermore, while Evgen'eva refutes other scholars' generalizations about the language of folk poetry inasmuch as they were based on a study of one genre only, her own study is subject to the same criticism. On the basis of the laments, she too generalizes about the variety and complexity of the language of folk poetry. Clearly each genre (*byliny*, historical songs, popular ballads, and so forth) must be studied separately; any generalizations about the language of folk poetry should take into account the conclusions reached about each separate genre.

[13] Ibid. 314.

[14] Ibid. 326–37.

The results of an original analysis of the epithet in Russian folk ballads are included below in Appendix A. The most frequently employed epithets in each of the three main groups of the Isačenko classification are listed with the most frequently modified substantives for each. On the basis of this analysis it is apprent that the epithet in Russian folk ballads has its source in concrete reality and is used to express man's basic sensory perceptions of that reality. Thus group (1a) is composed of the simplest colours (*belyi, zelenyi, chernyi*); group (1b) of the simplest categories of physical description (*vysokii, krasnyi, ostryi, temnyi, chistyi, yasnyi*) and of the simplest moral judgements, expressing approval (*dobryi, lyubimyi, milyi*) and disapproval (*zloi, lyutyi*); and group (2) of the basic materials of existence (*dubovyi, zolotoi, shelkovyi*).

The meaning of the epithet in Russian folk ballads is, for the most part, unambiguous. The words are generally monosemantic and lack emotional overtones. They derive their effect from their clarity and from the immediacy of their impact. The usual function of each epithet with regard to its substantive is the expression of the typical, constant, or ideal trait of that substantive. No new meaning is added by the epithet, nor is the meaning of the substantive limited or individualized in any way.

The folk ballads contain none of the so-called emotional or psychological epithets characteristic of nineteenth-century poetry, neither those which were used to describe events (*strashnyi, uzhasnyi, tainstvennyi*) nor those which describe characters and settings (*blednyi, zadumchivyi, mrachnyi, odinokii, pechal'nyi, pustynnyi, smutnyi, tikhii, unylyi*). This analysis has not revealed any variety or complexity in the epithets of Russian folk ballads; on the contrary, the range and usage of the epithet is very limited indeed. It is clear from the above that the epithet in folk ballads is much closer to the epithet in the *byliny* than to that in the laments.

The epithet as a stylistic device in literary ballads has attracted the attention of scholars in various European literatures, particularly in English literature.[15] Friedman, in his study of the English ballad revival, includes a brief section on the general aesthetics of folk

[15] See also Robertson, *L'Épithète* and C. Zgorzelski, *Duma, poprzedniczka ballady* (Toruń, 1949), 228–36.

ballads as opposed to those of literary ballads.[16] He maintains that, although late eighteenth- and early nineteenth-century poets took their initial inspiration from the traditional genre, they soon found that the techniques of folk literature were inapplicable in their own poetry. They adopted the verbal simplicity and economy of means of folk ballads, and even introduced certain folkloric idioms. But in general the language of folk ballads was thought to be too simple, allowing no room for physical and psychological description, for motivation and moralization, and, most of all, for individual style. While the anonymous authors of folk ballads tried to generalize about the nature of experience, poets since the Renaissance have sought striking original figures of speech to express their own individuality. Thus, Friedman concludes, folk ballads tended to ignore or de-emphasize precisely those elements which 'sophisticated' poets savour most and develop into their own stylistic systems.

An example of this contrast in aesthetic principles is provided by Kroeber's comparison of one English folk ballad with its literary imitation.[17] In 1709 Matthew Prior published what is probably the first English literary ballad, *Henry and Emma, a Poem, Upon the Model of the Nut-browne Maid*.[18] The most striking stylistic difference between the original and the imitation is that Prior's version contains numerous emotional epithets (*weary*, *tedious*, *happy*, *dejected*, *wounded*), whereas the vocabulary of the original is limited and stylized. Prior tends to present objects and ideas in terms of the emotions which they evoke in him.

Kroeber infers two reasons for such an important contrast between the two works: first, that Prior conceives of the story in terms of specific characters, and therefore uses epithets to particularize his narrative; and second, that since the author was in command of such a rich vocabulary, complete with metaphor and ambiguity, it was only natural for him to relate the simple story in his own language. Kroeber does not state the most important conclusion: that it was *only* through such epithets that Prior could express his own, original interpretation of the material in his own, individual style. *Henry and Emma* is Matthew Prior's 'translation' of *The Nut-browne Maid*, and the poet's personality is communicated primarily through his language.

[16] *The Ballad Revival*, 292–326.
[17] *Romantic Narrative Art*, 13–15.
[18] See above, Ch. I, p. 8.

A brief historical survey of the epithet in English literary ballads was included by Josephine Miles in *Eras and Modes in English Poetry*.[19] She begins with a discussion of Percy's alterations in the language of his *Reliques*, which tended to make emotions more explicit by the introduction of epithets such as *bold*, *doughty*, *gentle*, and *proud*. Both Percy's selection and his principles of editing became a guide for future ballad imitators, each of whom modified the original method and materials to suit his poetic practice. Thomas Chatterton, for example, preserves the basic ballad vocabulary, but introduces epithets such as *high* and *noble* as authorial evaluation. On the other hand, Walter Scott places much greater emphasis on observed colours and objects, and much less on emotional and moral judgements. In general, the use of the traditional epithets of folk poetry declined; Wordsworth and Coleridge's *Lyrical Ballads* (1798) represent an entirely new development in the history of the English literary ballad genre.

The results of a sample of 1,000 lines from English literary ballads by Scott and Southey are included in Appendix A. The most frequent epithets in each of the groups (1a), (1b), and (2) are listed along with the substantives most frequently modified by them. Miles's list of epithets which are used ten times or more per 1,000 lines of traditional English folk ballads is included for comparison.[20]

The survey demonstrates how rarely the epithets of English folk ballads and literary ballads coincide. The only folk epithets which occur with some frequency in the literary ballads are *fair* and *young*. The traditional folk epithets (*bonny*, *dear*, *good*, *handsome*) have been replaced by literary epithets with their various emotional connotations (*bright*, *cold*, *dark*, *holy*, *pale*).

For comparison with this survey of English folk epithets, the results of a sample of 1,000 lines from German literary ballads by Bürger, Goethe, Schiller, and Uhland are also included in Appendix A. The most frequent epithets in each of the groups (1a), (1b), and (2) are listed along with the substantives most frequently

[19] (Berkeley and Los Angeles, Calif., 1957), 100–23. See also her *Renaissance, Eighteenth-Century, and Modern Language in English Poetry: A Tabular View* (Berkeley and Los Angeles, Calif., 1960), which lists adj./n./v. frequency (per 10 lines) and major adjectives (10 times or more per 1,000 lines) for: Young, Thomson, Gray, Goldsmith, Wordsworth, Coleridge, Southey, Campbell, and others.

[20] *A Tabular View*, see chart 'Major Adjectives'.

modified by them. A list of epithets which are used four times or more in a small sample of traditional German folk ballads (350 lines) is included for comparison.

This survey indicates a greater coincidence of epithets in German folk ballads and literary ballads. All but one of the most frequent epithets in the folk ballads are employed in the literary ballads. But the literary ballads also show repeated use of literary epithets with their emotional connotations (*furchtbar*, *kühn*, *still*, *teuer*, *tief*).

Friedman's general conclusion regarding the opposition of aesthetic principles in folk ballads and literary ballads has been substantiated by this brief survey of epithets in English and German ballads. Epithets in folk ballads differ fundamentally from those in literary ballads in their range, frequency, and meaning. The concrete, unambiguous epithets of the traditional ballads are replaced in the literary imitations by emotional, connotative epithets which afford sophisticated poets the possibility of interpreting the events and of expressing their individuality through their style.

The epithet in eighteenth-century Russian poetry has attracted considerable attention from Soviet scholars. Although some valuable insights have emerged as a result of their work, their conclusions have generally been based on the analysis of a limited number of epithets and closer investigation has shown that many of their generalizations are unfounded.

Gukovsky studied early Petrine love-songs containing a mixture of various styles and linguistic elements.[21] Folk epithets such as *belyi golubchik*, *yasnyi sokol*, *syryi bor*, and *burnoe more* are combined with literary epithets such as *zhestokaya rana*, *zlaya fortuna*, *nechayannyi ogon'*, *ostraya strela*, and *prekrasnyi tsvet*. This mixture of styles was resolved by the middle of the eighteenth century with the establishment of Russian classicism in general, and with Lomonosov's stylistic reforms in particular.

Lomonosov's language, including his epithets, has been studied by Gukovsky[22] and I. Z. Serman.[23] The former argues that Lomonosov is the last great European Renaissance figure and that this fact is reflected in his attitude towards the 'word'. According

[21] *Russkaya literatura XVIII veka*, 33–7.
[22] Ibid. 107–16; and *Russkaya poeziya XVIII veka* (L., 1927), 14–19.
[23] *Literaturnoe tvorchestvo M. V. Lomonosova* (M.-L., 1962), 101–32.

to Gukovsky, Lomonosov transforms his words into abstractions, invents strong metaphors, and employs 'bold' epithets which destroy the logical connection between epithet and substantive. The organizing principle of Lomonosov's language is defined as adornment (*ukrashenie*), and the desired effect is described as a feeling of grandeur and majesty. While Gukovsky tends to generalize on little evidence, Serman reaches similar conclusions through an analysis of two epithets (*sladkii* and *zlatoi*) as they develop from concrete, descriptive epithets to emotional metaphoric epithets: from *sladkii sok* to *sladkii vek*, and from *zlataya dennitsa* to *zlataya vesna*.[27] Serman concludes that this one aspect of Lomonov's style became the main stylistic principle during the early nineteenth century, and that it is particularly evident in Batyushkov's poetry.[25]

An original analysis of a sample of 150 epithets taken from genres representative of Lomonsov's poetry yields results which contradict the conclusions of both Gukovsky and Serman.[26] Both scholars tend to exaggerate the importance of Lomonosov's epithets, particularly that of his 'emotional-metaphoric' epithets. In accordance with Lomonosov's own theory of poetic tropes, the epithet plays a secondary role in his stylistic system.[27] Gukovsky's frequently quoted abstract epithets (*velikolepnyi*, *velikodushnyi*, *nesravennyi*, *radostnyi*, *sladkostrunnyi*) are rarely used. The majority of the 150 epithets are not 'bold', nor are they employed particularly 'boldly'. Serman's two chosen epithets (*sladkii* and *zlatoi*) were used in the figurative sense well before Lomonosov, both by Kantemir in his satires (1730s) and by Trediakovsky in his translation of P. Tallement's *Voyage à l'île d'Amour* (1730).[28] By the late

[24] Ibid. 125–9.

[25] See Serman, 'Poeziya K. N. Batyushkova', *Uchenye zapiski LGU*, III. (1939), 229–83.

[26] The following is a list of the most frequent epithets with sample substantives:

великий/ светило, творец
вечный/ высота, права
небесный/ дверь, очи
прекрасный/лик, весна
приятный/ струны, зефиры
сильный/ лев, царица
сладкий/ плод, слова
счастливый/жизнь, путь
чистый/ голос, луч

[27] See 'Kratkoe rukovodstvo k krasnorechiyu', *PSS* VII (M.-L., 1952), 131.

[28] B. O. Unbegaun suggests that the abstract meaning of the epithet *sladkii* originates in Church Slavonic. See 'Le russe littéraire est-il d'origine russe?' in *Selected Papers on Russian and Slavonic Philology* (Oxford, 1969), 308.

eighteenth century Lomonosov's usage had become standard literary cliché, and was canonized by quotation in the Academy of Sciences' Dictionary (1789–94). These epithets operate on one of two levels only, either the literal or the figurative. There is no question of ambiguity or polysemanticism. If the desired effect is emotional, it is the result of the cumulative force of several metaphoric epithets in series, and produces either majesty and grandeur or clumsiness and bombast.

Sumarokov's use of the epithet has often been contrasted with that of Lomonosov. During the 1750s Sumarokov initiated a lengthy polemic, objecting to some of Lomonosov's metaphoric epithets such as *plamennye zvuki* or *prokhladnye teni*, and he composed general parodies of Lomonosov's verse called *Vzdornye ody*. Gukovsky maintains that for Sumarokov the 'word' represents a scientific term having precise, concrete meaning, and is related to only one specific concept.[29] According to Gukovsky, there is little semantic widening or transformation of the original meaning of words; the use of tropes is kept to a minimum, and when they are used both members of the poetic comparison are closely connected.

An original analysis of a sample of 100 epithets taken from Sumarokov's poetry shows the contrast with Lomonosov's language.[30] The difference in range between the two authors' epithets is partly the result of Sumarokov's constant development of one theme, that of happy or unhappy love, an experience common to all men. But both Lomonosov and Sumarokov use epithets in the same way: unambiguously and monosemantically. Gukovsky's description of Sumarokov is more accurate than his analysis of Lomonosov; however, he does overlook Sumarokov's abstract epithets, which he said were characteristic of Lomonosov's style (*blagopoluchnyi*, *blagoslovennyi*, *velikii*, *radostnyi*). Serman, in his study of Lomonosov, also overlooks the fact that Sumarokov em-

[29] *Russkaya poeziya*, 19–32; and *Russkaya literatura*, 142–4, 165–9.

[30] The following is a list of the most frequent epithets with sample substantives:

драгой/ дни, жизнь
злой/ жизнь, печали, рок
лютый/ болезнь, судьбина
нежный/ любовь, глас
печальный/ сердце, мысль
прекрасный/ нимфы, весна
приятный/ взор, жизнь
сладкий/ дни, век, песни

ploys the epithets *zlatoi* and *sladkii* in precisely the same metaphoric way as does Lomonosov (*zlatoi vek, zlatye dni, sladkaya zhizn', sladkaya nadezhda*).

Gukovsky also studied the poetry of M. N. Murav'ev,[31] and his conclusions have since been supported by L. I. Kulakova.[32] Their interpretation is based, to a large extent, on the re-examination of Murav'ev's work by Karamzin, Batyushkov, and Zhukovsky in the early nineteenth century.[33] Gukovsky maintains that the new subjective world-view and aesthetic principles of nineteenth-century poetry have their origin in Murav'ev's work. His poetic vocabulary was gradually narrowed to words of a particular emotional nature—what Gukovsky calls *sladostnaya leksika.* These words were employed exclusively for their emotional, evocative value to allude to the inner, spiritual condition of the poet himself. Gukovsky places the epithet at the centre of this new style; thus the epithet was no longer used to describe external objects and phenomena, but to characterize the relationship between the subject and these objects.

An original analysis of a sample of 100 epithets taken from genres representative of Murav'ev's poetry demonstrates the continued importance of eighteenth-century diction (*nebesnyi, nezhnyi, sladkii*).[34] Many of the most typical epithets used by Lomonosov and Sumarokov, such as *vechnyi, pyshnyi, zloi, lyutyi,* and *lyubeznyi,* are among those most frequently employed by Murav'ev. There is, however, a significant increase in the use of what were to become some of the most common epithets in early nineteenth-century poetry (*tainyi, temnyi,* and especially *tikhii*).

[31] 'U istokov russkogo sentimentalizma', in *Ocherki po istorii russkoi literatury i obshchestvennoi mysli XVIII veka* (L., 1938), 252–98.

[32] M. N. Murav'ev, *Stikhotvoreniya,* 5–49.

[33] See above, Ch. II, p. 23.

[34] The following is a list of the most frequent epithets with sample substantives:

высокий/	трон
небесный/	свод, красота, певец
нежный/	весна, мечты
полночный/	час, брега
священный/	волна, лес
сладкий/	покой, глас
тайный/	стезя, сени
темный/	ночь, прохлада
тихий/	трепет, пространство, светлость

The epithets *polunochnyi* and *svyashchennyi* were introduced in the description of settings, and emotional epithets such as *spokoinyi* and *utomlennyi* began to appear in Murav'ev's lyrics.[35]

Thus, while it is true that Murav'ev introduces elements of what might be called the 'new subjective aesthetics', Gukovsky and Kulakova overstate their case. Murav'ev must be seen as a transitional figure whose poetry demonstrates the striking contrast between the norms of conventional eighteenth-century usage and the new aesthetic principles beginning to influence the language of Russian poetry.

Gukovsky also studied Derzhavin's diction and concludes that he was 'more a realist, than a romantic', since his words describe external objects and facts rather than his own subjective experience.[36] More recently Derzhavin's epithets were classified by N. B. Rusanova, who divides them into two groups: (1) those which describe man's sensory perception of the external world (visual, aural, tactile, and so on); and (2) those which describe his intellectual perception of the external world (epithets of the first group used figuratively).[37] Rusanova draws no conclusions about the significance of Derzhavin's use of the epithet in the development of Russian poetic style.

Finally, Karamzin's language has been compared to Derzhavin's. Gukovsky maintains that Karamzin's epithets, unlike Derzhavin's, are used to characterize the subjective relationship between the poet and external phenomena.[38] L. V. Gerasimova classifies Karamzin's sensory and psychological epithets, sentimental clichés, allegorical and folkloric expressions, and concludes with a comparison of the epithet in Karamzin's poetry with that in his prose.[39]

From its relatively insignificant role in the classical styles of Lomonosov and Sumarokov, the epithet increased in importance in Russian poetry of the late eighteenth century. Murav'ev's language reflects the transition from objectivity and clarity to the new subjective aesthetics. Derzhavin's lingering classicism, or

[35] See above, pp. 23–6 on the language of Murav'ev's literary ballads.

[36] 'Vokrug Radishcheva', in *Ocherki*, 200–17.

[37] 'Epitety Derzhavina', in *XVIII vek*, VIII (L., 1969), 92–102.

[38] *IRL* V. 55–105.

[39] 'Epitety v proizvedeniyakh Karamzina', in *XVIII vek*, 290–8. See above, pp. 26–30 on the language of Karamzin's literary ballads.

what Gukovsky calls his 'proto-realism', represents a deviation from the mainstream of stylistic development. Progress towards total subjectivity, continued by Karamzin, reaches its culmination in the poetry of V. A. Zhukovsky.

Among the first studies of Zhukovsky's epithets was an introductory article by M. I. Sukhomlinov which appeared in the fifth edition of the poet's collected works (1846).[40] He lists Zhukovsky's 'favourite images' with examples from the lyrics, including a limited number of the most frequent epithets: *sladkii, sladostnyi, milyi, yunyi, unylyi,* and *tikhii.* In 1893 V. Istomin published a 'mechanical' analysis of Zhukovsky's language in which he refers to the 'constant use of epithets which convey living characteristics to objects'.[41] He cites several examples, including *boi yaryi, sladkopamyatnyi zavet, gromozvuchnoe urá,* and *grustnaya mrachnost'.* The first volume of L. A. Bulakhovsky's study of the Russian literary language contains lists of Zhukovsky's epithets in his elegies, ballads, *povesti,* and other genres.[42] None of these three works contains any stylistic analysis of the epithets.

The most important contribution to the study of Zhukovsky's epithets was made by Gukovsky in the first chapter of his projected history of Russian realism.[43] He argues that poetic art, in Zhukovsky's world-view, was intended to express the internal life of consciousness, the 'inexpressible spiritual emotions', and not the objective world of nature. Gukovsky analyses the lyric *Nevyrazimoe* (1819) as a statement of Zhukovsky's artistic credo and the elegy *Vecher* (1806) as an earlier example of his poetic practice, in order to demonstrate how the 'word' was losing its generally accepted terminological meaning. Gukovsky draws an analogy with music: words must sound like music, producing emotional overtones and a haze of associations. The poet produces a musical-verbal stream with words instead of notes, but the melody swallows up the sense delimitations of individual words, and they only have meaning in the unified stream. Meaning, according to Gukovsky, is located not in dictionary definitions but in the soul of the reader; not in the

[40] 'Yazyk i slog Zhukovskogo', *Stikhotvoreniya* (SPb., 1849).

[41] 'Glavneishie osobennosti yazyka i sloga proizvedenii V. A. Zhukovskogo (1783–1852)', *Russkii filologicheskii vestnik,* No. 3 (1893), 1–48.

[42] *Russkii literaturnyi yazyk pervoi poloviny XIX veka* (Kiev, 1941).

[43] *Pushkin i russkie romantiki,* 13–173.

words but between the words, in the consciousness which perceives them and joins them into verbal melody. The result is that all words are made subjective; thus, the whole objective world is made subjective.

Within this general aesthetic framework, Gukovsky points to the abundance and predominance of epithets in Zhukovsky's poetry, and concludes that the epithet is the key to the poet's subjective method. He defines the use of the epithet as 'lyrical', that is, it adorns and evaluates rather than describing or defining. These epithets lose their attachment to specific substantives, become independent, and introduce the element of *bespredmetnost'* into the language.

Gukovsky analyses specific epithets in several of Zhukovsky's lyrics. For example, *tikhoe nebo* in *Nevyrazimoe* (1819)[44] is said to be typical of Zhukovsky's epithets inasmuch as the 'object-defining' meaning of the adjective is lost; the phrase is not a metaphor, since no comparison is implied. However, Gukovsky notes that, since this epithet can also be applied to a human being (*tikhii chelovek*), Zhukovsky's *tikhii*, although it seems to describe an external object (*nebo*), in fact refers to the subject, the poet who perceives the sky.

Several problems emerge from Gukovsky's analysis. The fundamental one is related to his general approach to Zhukovsky's world-view. The poet believed, according to Gukovsky, that the objective world was ephemeral and that logic and reason could produce only falsehood. Thus, even a critic's logical approach to that world-view would necessarily distort its meaning. And since style is defined by Gukovsky as the aesthetic aspect of the poet's world-view, one must conclude that a logical approach to the poet's style would also distort its meaning.

Gukovsky's approach is not logical: it is emotional and impressionistic. He indulges in vague generalizations rather than actual analysis; he examines only three poems closely, and asserts that his conclusions are valid for most of Zhukovsky's lyrics and all of his ballads; his examples treat only six epithets (*zlatoi*, *legkii*, *sladkii*, *temnyi*, *tikhii*, *yasnyi*); nevertheless he maintains that his findings can be applied to numerous others. Gukovsky's method suffers from two additional biases. First, he was a literary critic, not a

[44] Ibid. 50.

linguist; his conclusions, therefore, overlook complex semantic factors. Second, he seems to be influenced by the Russian symbolists' mystical concept of the 'word', as for example, in his analysis of *Nevyrazimoe*; and he seems to be prejudiced by the symbolists' interpretation of Zhukovsky's role in the history of Russian poetry.[45]

In 1951 Gukovsky's theory was challenged by a linguist, V. P. Petushkov, who defended a thesis on the adjective in Zhukovsky's poetry.[46] He studied the lyrics written between 1802 and 1821 and discovered that adjectives constitute 12·5 per cent of the autonomous or 'auto-semantic' (*znamenitel'nye*) words. Of the 981 total uses of adjectives in the sample, Petushkov found that 52 per cent of the examples are limited to only 81 epithets; that of this same 52 per cent approximately half the examples are limited to only 21 epithets. In other words, approximately one-quarter of the total uses of Zhukovsky's epithets is limited to 21 words.[47]

Petushkov rejects Gukovsky's conclusion that it was Zhukovsky who introduced polysemanticism into Russian literature. He surveys the epithet in Old Russian texts and in eighteenth-century poetry and concludes that Zhukovsky's epithets are employed in the same basic way, only more subjectively. Thus what Zhukovsky introduced in his work was not so much the 'expansion of the significance of the word' (*rasshirenie mnogoznachnosti slova* or *Bedeutungsweiterung*), but the 'hypertrophied voluminosity of the significance of the word' (*gipertrofirovannaya ob''emnost' mnogoznachnosti slova*)—in other words, the 'slurring of the semantic definiteness' or the 'deprivation of the concrete weightiness' of the word.[48] The result of all this, according to Petushkov, is that Zhukovsky's poetry became vague, subjective, mystical, and 'symbolic'.

[45] Blok in his *Autobiography* (1915) refers to Zhukovsky as the first source of his poetic inspiration, and in an *Autobiographical Questionnaire* lists Zhukovsky with Fet and Solov'ev as the greatest influences on his work. Zhirmunsky argues that the roots of Russian symbolism were located in Russian romantic lyrics, especially those of Zhukovsky; see *Valerii Bryusov i nasledie Pushkina* (P., 1922).

[46] 'Imena prilagatel'nye v poezii V. A. Zhukovskogo: Opyt stilisticheskogo analiza', unpublished Candidate's Thesis (LGPI, 1951).

[47] The following epithets were used more than 100 times each in the sample: *milyi, prekrasnyi, syatoi, tikhii;* the following epithets more than 50 times each in the sample: *bozhii, vernyi, veselyi, groznyi, zemnoi, mladoi, nebesnyi, poslednii, svetlyi, svyashchennyi, sladkii, strashnyi, tainyi, uzhasnyi, unylyi, chistyi, yasnyi.*

[48] 'Imena prilagatel'nye', 158–9.

Petushkov then analyses specific epithets. One of them, *tikhii*, was used by Zhukovsky 118 times in full form and 12 times in short form in the lyrics of this period. Petushkov found that Zhukovsky uses the epithet only in its 'ordinary' meanings (literal and figurative), namely those meanings listed in the Academy of Sciences' Dictionary (1789–94). Furthermore, he noted that approximately half the uses of the word are in religious contexts. For example, Petushkov interprets the phrase *tikhoe nebo* from *Nevyrazimoe* either as a metaphor ('the sky as a quiet harbour') or as an indication of the poet's subjective emotions.[49]

Petushkov also investigates those expressions in which one epithet could be replaced by another, without any change in the semantic value of the expression: *tikhii blesk*, *mirnyi blesk*, *svezhii blesk*, *priyatnyi blesk*. He concludes that such ease of substitution proves that each epithet retained little specific meaning; therefore, polysemanticism, or the simultaneous existence of multiple meanings, could not exist under the circumstances. Petushkov's thesis is that Zhukovsky employed words as conventional, approximate symbols which could represent the inexpressible, mysterious essence of external phenomena.

While Gukovsky's analysis is limited because he was too much the literary critic, Petushkov's suffers even more because he was too much the linguist. The emphasis is on the language alone, and not on the relationship between the words and the total effect of a given phrase, line, or poem. In fact not even the immediate context of the epithet is considered. Petushkov's case for the existence of polysemanticism in Old Russian literature and in eighteenth-century poetry is insubstantial. The examples given are few, and his comments on specific epithets include only three examples: *tikhii*, *milyi*, and *prekrasnyi*. Finally, Petushkov adopts a very narrow definition of polysemanticism as the acquisition by a word of specific new meanings; Gukovsky, on the other hand, had implied only vague emotional overtones and a haze of associations. For the purposes of his argument, Petushkov assumed that Gukovsky was using the term in its narrow sense; he then examined the material linguistically and failed to discover any polysemanticism. Neverthel ess,his conclusions are remarkably close to those reached by Gukovsky.

[49] Cf. Gukovsky's conclusions about the same example, cited above.

A comprehensive investigation of the sources and meanings of Zhukovsky's epithets is included in Appendix B. In this analysis, epithets in Zhukovsky's ballads are compared with epithets in traditional Russian folk ballads, in Western European literary ballads, in eighteenth-century Russian poetry, and in early (pre-Zhukovsky) Russian literary ballads in order to determine the originality of Zhukovsky's epithets and to define his contribution to the development of Russian poetic style.

Forty of the most frequent and characteristic epithets have been selected and divided into the three groups of the Isačenko classification: (1a) qualitative absolute (8 epithets); (1b) qualitative relative (28 epithets); and (2) relative (4 epithets). For the epithets in groups (1a) and (2) examples are selected from the ballads in order to present the different ways in which these epithets are used. Typically, each of these epithets crosses the boundary from (1a) qualitative absolute or (2) relative to (1b) qualitative relative epithets. The charts also provide selected examples of these epithets as used in traditional Russian folk ballads and in early Russian literary ballads, as well as equivalent epithets from English and German literary ballads. When required, each epithet is followed by comments on Zhukovsky's usage.

The epithets in the largest and most important (1b) group are presented in greater detail. Examples for each of these epithets are listed in full from all of Zhukovsky's forty literary ballads are subdivided into their various meanings on the basis of context. The charts also provide material for comparison: (1) the definition of each epithet from the Academy of Sciences' Dictionary (1789–94); (2) selected examples of eighteenth-century Russian usage from the Academy of Sciences' Dictionary of Eighteenth-Century Russian (in preparation), supplemented by further examples from an original survey; these are arranged by thirds of the eighteenth century; and (3) selected examples from traditional Russian folk ballads, early Russian literary ballads, and equivalent epithets from German and English literary ballads. Each epithet is followed by comments on its frequency, source, and usage in Zhukovsky's ballads.

Russian scholars view the literary ballad as the culmination of the movement towards *narodnost'* which began in Russian literature in the late eighteenth and early nineteenth century. They emphasize the influence of folklore on Zhukovsky's ballads, in particular, that of folkloric language on his literary language. But a comparison of the epithet in folk ballads and in Zhukovsky's ballads results in very different conclusions.

Firstly, it is true that many of the most frequent epithets in folk ballads are also the most frequent epithets in Zhukovsky's ballads. In group (1a), of the four most frequent epithets in folk ballads (*belyi, zelenyi, rodnoi, chernyi*), three occur frequently in Zhukovsky's ballads (*belyi, rodnoi, chernyi*). In group (1b), of the eight most frequent epithets in folk ballads (*vysokii, dobryi, krasnyi, lyutyi, temnyi, chistyi, shirokii, yasnyi*), five occur frequently in Zhukovsky's ballads (*vysokii, temnyi, chistyi, shirokii, yasnyi*). In group (2) of the four most frequent epithets in folk ballads (*bozhii, dubovyi, zolotoi, shelkovyi*), two occur frequently in Zhukovsky's ballads (*bozhii, zolotoi*).

However, this correspondence of epithets in folk ballads and in Zhukovsky's ballads is not a basis on which to assume the influence of folk language on Zhukovsky's literary language. Folk ballads employ the basic descriptive concepts of language: colours (1a), simple physical description and moral judgements (1b), and materials (2).[50] These concepts are an essential component in the language of any genre of folk or sophisticated literature. Therefore, a correspondence of epithets is only natural and does not constitute evidence of influence.

Secondly, it is true that many fixed and so-called 'relatively fixed' epithets in folk ballads are also used in Zhukovsky's ballads. In group (1a) the following fixed epithets are common to folk ballads and Zhukovsky's ballads: *belyi* + *lebed', plat, golubchik*; *glukhaya polnoch'*; *chuzhaya strana*; *chernyi voron*. In group (1b) the following fixed epithets are common to folk ballads and Zhukovsky's ballads: *vernyi sluga*; *veselyi pir*; *goryuchie slezy*; *groznyi* + *son, tuchi*; *dal'nyaya storona* (Zhukovsky: *strana*); *dobryi kon'*; *dremuchii les*; *krasnaya deva* (Zhukovsky: *devitsa*); *nezhnye ruki*; *svyatye moshchi*; *strashnyi son*; *temnyi* + *les, noch'*; *chistoe pole*; *shirokii* + *dvor, doroga*; *yaryi vosk*.[51] In group (2) the following fixed epithets are common to folk ballads and Zhukovsky's ballads: *zolotoi* + *venets, krest, persten', uzda; nebesnyi tsar'*.

[50] See above, p. 81.

[51] Cf. *gor'kii* + *uchast', dolya* and *zvonkie gusli* in folk ballads, with *gorkii* + *sud'bina, zhrebii* and *zvonkie struny* in Zhukovsky's ballads.

But even this correspondence of fixed epithets in folk ballads and in Zhukovsky's ballads fails to support the view that folkloric language influenced Zhukovsky's literary language. Newly available evidence on the history of the Russian literary language in the eighteenth century indicates that almost without exception all the folk epithets which occur in Zhukovsky's ballads were in common use.[52] By the end of the eighteenth-century and in the beginning of the nineteenth century their use represents only a superficial attempt at folkloric colour and results in conventional stylization, bearing little resemblance to the language of genuine folk poetry.[53]

Thus there is no evidence to suggest any substantive relationship between the epithet in folk ballads and in Zhukovsky's literary ballads. In fact, the epithets can only legitimately be compared in terms of their coincidental function: as in folk ballads, the epithet in Zhukovsky's literary ballads tends to add no new meaning to the expression. It simply identifies the typical, constant trait of the qualified substantive.

Whereas Russian criticism overemphasizes the influence of folklore, it minimizes the influence of Western European literature on the language of Zhukovsky's ballads. A comparison of the texts of the ballads with their original sources demonstrates that approximately 20–25 per cent of Zhukovsky's epithets were 'translated' from his foreign sources.[54] Of this percentage, approximately half the epithets were translated from English, and half from German. The remaining 75–80 per cent of Zhukovsky's epithets were supplied by him when no epithet was present in the source.

In both the English and the German literary ballads which served as Zhukovsky's models, the range of synonymous epithets is much greater than that in Zhukovsky's ballads.[55] With fewer synonyms available, Zhukovsky found it necessary to repeat the same epithets more frequently than did the authors of the foreign sources.[56]

The use of English and German epithets differs considerably

[52] Academy of Sciences' Dictionary of Eighteenth-Century Russian (in preparation).

[53] See above, Ch. II, p. 36.

[54] This figure excludes *Svetlana*, *Eolova arfa*, *Akhill*, *Gromoboi*, and *Vadim* which have no immediate sources. It includes, however, those epithets which replaced, rather than translated, epithets in the original source: e.g. *wild* (Ger.). *weit*, *longue* are replaced by *gustoi*; *little*, *holy*, *halb sichtbarlich* by *svetlyi*.

[55] See Appendix B, p. 232.

[56] See Appendix B, p. 232.

from that of Zhukovsky's epithets. In English ballads epithets tend to be more concrete and are rarely applied to abstract concepts or to psychological-emotional substantives. For example, the epithet *bright* is applied to *eyes, arms, lady, silver* (cf. Zhukovsky's *svetlyi + sumrak, chas, zhizn'*); *dark* is applied to *night, eyes, brow, waters* (cf. Zhukovsky's *temnyi + glubina, mogila, chuvstvo*); and *pale* is applied to *face, cheek, brow, light, hue* (cf. Zhukovsky's *blednyi + tolpa, plamen', post*). The epithet in English literary ballads remains closer to that in the traditional folk ballads which served as direct models for imitation by English poets. Their use of the epithet in the literary ballad had little influence on Zhukovsky's diction.

In German literary ballads of the late eighteenth century, epithets became less concrete and were applied to abstract concepts and more often to psychological-emotional substantives. For example, the epithet *dunkel* is applied to *Knäuel, Gefühl, Hain* (cf. Zhukovsky's *temnyi*); *still* is applied to *Hochzeitbettchen, Weiner, Antlitz, Hoffnung* (cf. Zhukovsky's *tikhii + zhelan'e, siyan'e, radost'*); and *süss* is applied to *Mund, Klang, Lieder, Freundin* (cf. Zhukovsky's *sladkii + smyaten'e, pesny, zvuki*). Although German poets actually had models of traditional folk ballads for imitation, their more abstract psychological epithets differ significantly from those in the traditional ballads. However, the epithet in German literary ballads remains 'objective', that is, it continues to relate to the object or the abstract concept; it does not become 'subjective', relating only to the consciousness which perceives the phenomena. The language of the German literary ballads exerted a considerable influence on Zhukovsky's diction. The crucial difference lies in the total subjectivity of the Russian epithets. After Zhukovsky's visit to Weimar in September 1827 Goethe recognized this fact in his judgement: 'Auch Schukoffsky hätte weit mehr aufs Objekt hingewiesen werden müssen.'[57]

In comparison with the epithet in Western European literary ballads, Zhukovsky's epithets are far more frequent; they have their primary source in the poet's own imagination; they have fewer synonyms, and therefore are repeated more often; and finally, in their total subjectivity they differ substantially in meaning from the German and English sources.

[57] Neumann, *Geschichte*, 71.

In the language of eighteenth-century Russian poetry epithets began to acquire figurative meanings and were more often applied to abstract substantives. The grammatical and logical connection between epithet and object was still maintained. Among the most common figurative epithets and substantives in eighteenth-century poetry are: *vysokii* + *dukh*, *mysli*; *glubokii* + *vechnost'*; *nezhnyi* + *lyubov'*, *krasota*; *sladkii* + *vostorg*, *vremya*; *temnyi* + *ponyatie*, *zavist'*; *tikhii* + *zefiry*, *serdtse*; *tyazhkii* + *neschast'e*; *chistyi* + *serdtse*, *sovest'*.

During the later part of the eighteenth century certain epithets, such as *dikii*, *nezhnyi*, *sladkii*, and *uzhasnyi*, came to be used in poetry much more frequently. Others acquired distinct emotional overtones which can be characterized: for example, *blednyi* + fear, death; *mrachnyi* + gloom; and *temnyi* + mystery, death. But far more epithets, particularly during the last third of the century, acquired vague emotional overtones and were applied to a wider range of substantives, including abstract and emotional concepts. The most common of these epithets and substantives were: *glubokii* + *melankholiya*; *zadumchivyi* + *luna*; *milyi* + *taina*, *mechta*; *nezhnyi* + persons; *pechal'nyi* + *luna*, *lira*, *unynie*, *dusha*; *sladkii* + *volnen'e*, *zadumchivost'*; *tikhii* + *tuman*, *dolina*, *chuvstvo*, *dusha*; *unylyi* + *lesa*, *dukh*, *dusha*; and *chistyi* + *dusha*, *chuvstva*.

In all these expressions the logical connection between epithet and substantive was beginning to dissolve. Poets were becoming more concerned with the over-all, general impression of their phrases and lines, and less interested in the meaning of their individual words. Epithets were employed primarily to create mood or atmosphere and to produce an emotional effect on the reader's consciousness. These late eighteenth-century developments are most clearly reflected in early Russian literary ballads, particularly in those by Murav'ev and Karamzin.

Zhukovsky's poetic practice undoubtedly emerges from that of the eighteenth century; moreover, his language was very much influenced by the Russian classical tradition. In his literary ballads Zhukovsky uses certain epithets in a specifically eighteenth-century manner, such as *gorkii*, *prekrasnyi*, *prelestnyi*, *priyatnyi*, *bozhii*, *zemnoi*, *nebesnyi*, *plamennyi*, *rokovoi*, and *tsarskii*. However, the changes in the use of epithets in the late eighteenth century also influenced Zhukovsky's poetry. In his ballads such epithets as *bednyi*, *bezmolvnyi*, *bezmyatezhnyi*, *bezotvetnyi*, *nevinnyi*, *nevozratnyi*, *neizbezhnyi*, and *tomnyi* came to be used frequently. But in spite of Zhukovsky's heavy debt to eighteenth-century Russian, the epithets in his literary ballads in their frequency, meaning, and application represent a new development in the history of Russian poetic style.

Zhukovsky uses the epithets of the (1a) qualitative absolute and (2) relative groups in the conventional eighteenth-century manner. However, each of the epithets selected from the sample crosses the boundary from (1a) or (2) to the larger (1b) qualitative relative group. In other words, each epithet becomes an instrument for the poet to interpret or evaluate the phenomena he is supposed to be describing. For example, in group (1a) *belyi* acquires overtones of sanctity and occurs in religious contexts (*belaya odezhda*); *chernyi* acquires overtones of mystery and foreboding, and is used in the description of ballad settings (*chernaya puchina*); *rodnoi* comes to indicate spiritual similarity (*rodnaya dusha*) and emotional patriotic feeling (*rodnaya strana*, *zemlya*); and *chuzhoi*, as the opposite of *rodnoi*, betokens spiritual dissimilarity and alienation (*chuzhoi breg*). As for group (2), *grobovoi* acquires overtones of mystery and melancholy (*grobovoi golos*); *zlatoi* connotes beauty and spirituality (*zlataya yunost'*); and *pustynnyi* acquires overtones of vagueness and desolation (*pustynnoe otdalenie*).

The group of qualitative relative epithets (1b) is by far the largest and most important; it is in the application of these epithets that Zhukovsky is the most original. The epithets in group (1b) are used not so much to describe or characterize objects or concepts as to convey the poet's subjective impressions about these objects and concepts. In fact, Zhukovsky's epithets come to refer almost exclusively to the poet's consciousness which perceives the phenomena, and they are used to evoke imaginary associations in the reader's consciousness which enable him to share the poet's own experience. For example, the epithets *veselyi*, *zadumchivyi*, *pechal'nyi*, and *unylyi* are used to refer to their respective emotions: (a) as experienced by objective characters (*veselaya Lyudmila*, *zadumchivyi rybak*, *pechal'nyi Milon*, *unylyi pevets*); (b) as expressed in these characters' appearance or words (*veselaya pesnya*, *zadumchivye ochi*, *pechal'noe litso*, *unylyi golos*); and (c) as evoked in the poet's consciousness by external phenomena (*veselaya priroda*, *zadumchivyi zvon*, *pechal'nyi sumrak*, *unylyi les*).

Gukovsky wrote in reference to the epithet *sladkii*: '. . . in Zhukovsky's system this epithet, in being transferred from the object to the subject, . . . acquired the possibility of linkage with any object or action. . . .'[58] The implications of this statement must be explored. As the subjectivity of Zhukovsky's epithets increases, the logical, conventional connection between epithet and substantive is destroyed. Thus epithets can be connected with almost any object or concept. In other words, as a result of this greater applicability, the meaning of each epithet becomes more indeterminate. As the meaning becomes more indeterminate, so the applicability of the epithet continues to increase.

The applicability of *strashnyi* and *uzhasnyi*, for example, increases to include sights, sounds, persons, places, time, events, emotions, and so on; consequently the terminological meaning of these epithets becomes more indeterminate; (*strashnyi* + *sumrak, khor, utes, mig, mshchen'e; uzhasnyi* + *mrak, tishina, ad, den', delo*). The evidence of the ballad manuscripts demonstrates the near equivalence of these two epithets, and further reveals their ability to replace such seemingly specific epithets as *groznyi* and *dikii*. In fact these four epithets are used in the same way by Zhukovsky to create the emotionally charged atmosphere characteristic of a ballad. They refer less to objective phenomena than to the subjective experiences of horror, terror, anxiety, and fear to be shared by the poet and reader. Similarly, the applicability of the epithet *svyatoi* is extended to include persons, places, time, holy objects, and religious concepts, with a corresponding increase in the indeterminateness of its meaning (*svyatoi* + *anakhoret, skala, chas, fimiam, zhizn'*). The ballad manuscripts demonstrate that *svyatoi* can even replace *zlatoi* as an equivalent indicating some vague emotional approval of the object described.

Zhukovsky's epithets acquire vague overtones, most often of fear, death, mystery, evil, emotional warmth, and sanctity. The more overtones an epithet acquires, the more easily it can be applied to abstract substantives, and the more indeterminate its meaning becomes. Expressions such as *vysokaya dal'*, *miloe smyaten'e*, *tainaya skorb'*, and *tikhaya glubina* serve as examples of Zhukovsky's most striking combinations.

The originality of Zhukovsky's epithets, then, resides in their

[58] *Pushkin i russkie romantiki*, 62.

total subjectivity and in the complex interrelationship between their applicability and their indeterminateness. In his study of poetic language, Tynyanov wrote: 'The word does not have one fixed meaning. It is a chameleon: not only different shades (*ottenki*), but sometimes even different colours (*kraski*) appear'.[59] Potebnya's formulation neatly summarizes the results of this investigation: 'Every new application of a word . . . is the creation of a word'.[60] Zhukovsky's epithets laid the foundation for the vocabulary of Russian romantic poetry. Therein lies his major contribution to the development of Russian poetic style.

[59] *Problema stikhotvornogo yazyka* (L., 1924), 48.
[60] *Slovo*, VIII (1918), 26.

V

POLEMICS

Зачем кусать нам груди кормилицы нашей?
—Пушкин[1]

BETWEEN 1815 and 1825 Zhukovsky stood at the centre of the empassioned polemics in Russian literary criticism. The genre of the literary ballad, the poets who imitated Zhukovsky's style, and finally Zhukovsky himself were subjected to thorough critical scrutiny. Members of the most diverse literary circles participated in the debate. On the 'conservative' side, A. A. Shakhovskoi, one of the leading figures in the Beseda lyubitelei russkogo slova, and Kyukhel'beker, Gnedich, Somov, Del'vig, and Griboedov, members of the Vol'noe obshchestvo lyubitelei rossiiskoi slovesnosti, led a series of attacks on the new genre and on its creator. To counter the assault, Arzamas was formed by the 'progressives': Batyushkov, Vyazemsky, Pushkin, A. F. Voeikov, A. I. Turgenev, the minor critics D. V. Dashkov and D. N. Blyudov, and Zhukovsky himself. The Vol'noe obshchestvo lyubitelei slovesnosti, nauk i khudozhestv, which included amongst its members Ostolopov, Kamenev, A. E. Izmailov, and S. S. Bobrov, occupied a middle position in the struggle. Merzlyakov read an attack on the literary ballad during a meeting of the Obshchestvo lyubitelei rossiiskoi slovesnosti at Moscow University. The discussion found expression in various forms: poetry, comedy, critical reviews, exchanges of letters, and epigrams. This chapter is an attempt to survey the polemics which began shortly after the publication of Zhukovsky's *Lyudmila* in 1808, gather strength during the next decade, and reached their climax in 1825.

During the early 1810s Zhukovsky was the subject of lengthy verse *poslaniya* addressed to him by A. I. Turgenev, A. F. Voeikov,

[1] *PSS* XIII. 135 (Letter to Ryleev, January 1825).

M. V. Milonov, and V. L. Pushkin.[2] In each of these works Zhukovsky's first efforts at writing verse were sympathetically received, and he was commended for his salutary influence on the development of Russian literature.

The earliest discordant note in the symphony of praise was sounded in 1810 by Zhukovsky's close friend Batyushov in the poem *Prividen'e*,[3] a free translation of Parny's elegy, *Le revenant*. Batyushkov sets out to describe what sort of a loving apparition he would become after his own death, if only the dead could be resurrected. Then he continues:

> . . . но из могилы,
> Если можно воскресать,
> Я не стану, друг мой милый,
> Как мертвец тебя пугать.
> В час полуночных явлений
> Я не стану в виде тени,
> То внезапу, то тишком
> С воплем в твой являться дом.[4]

This passage is clearly intended as a friendly polemic with Zhukovsky's description of the lover's ghost in *Lyudmila*.[5] The nouns *mertvets* and *ten'*, the adverbs *vnezapu* (cf. Zhukovsky's *vdrug*) and *tishkom* (cf. Zhukovsky's *tikhii*), and the entire line 'V chas polunochnykh yavlenii' (cf. *Lyudmila*, 16: 2, 'V chas polunochnykh videnii') are all borrowed from Zhukovsky's diction so that Batyushkov can demonstrate how he would *not* describe his own apparition.

In *Moi penaty* (1811–12) and in the *poslanie*, *K Zhukovskomu* (1812), Batyushkov characterizes his friend's poetry more sympathetically. He depicts Zhukovsky as a poet of elegies and ballads, whose favourite themes are sadness and joy, melancholy and friendship. But in another *poslanie* written during the same period,

[2] See *Poety 1790–1810-kh godov*, *Biblioteka poeta*, *Bol'shaya seriya*, 2-oe izd. (L., 1971).

[3] *Vestnik Evropy*, No. 6 (1810), 108–10.

[4] K. N. Batyushkov, *Polnoe sobranie stikhotvorenii*, *Biblioteka poeta*, *Bol'shaya seriya*, 2-oe izd. (M.-L., 1964), 119.

[5] See I. Z. Serman, *Konstantin Batyushkov* (N.Y., 1974), 69-71.

Otvet Turgenevu (1812 ?),[6] Batyushkov once again expresses some gentle irony in his attitude towards the ballads:

Под знаменем Киприды
Сей новый Дон-Кишот
Проводит век с мечтами:
С химерами живет,
Беседует с духами,
С задумчивой луной,
И мир смешит собой.[7]

A similar satirical description of Zhukovsky as a *balladnik* is included in the earliest version of A. F. Voeikov's unofficial and unpublished series of stanzas called *Dom sumasshedshikh* (1814–17). In later redactions of this work Zhukovsky's name was replaced by the ironic 'Balladin':

Вот Жуковский, в саван длинный
  Скутан, лапочки крестом,
Ноги вытянув умильно
  Черта дразнит языком.
Видеть ведьму вображает:
  И глазком ей подмигнет,
И кадит и отпевает,
  И трезвонит, и ревет.[8]

Like Batyushkov, Voeikov gently caricatures the Gothic paraphernalia of Zhukovsky's early ballads: the shrouds, demons, and witches of *Lyudmila* and *Svetlana*. More incisive verse parodies of Zhukovsky's ballads were composed and circulated in the late 1820s and early 1830s by Pushkin and Lermontov,[9] and by Del'vig, Izmailov, K. A. Bakhturin, V. A. Protashinsky, and others.[10] The real polemic, however, was being enacted elsewhere: on the stage.

On the evening of 23 September 1815 in the Malyi teatr in St. Petersburg, there took place the premiere of a new play by A. A. Shakhovskoi called *Urok koketam, ili Lipetskie vody*. The author, a

[6] *Opyty v stikhakh i proze*, II (SPb., 1817), 153–6.
[7] *K. N. Batyushkov*, 144.
[8] *Poety 1790–1810-kh godov*, 796.
[9] See below, Chs. VII and VIII.
[10] See *Russkaya stikhotvornaya parodiya, Biblioteka poeta, Bol'shaya seriya* (L., 1960), and *Mnimaya poeziya*, ed. Yu. Tynyanov (M.-L., 1931).

member of Admiral Shishkov's Beseda, had previously expressed his 'conservative' views on the subject of contemporary Russian literature. His earlier comedy, *Novyi Stern* (1805), had been directed against sentimentalism; its hero, Count Pronsky, was intended to be a caricature of Karamzin. The first canto of Shakhovskoi's poem *Raskhishchennye shuby* (1815) contained a mocking reference to Zhukovsky's *sto zhalostnykh ballad*.[11] In his new comedy, *Urok koketam*, Shakhovskoi launched a savage attack on the ballad genre and on its creator: in the pitiful figure of the *balladnik* Fialkin, Shakhovskoi created a brilliant caricature of Zhukovsky.

Soon after Fialkin's first appearance on stage (II. v), he boldly asserts that his own genius was inspired by the fashionable genre of the literary ballad.[12] His speech contains numerous expressions which suggest the vocabulary of Zhukovsky's lyrics and ballads: *naivnost' raiskaya*; *fimiam*; *um chudesnyi*; *dusha nebesnaya*; *raiskaya vest'*. In the next scene Fialkin enters, 'sighing from afar', to recite one of his ballads for his patroness, the Countess Leleva; it is a witty parody of Zhukovsky's 'classical' ballad *Akhill* (1814):

Пел бессмертный славну Трою,
Пел родных Приама чад;
Пел Ахилла, жадна к бою,
Пел Элены милый взгляд.
Но чувствительность слезами
Излила глаза певца.
Ах! мы любим не глазами,
Для любви у нас сердца;
И бессмертный под сетями
У бессмертного слепца.[13] (II. vi)

Although the Countess tells Fialkin that the ballad is *ochen' mil*, she exclaims in an aside to the audience: 'Chto za vzdor!' Fialkin explains that his ballad might have lost something during his recitation; he then chases the Countess off stage, shouting 'Ballada

[11] A. A. Shakhovskoi, *Komedii, stikhotvoreniya, Biblioteka poeta, Bol'shaya seriya*, 2-oe izd. (L., 1961), 91.

[12] One of Fialkin's lines ('Ya vybral modnyi rod/Ballad') could almost have been a paraphrase of Zhukovsky's admission in a letter to A. I. Turgenev in 1813: 'Ballady moi izbrannyi rod poezii.' See above, p. 39.

[13] Shakhovskoi, *Komedii*, 164.

vam' and imploring her to hear out the rest of his forty-eight stanzas.

When Fialkin returns (v. ii), it is so that Shakhovskoi can direct his criticism against the Gothic paraphernalia of Zhukovsky's literary ballads. The *balladnik* confesses that his own knowledge of corpses is derived from his readings in contemporary Russian ballads; his description contains a healthy assortment of Zhukovsky's favourite motifs and expressions:

. . . ими [мертвецами] я свой нежный вкус питаю;
И полночь, и петух, и звон костей в гробах,
И чу! . . . все страшно в них; но милым все приятно,
Все восхитительно! хотя невероятно.[14]

The unfortunate Zhukovsky happened to be present at the first performance of Shakhovskoi's comedy. The event is recalled by the memoirist F. F. Vigel': 'One could imagine the predicament of poor Zhukovsky, at whom several indiscreet glances were directed! One could imagine the astonishment and fury of the friends sitting around him! The glove had been thrown down; Blyudov and Dashkov, still in their tumultuous youth, hurried to pick it up'.[15] Blyudov responded with a satirical sketch about Shakhovskoi called *Videnie v kakoi-to ograde*. Dashkov followed suit with two satirical attacks on the comedy: *Pis'mo k noveishemu Aristofanu* and *Venchanie Shutovskogo*. Vyazemsky joined in the attack with his satirical *Pis'mo s Lipetskikh vod*. In it he referred to the characters of Shakhovskoi's play as 'soulless creatures' and 'facetious Lilliputians'; Fialkin was described as an 'obvious idiot'.[16] Vyazemsky also composed a cycle of epigrams directed against the playwright entitled *Poeticheskii venok Shutovskogo*. In 1819 Bestuzhev, in an article published in *Syn otechestva*, criticized the style, structure, and language of *Urok koketam*, and concluded that 'fortunately the clouds of such comedies cannot eclipse true talent'.[17]

A major consequence of the polemic surrounding Shakovskoi's play was the formation of the literary society Arzamas by Zhukovsky's closest friends. At the first meeting in 1815 each member of

[14] Ibid. 238.
[15] *Zapiski*, IV. 171–2.
[16] *Rossiskii muzeum*, No. 12 (1815), 257 ff.
[17] No. 6 (1819), 263 ff.

the group took a nickname from one of Zhukovsky's ballads, either a title, a character, or a phrase: A. I. Turgenev was called *Eolova arfa*; Pushkin was nicknamed *sverchok* (from *Svetlana*); Zhukovsky was known as *Svetlana*; Dashkov as *Chu*!; and V. L. Pushkin as *Vot*.[18]

Zhukovsky refrained from engaging in the debate, except in his minor satirical works directed against the members of the Beseda. For example, in *Pred sudilishche Minosa* (1815) he refers to his literary enemies as *skoty* and parodies the fables written by D. I. Khvostov, one of Shakhovskoi's supporters. In *Plach o Pindare* (1815) Zhukovsky's wit is directed against the entire Beseda, in particular, Khvostov and the poetess A. P. Bunina. However, Zhukovsky's real attitude is reflected in a letter written during the autumn of 1815, sent from St. Petersburg to his family in Belev:

There is an author here . . . [called] Shakhovskoi. It is well known that authors are not admirers of other authors. And therefore he is not an admirer of mine. He decided to write a comedy in which he makes fun of me. My friends intervened. . . . Now there is a terrible war on Parnassus. They are fighting around me and for me, but I remain silent, and it would be better if everyone remained silent. . . .[19]

M. N. Zagoskin responded to the attacks on Shakhovskoi with a comedy entitled *Komediya protiv komedii, ili Urok volokitam*, first performed on 3 November 1815. The hero Izborsky praises the virtues of Shakhovskoi's play: 'Write what you will: both prose and verse; in spite of it all, the comedy [*Urok koketam*] is splendid: it honours our literature. I think that it has some passages worthy of Molière'.[20] Izborsky then directs his attention to the ballad genre; he criticizes the untalented imitators of Zhukovsky who, by writing only about corpses and ghosts, would eventually lower the standard of Russian poetry.[21] Zagoskin's comedy, in turn, was

[18] See *Arzamas i Arzamasskie protokoly*, ed. M. S. Borovkova-Maikova (L., 1933).

[19] Shakhovskoi, *Komedii*, 774–5. Karamzin expressed similar sentiments in a letter to A. I. Turgenev dated October 1815: 'Let Zhukhovsky answer only with new and beautiful verse; Shakhovskoi will never catch him up'.

[20] *PSS* VI (P., n.d.), 210.

[21] Ibid. 213.

followed by a series of reviews, letters, and epigrams attacking the playwright.

In 1817 Griboedov and Katenin collaborated in the writing of a satire called *Student*, which was never performed and which remained unpublished until 1858.[22] The main character, Benevol'sky, is a composite caricature of Zhukovsky, Batyushov, and Zagoskin (whose personal pseudonym in the journal *Severnyi nablyudatel'* was in fact Benevol'sky). The play also contains critical references to Karamzin, A. E. Izmailov, and other of Zhukovsky's supporters. Some of the hero's lines echo particular lyrics of Zhukovsky and Batyushkov; other lines parody more general features of the poets' diction:

> . . . в голове моей, в сердце такое что-то неизбяснимое, мир незнаемый, смутная будущность.[23]

> . . . которая часто появлялась мне в сновидениях, светла, как Ора, легка, как Ириса,—величественный стан, сафирные глаза, русые, льну подобные, волосы. . . .[24]

Benevol'sky cannot express himself without using a great number of epithets, most of which are borrowed from Zhukovsky's vocabulary: *sumrachnaya dal'*, *mrachnye mysli*, *zlatoi chas*, *milyi tsvet*, *tomnyi vzor*.

These comedies and the polemics which surrounded them demonstrate the central importance of Zhukovsky's position in Russian literary criticism during the 1810s. When in 1816 critical attention was focused on specific ballads, the issues in the debate became more clearly defined.

Zhukovsky's first ballad *Lyudmila*, a free translation of Bürger's *Lenore*, was published in *Vestnik Evropy* in 1808. In 1816 P. A. Katenin translated the same ballad under the title of *Ol'ga* and sent a copy to Zhukovsky, who forwarded it to Gnedich with the following letter: 'This work, in spite of its many faults, demonstrates that in time he [Katenin] will write well. If he had less self-confidence and decided to write not only for transient praise, then

[22] The manuscript was discovered and published by E. N. Serchevsky in *A. S. Griboedov i ego sochineniya* (SPb., 1858).

[23] A. S. Griboedov, *PSS* I (SPb., 1911), 68.

[24] Ibid. 82.

he would be a good author. He definitely has talent.'[25] The publication of *Ol'ga* in *Vestnik Evropy* and *Syn otechestva* later that year provoked a storm of controversy concerning specific features of Katenin's style in comparison with Zhukovsky's which foreshadowed all future criticism of the literary ballad genre.[26]

Gnedich published the first review of Katenin's *Ol'ga*. He begins with lavish praise for Zhukovsky's *Lyudmila*, which he considers to be an 'original Russian ballad', since it had borrowed only its theme from Bürger's work. The local colour, tone, feeling, and 'popular language', he claims, are all original to Zhukovsky; in some passages Zhukovsky's Russian version is alleged to be preferable to the German. Gnedich then compares *Ol'ga* with Bürger's *Lenore*, and finds Katenin's version full of sins against grammar, logic, euphony, and good taste. He singles out several unacceptable colloquial forms (*svetik*, *vplot'*, *sporo*, *svoloch'*) and vulgarisms,[27] and finds Bürger's original 'simpler, stronger, and better' than Katenin's translation. The review concludes with an ironic attack on the entire ballad genre: 'What wonderful devils he [Katenin] found for his ballads! *Vivent les ballades*! And after this they dare to attack them? And after this they tell me that ballads have no moral purpose.'[28]

Griboedov came to Katenin's defence. In an article also published in *Syn otechestva* that year he takes exception to Gnedich's analysis of Katenin's errors in grammar, logic, and taste, and answers each of the specific accusations in turn.[29] He then directs his attention to Zhukovsky's *Lyudmila* and criticizes expressions such as *Pyl' tumanit otdalen'e* as incorrect usage, *nadezhda-sladost'* as tautology, and the excessive use of *chu*! and *slyshish'*! Furthermore, he questions the logical meaning of Zhukovsky's version, arguing that Lyudmila is depicted as too humble and as totally undeserving of punishment; that the corpse is too *milyi*; that the heroine embraces the hero even after she knows that he is a

[25] *SS*, IV. 569.

[26] *Vestnik Evropy*, No. 9 (1816); and *Syn otechestva*, No. 24 (1816).

[27] For example, Lenore's question about the bridal bed ('Hat's Raum für mich?') is rendered by Katenin as 'V nei ulyazhetsya l' nevesta?' Gnedich points out that a *nevesta* who could ask such a question has no place in the original or in any translation. Zhukovsky characteristically omits Lenore's question in his version.

[28] *Syn otechestva*, No. 27 (1816), 21.

[29] Ibid., No. 30 (1816), 150–60. Griboedov asks whether the *nevesta* should have asked: 'Predat'sya toshchim mechtaniyam lyubvi ideal'noi?'

corpse; and so on. Griboedov concludes with a reply to Gnedich's attack on the genre; he defends the ballad and argues that he can see no reason why ballad-writers should have to apologize for their choice of form.

Gnedich's initial article on Katenin also provoked a response from Batyushkov. In a letter to Gnedich written in August 1816, Batyushkov thanks him for his criticism of *Ol'ga* but objects to his attack on the ballad in general; he maintains that 'all genres are worthy'. Furthermore, Batyushkov advises Gnedich not to answer Griboedov's criticism; rather he should simply demonstrate that Zhukovsky was the greater poet: 'then all Griboedovs would disappear.'[30]

Griboedov did disappear shortly thereafter—on a diplomatic mission to Persia—and there this phase of the polemics almost ended. However, in 1822 Katenin, in a review of Grech's *Opyt kratkoi istorii russkoi literatury*, attacks the critic for overlooking his ballads. Katenin declares that his *prostonarodnye ballady* deserved more attention as 'totally original work, not borrowed from anywhere'.[31] Katenin was soon answered by Bestuzhev, who states that he finds no originality whatsoever in any of Katenin's works; furthermore, he points out that there are obvious borrowings from Derzhavin in at least one of his ballads (*Leshii*).[32] Katenin's faithful disciple, N. N. Bakhtin, came to his friend's defence. He replies to the objections raised by Bestuzhev, and even returns to the original accusations made by Gnedich in 1816. Bakhtin then criticizes Zhukovsky's *Lyudmila*, and concludes with an eloquent defence of Katenin as the better poet of the two.[33]

Katenin was never able to forget the dispute. In 1831, when he read Zhukovsky's second translation of Bürger's *Lenore*, he thought no more of it than he had of the earlier *Lyudmila*. He wrote to Bakhtin: 'The translation is rubbish, and perhaps its only merit is that it preserves the metre of the original precisely.'[34] In another letter to Bakhtin in 1833 Katenin wrote: 'Both the words of

[30] *Sochineniya*, III (SPb., 1886), 389.
[31] *Syn otechestva*, No. 13 (1822), 260.
[32] Ibid., No. 20 (1823), 253–69.
[33] *Vestnik Evropy*, No. 3–4 (1823), 193–214.
[34] *Russkaya starina*, CXLVII (1911), 355. It should be noted that under the influence of Zhukovsky's retranslation, Katenin reworked his *Ol'ga* and made some corrections to it. See below, Ch. VI, p. 128.

Griboedov in the debate with Gnedich, and the action of Zhukovsky, who acknowledged by his second translation that his first was inadequate, justified my writing of *Ol'ga*, in spite of the existence of *Lyudmila*.'[35]

The *Lyudmila/Ol'ga* controversy and its aftermath are indicative of the next phase of the polemics. Beginning in 1816 more critics and writers were forced to take sides: Gnedich, Batyushkov, and Bestuzhev supported Zhukovsky; Griboedov, Bakhtin, and, above all, Katenin supported Katenin. Furthermore, criticism was no longer limited to details of grammar, logic, taste, and so on; rather, the more general themes of *narodnost'*, creative originality, and the validity of the ballad genre were raised; these issues were to dominate the critical debate during the next decade.

During the years immediately following the 1816 phase of the polemics it is possible to detect a change in the general critical attitude towards the genre of the literary ballad and towards its creator. Anonymous reviews in various periodicals and the memoirs of Zhukovsky's contemporaries testify to the poet's early popularity. But, first in private correspondence and then in published articles, even Zhukovsky's supporters began to express their growing dissatisfaction with his limitations.

The reviews of Zhukovsky's poetry and prose published in *Syn otechestva* from 1816 to 1818 contain only approbation. An article on *Dvenadtsat' spyashchikh dev* pays tribute to the ballad's 'easy, free versification', its 'descriptive or pictorial poetry', and its 'vivid depictions of the majestic and the terrible'.[36] The reviewer of the second edition of Zhukovsky's poetry (1818) writes that he 'belongs to the small group of our true poets'.[37] N. I. Grech, recalling in his memoirs Zhukovsky's appearance on the literary scene, describes the overwhelming enthusiasm universally shared for his early work: 'Any doubt about the perfection of his [Zhukovsky's] verse was considered a crime.'[38] Another memoirist, F. F. Vigel', expresses similar sentiments about the poet's personality: 'To know Zhukovsky and not to love him was absolutely impossible.'[39]

[35] *Russkaya starina*, CXLVII (1911), 365. See also Katenin's article in *Moskovskii telegraf*, No. 11 (1833), 450–1.

[36] *Syn otechestva*, No. 32 (1817), 230–2.

[37] Ibid., No. 36 (1818), 225.

[38] *Zapiski o moei zhizni* (M.-L., 1930), 493.

[39] *Zapiski*, II. 54.

Kyukhel'beker, who was later to criticize the language of Russian poetry for its monotony, particularly for its excess of epithets, and who was to extol Katenin's ballads, in 1817 was one of Zhukovsky's most avid supporters. In a survey of Russian literature he commends Zhukovsky for his transformation of the 'external form and internal spirit' of Russian poetry, and for his introduction of 'the German spirit'.[40] In an article on Batyushkov, Kyukhel'beker compares the two poets and finds them equally talented, though different: while Batyushkov was influenced by Italian and French verse, Zhukovsky had become the 'Russian Scott, Byron, and Goethe'.[41] As late as 1820 Kyukhel'beker was still defending Zhukovsky against an anonymous attack published in *Nevskii zritel'*.[42]

A similar comparison of Batyushkov and Zhukovsky as poets was drawn by Bestuzhev in his general review of Russian literature in 1823. Bestuzhev, who was later to berate Russian poets for their lack of originality, is full of praise for Zhukovsky: 'The soul of [Zhukovsky's] reader is troubled by mournful emotions, but indescribably pleasant ones. Thus do the vague sounds of the Aeolian harp, vibrating in the sighs of the wind, reach our hearts.'[43] Bestuzhev cites the variety of Zhukovsky's descriptions. While admitting that there may be a little too much German atmosphere and mysticism, he asserts that these are but minor faults in the creator of such masterpieces as *Lyudmila* and *Svetlana*.[44]

As early as the mid-1810s Batyushkov, to whom Zhukovsky was so often compared, was becoming concerned about his friend's limitations. Although he published an article lauding Zhukovsky's 'passionate imagination' and his ability to convey 'the profound sensations of his strong and noble soul',[45] privately, in 1814 in a letter to Zhukovsky, he expresses his deep anxiety: '[A. I.] Turgenev told me that you are writing a ballad. Why not write a *poema*? . . . What a queer fish you are! You possess everything needed to achieve lasting fame based on important work. You have the imagination of Milton, the tenderness of Petrarch . . . and you

[40] *Vestnik Evropy*, No. 17–18 (1817), 157.

[41] Ibid., No. 23–4 (1817), 204–8.

[42] *Nevskii zritel'*, I (Feb. 1820), 106–28.

[43] *Polyarnaya zvezda* (1823), 22.

[44] See also an anonymous review in *Vestnik Evropy*, No. 23–4 (1817), 193–204: "God preserve us from this German spirit."

[45] Ibid., No. 10 (1816), 93–104.

write ballads. Leave the trifles to us. Take up something worthy of your talent.'[46]

A different sort of concern was expressed by another of Zhukovsky's followers, Vyazemsky, in his letters to A. I. Turgenev in 1819. He maintains that Zhukovsky's poetry was prone to a certain monotony of 'patterns, forms, and phrases':[47] 'The poet must pour his soul into various vessels. Zhukovsky, more than others, has to guard against monotony.'[48]

Another former supporter and ex-ballad-writer, Merzlyakov, launched a vitriolic attack on the ballad genre at a public meeting of the Obshchestvo lyubitelei rossiiskoi slovesnosti at Moscow University on 22 February 1818. He read out, in Zhukovsky's presence, the text of his *Pis'mo iz Sibiri*, excerpts of which were later published in *Vestnik Evropy*.[49] The memoirist M. A. Dmitriev recalls the plight of the unfortunate Zhukovsky:

> The leading lights of Moscow society were assembled for the meeting of the Obshchestvo. . . . Imagine everyone's astonishment when Merzlyakov . . . suddenly began to read out his 'Letter from Siberia' against . . . the ballads of Zhukovsky—who was sitting at the table with all the other members. . . . Zhukovsky had to endure the reading until the end; the chairman was on pins and needles; it was impossible to stop the speaker. What a most unpleasant surprise both for the members and for the public![50]

Merzlyakov criticizes the Russian literary ballad for two reasons: firstly, it contravenes the rules of classical poetics with its improbable content, its lack of form, and its absence of purpose; secondly, the ballad's foreign origin and alien spirit betray the great tradition of Russian poetry. Merzlyakov remained a true classicist, both in his own efforts at writing literary ballads during the 1790s[51] and in his classical criticism of Zhukovsky's distinctly non-classical ballads in the 1810s.

A critic who shared Merzlyakov's classical position, A. G. Glagolev, turned his attention in 1820 to Zhukovsky's imitators.

[46] *Sochineniya*, III. 306. See also Batyushkov's letters to Vyazemsky and Gnedich in 1817.
[47] *Ostaf'evskii arkhiv*, I (SPb., 1899), 227.
[48] Ibid. 305.
[49] *Trudy Obshchestva lyubitelei rossiiskoi slovesnosti*, XI (1818), 52–70.
[50] *Melochi*, 167–9.
[51] See above, Ch. II, pp. 30–3.

His criticism was occasioned by the publication in *Syn otechestva* of P. A. Pletnev's ballad *Mogil'shchik*.[52] In a letter to the editor of *Vestnik Evropy* Glagolev points out the errors in Pletnev's grammar and logic, and denounces the ballad's Gothic motifs and pervasive morbidity: 'What is the goal of this ballad? What is its use? Where is the enjoyment? Is this the language of the gods?'[53] In response to an anonymous defence of Pletnev,[54] Glagolev extends his attack to German romanticism, which, he claims, is threatening to destroy the traditions of Russian classicism. While Russian literature would always be grateful to Zhukovsky for the introduction of English and German themes, Glagolev argues that the poet's successors have 'entered into the immeasurable abyss of mysticism and romanticism'.[55]

The attacks by Merzlyakov and Glagolev, both launched from the position of classical aesthetics, were aimed principally at the ballad genre and at Zhukovsky's imitators. In 1821, however, criticism began to be directed at Zhukovsky himself, namely at the language of his ballad *Rybak* (1820),[56] a translation of Goethe's *Der Fischer*.

O. M. Somov initiated this phase of the polemics with a savage attack on the content and style of Zhukovsky's translation. He belittles the subject of the ballad and criticizes the author's language, in particular, his epithets: '*Dusha* (one must assume of the fisherman) *polna prokhladnoi tishinoi*. In the figurative sense this means that ecstasy, reverence fill his soul; . . . but neither *tishina* nor *shum* has the capacity to fill a soul. And how can *prokhladnaya* be a quality of *tishina*? Therefore we must also have *teplaya tishina*, *znoinyi shum*, and so on.'[57] Somov takes exception to almost every epithet in Zhukovsky's version:

[*Vlazhnaya glava*] What? the head of the maiden is composed of *vlaga*? . . . *Rodnoe dno*. What a strange *rodstvo*! . . . *Kipuchii zhar* is good too. . . . Where is this *znoinaya vyshina*, Mister Author? . . . *Gorit svezheyu krasoi*; that is so astonishingly complicated, isn't it? . . .

[52] *Syn otechestva*, No. 17 (1820), 217–18.

[53] *Vestnik Evropy*, No. 11 (1820), 215. In the same article Glagolev refers to *Ruslan i Lyudmila* as a parody of Kirsha Danilov by some unknown *piit*.

[54] *Syn otechestva*, No. 31 (1820), 228–32.

[55] *Vestnik Evropy*, No. 16 (1820), 283–96.

[56] *Syn otechestva*, No. 36 (1820); see above, Ch. III, pp. 47–9.

[57] *Nevskii zritel'*, V (Jan. 1821), 60.

Prokhladno-goluboi svod neba! that is also very complicated. In time we shall compose new tones of colour and will say: *vetreno-ryzhii, dozhdlivo-zheltyi, merzlo-sinii, znoino-zelenyi*, etc., etc.[58]

Somov's objections to Zhukovsky's semantic system are invaluable inasmuch as they help to clarify the nature of the poet's stylistic innovations. Specific epithets are criticized because they do not make rational, logical sense. Thus Somov totally rejects Zhukovsky's emotional language precisely because it obscures the objective terminological meaning of his words.[59]

The critic F. V. Bulgarin answered Somov with a defence of Zhukovsky's translation. He makes the argument that the content of *Rybak* is rooted in the tradition of the Russian *skazka*, and at the same time maintains that the language of the Russian version is very close to that of the German original. Expressions such as *prokhladnaya tishina* and *vlazhnaya glava* are interpreted as examples of Goethe's (and Zhukovsky's) new and original use of language. Bulgarin concludes: 'Klopstock, Schiller, Goethe, Byron, Derzhavin, and Zhukovsky abound in these bold bursts of creative imagination. New sensations and thoughts give birth to new expressions.'[60] Bulgarin was incredibly perceptive. These new sensations and thoughts could not be translated into the objective, terminological language which Somov was demanding. A new subjective, emotional language had to be invented, and Zhukovsky was to be its creator.

Somov answered Bulgarin. He asserts that a critic always has the right to demand that poetry make logical sense when 'translated' into objective language. He supplies a literal rendition of Goethe's *Der Fischer* and demands: 'Where then is the *prokhladnaya tishina* in his soul and the *vlazhnaya glava*? Where is the *rodnoe dno* and *kipuchii zhar*, *znoinaya vyshina* and *prokhladno-goluboi svod*

[58] Ibid. 61–3. Somov includes an amusing parody using his new compound expressions:

Октябро-непогодно-бурна,
Дико-густейша темнота,
Сурово притворно-сумбурна,
Збродно-порывна глухота,
Мерцает в скорбно-желтом слухе,
Рисует в темно-алом духе,
Туманно-светлый небосклон.

[59] See above, Ch. IV.

[60] *Syn otechestva*, No. 9 (1821), 71–2.

neba?'[61] Somov admits that he too had been an admirer of Zhukovsky's poetry until 'Western, alien *tumany* and *mraki*' obscured the poet's senses; now 'everything is German, except for the letters and the words'.[62]

With Somov's answer, this phase of the polemics was almost concluded. A humorous announcement for subscriptions to 'The Collected Works of O. M. Somov' was published by Voeikov. Somov's works were supposed to include a 'Eulogy to the author written by himself', 'Translations from languages of which the translator has no knowledge', and 'Collections of misprints copied from the works of Batyushkov, Zhukovsky, Krylov, etc.'[63] Shortly thereafter a minor poet, Ya. I. Rostovtsov, wrote a defence of Zhukovsky in verse entitled *K zoilam poeta* ('S pevtsa vam ne sorvat' venka').[64] But it was Bestuzhev who pronounced the final succinct judgement:

> Балладу поместил я в число образцовых переводов, а критику на нее между уродцами.[65]

Criticism of the new subjective language of Russian poetry, in particular of its epithets, had begun as early as 1820. An anonymous reviewer, referring to Zhukovsky's ballad *Uznik*, writes: 'I will not comment on the expression: *nebesno-tainoe*, because, for me, it is *sovershenno-neponyatnoe*.'[66] Kyukhel'beker, in his survey of Russian poetry in 1824, provides a full list of the most frequently repeated combinations of epithets and substantives:

> Картины везде одни и те же: луна, которая разумеется, уныла и бледна, скалы и дубравы, где их никогда не бывало; лес, за которым сто раз представляют заходящее солнце; вечерняя заря; изредка длинные тени и привидения, что-то невидимое, что-то неведомое, пошлые иносказания, бледные, безвкусные олицетворения; . . . в особенности же туман: туманы над водами, туманы над бором, туманы над полями, туман в голове сочинителя.[67]

[61] *Nevskii zritel'*, V (Mar. 1821), 283.
[62] Ibid. 277–9.
[63] *Syn otechestva*, No. 11 (1821), 195–6.
[64] Ibid., No. 12 (1821), 232–3.
[65] Ibid., No. 13 (1821), 263.
[66] Ibid., No. 20 (1820), 25.
[67] *Mnemozina*, II (1824), 37–8.

In 1825 Kyukhel'beker again refers to the abundance of epithets in contemporary Russian poetry, citing Katenin's ballads as the only exception: 'So! our literature is young: but we had and still have poets (though very few) with bold imagination, laconic style—not diluted by a flood of melodious, empty epithets.'[68]

In a similar vein, Vyazemsky writes in a review of Zhukovsky's prose tale *Mar'ina roshcha* (1809): 'In his style, one senses youth, but a promising youth—particularly in his lack of restraint in adjectives, which is the usual fault of young writers and of young literatures in general.'[69] This is followed by an interesting confession: 'The truth is I am not an enemy of adjectives; I regard them as one of the means of expressing thoughts left to us: all nouns have been uttered; it remains for us to qualify [*ottenivat'*] them anew with adjectives.'[70]

The most sophisticated criticism of the new stylistics is contained in an anonymous review entitled 'Mysli o Sumarokove i drugikh pisatelyakh' published in 1828. Contemporary poetry, according to the writer, is based on the domination of imagination over reason. The obscurity of the emotional language is the result of the elimination of necessary verbs, the use in translations of syntactic calques from the language of the original, the striving after excessive euphonic effects, and, finally, the modification of substantives by unsuitable epithets. As examples of the last feature, he cites such expressions as *krasno-rechivaya reka*, *dushistaya ten'*, *rodnaya gora*, and *svyatoi polden'*.[71]

From their first attacks on the ballad genre, to their attacks on Zhukovsky's imitators, and finally on the poet himself, the polemics of the late 1810s and early 1820s help to reveal the nature of Zhukovsky's innovations in the language of Russian poetry. However, the climax in the polemics in 1825 suddenly reduced Zhukovsky from the most outstanding figure in the contemporary literary scene to an important figure in Russian literary history.

As early as 1823 impassioned pleas were made for the creation of a national Russian poetry, independent of the influence of foreign literatures. Somov, in his articles on romanticism, com-

[68] *Syn otechestva*, No. 17 (1825), 71.
[69] *Moskovskii telegraf*, No. 23 (1826), 172.
[70] Ibid. 173.
[71] *Otechestvennye zapiski*, No. 96 (1828), 75–6.

plains of the monotonous elegiac tone of contemporary poetry, and declares: 'Let there shine forth in their elevated songs, as in a pure stream, the spirit of our people and the qualities of our rich and majestic language. . . .'[72] Kyukhel'beker in 1824 makes a more emotional entreaty: 'Let there be created for the glory of Russia a truly Russian poetry; then let holy *Rus'* become the greatest power in the universe, not only in the political world, but also in the moral sphere'.[73] Early in 1825 Bestuzhev asks, almost despairingly: 'When will we ever get on to the right track? When will we begin to write in genuine Russian? God only knows!'[74]

Dissatisfaction with the 'new poetry' was widespread; appeals for national Russian verse were becoming more strident. When in 1825 Pletnev wrote an article praising Zhukovsky's talent and taste, concluding that he was 'the first poet of the golden age of our literature',[75] he provoked what was to be the last phase of the literary polemics surrounding Zhukovsky.

Bulgarin, who previously defended Zhukovsky's *Rybak* against Somov's objections, now violently disagrees with Pletnev: '. . . our age is not yet golden, and Zhukovsky is not the first poet of our age'.[76] Bulgarin condemns Zhukovsky for his lack of originality and for the inadequacy of his translations. He agrees that in his introduction of German and English themes Zhukovsky had performed a useful function; but unfortunately he had outlived his usefulness. Bulgarin hints that 'another poet' had already appeared to replace him.

Bulgarin was answered in an article by Vyazemsky. Having previously expressed his own anxiety in letters to A. I. Turgenev about the monotony of Zhukovsky's verse, Vyazemsky now defends Zhukovsky against Bulgarin's criticism, specifically against the charge of monotony. He concludes with a reasonable attempt to formulate the relationship between Zhukovsky and that 'other poet' alluded to by Bulgarin, a theme which was to bring that other poet into the polemics in 1825. Vyazemsky wrote: 'Pushkin is the consequence (*sledstvie*) of Zhukovsky.'[77]

[72] *O romanticheskoi poezii*, III (SPb., 1823), 102.
[73] *Mnemozina*, II (1824), 42.
[74] *Polyarnaya zvezda* (1825), 9.
[75] *Severnye tsvety* (1825), 34.
[76] *Syn otechestva*, No. 2 (1825), 204.
[77] *Moskovskii telegraf*, No. 4 (1825), 350.

The relationship between Zhukovsky and Pushkin is extraordinarily complex; too often individual statements made by each poet have been interpreted as definitive, when in fact they express only one aspect of the relationship. In 1820 when Zhukovsky read *Ruslan i Lyudmila* he sent his portrait to Pushkin with the inscription: 'To the conquering student (*uchenik*) from his conquered teacher'.[78] Pushkin's letters to Vyazemsky and Gnedich in 1822 are filled with pleas for Zhukovsky to stop translating and instead to start writing original works: 'God grant that he may begin to create.'[79] When Pushkin received the third edition of Zhukovsky's poems in 1824, he expressed his bitter disappointment in a letter to L. S. Pushkin: 'I received the Zhukovsky. The deceased was a good fellow [*Slavnyi byl pokoinik*], God grant him the heavenly kingdom.'[80] However, in 1831 Pushkin's letter to Pletnev conveyed the feelings with which he awaited Zhukovsky's latest works, still hoping that he would compose something original: 'I await his new ballads with impatience. . . . But you did not say what sort of ballads they are, translations or original works'.[81] His letters to Vyazemsky written later that year recapture his excitement when he finally received the poems:

> But here is some good news for you: Zhukovsky really has written twelve delightful ballads. . . .[82]

> Zhukovsky also translated an unfinished ballad by Walter Scott, *The Pilgrim*—and has added his own ending: charming![83]

> Zhukovsky has poetic diarrhoea, and although it has subsided, he is still [squirting] hexameters.[84]

When Pushkin entered the debate in 1825 his primary concern was to see that justice be done: Zhukovsky should be accorded what praise was rightfully his, and the relationship between the two poets should be clarified. In a letter to Ryleev in January 1825 Pushkin reacted against the growing wave of anti-Zhukovsky

[78] L. P. Fevchuk, *Lichnye veshchi A. S. Pushkina* (L., 1970), 28.
[79] *PSS* XIII. 48.
[80] Ibid. 98.
[81] Ibid. XIV. 162–3.
[82] Ibid. 170.
[83] Ibid. 175.
[84] Ibid. 208. Gogol' was equally enthusiastic about Zhukovsky's ballads and *skazki* of 1831; see his letter to A. S. Danilevsky of 2 Nov. 1831.

criticism. He shared neither the lavish praise expressed in Pletnev's article nor the criticism voiced by Bulgarin. He wrote: 'Why should we bite the breast of our wet-nurse? . . . Whatever you say, Zhukovsky has had a decisive influence on the spirit of our literature; and in addition, the style of his translations will always stand as a model.'[85] In a letter to Vyazemsky in mid-1825, Pushkin responded to the first formulation of the relationship between himself and Zhukovsky. In particular, he took exception to the word 'consequence': 'I am not his [Zhukovsky's] consequence (*sledstvie*), but rather his student (*uchenik*).'[86] In other words, Pushkin repeats that term used by Zhukovsky in his portrait inscription of 1820. Pushkin views the relationship as an active one: his poetry is not simply the 'result' of Zhukovsky's achievement; rather he sees himself as the conscious artist who, having studied Zhukovsky's style, could recognize its excellence: 'No one has had and no one will have a style which equals his in power and variety.'[87] Beginning his own literary career with imitations of that style, Pushkin went on to parody his teacher and finally to create his own original style which, in its 'power and variety', far surpassed that of Zhukovsky.[88] But never did Pushkin deny or reject Zhukovsky's significance either in his own poetic growth, or in the development of Russian literature.

After 1825 Zhukovsky and his ballads were no longer controversial. Other poets and other issues dominated the literary scene. Zhukovsky's influence had been exaggerated by some, underestimated by others, and correctly assessed only by Pushkin. As early as 1832 N. A. Polevoi wrote a comprehensive article entitled 'Ballady i povesti V. A. Zhukovskogo', published in *Moskovskii telegraf*, in which he tried to generalize about the poet's achievement. He criticizes Zhukovsky for his monotony, his lack of *narodnost'*, and for the faithfulness 'in essence, not in expression' of his translations. Polevoi maintains that Zhukovsky's originality is to be found principally in the 'musicality of his poetry', its *pevkost'* or *sladkozvuchie*: 'His sounds are a melody, the quiet murmuring of a

[85] *PSS* XIII. 135. Ryleev answered Pushkin on 12 Feb. 1825. He agreed that Zhukovsky's influence on Russian was beneficial, but considered that his 'influence on the spirit of our literature' was harmful.
[86] Ibid. 183.
[87] Ibid. 183.
[88] See below, Ch. VII.

stream, the light breath of the zephyr through the strings of the Aeolian harp.'[89]

When Polevoi's article was reprinted in his *Ocherki russkoi literatury*, Belinsky wrote a review of it in which he made the first of his several statements about Zhukovsky's role in the history of Russian literature. He takes exception to Polevoi's criticism and, by clever argument, manages to transform all Zhukovsky's alleged faults into commendable virtues. The 'monotony' of his poetry is not to be interpreted in a prejorative sense but rather in a 'profound' one. Zhukovsky's greatness, according to Belinsky, lies precisely in his *odnostoronnost'*. Nor is his lack of *narodnost'* a defect; it is his 'honour and glory'. The so-called inaccuracy of Zhukovsky's translations is simply a result of the fact that he was a poet, not a translator; he always remained faithful to himself.[90]

In various articles written during the years 1841–3 Belinsky develops the theme of Zhukovsky as the first Russian romantic poet:

He introduced romanticism to us, without which we would not have any poetry today.[91]

. . . Zhukovsky is the literary Columbus of *Rus'*, who discovered for her the America of romanticism in poetry.[92]

Zhukovsky translated into Russian not Schiller, or any other German or English poets; no, Zhukovsky translated into Russian the romanticism of the middle ages. . . .[93]

Just as Zhukovsky had been removed from the centre of the contemporary scene and assigned his place in literary history by Pushkin, Polevoi, and Belinsky, so too had the ballad genre been excluded from the arena of controversy. In 1836 Belinsky wrote in a review of K. S. Aksakov's verse parodies: 'There was a time when the ballad was in the front ranks of youthful romanticism and marched into battle first, holding its victorious banner aloft; but now it has become a purely classical form; as in parliaments, the left becomes the right.'[94] In his articles on Pushkin in 1843 Belinsky wrote: 'In our prosaic age the reading of marvellous ballads no longer provides any pleasure, but produces apathy and boredom.'[95]

[89] *Ocherki russkoi literatury*, I (SPb., 1839), 138.
[90] *PSS* III. 507. [91] Ibid. V. 548. [92] Ibid. VI. 460.
[93] Ibid. VII. 167. [94] Ibid. II. 198–9. [95] Ibid. VII. 177.

VI

ZHUKOVSKY'S IMITATORS

И потом собачий вой их баллад . . .
—Бестужев[1]

The genre of the literary ballad as popularized by Zhukovsky during the early nineteenth century attracted a multitude of of imitators. P. A. Katenin, whose *Ol'ga* played an important role in the polemics of 1816,[2] wrote five more ballads from 1814 to 1817. The ballad 'epidemic' reached its peak between 1817 and 1820: N. F. Grammatin, N. F. Ostolopov, P. A. Pletnev, V. L. Pushkin, D. Glebov, M. Zagorodsky, A. Durop, M. Makarov, A. I. Meshchevsky, and many others wrote ballads with such titles as *Uslad i Vsemila*, *Edvin i Klara*, *Lyudmila i Uslad*, *Edgar i Vaina*, *Prividen'e*, *Mogil'shchik*, and so on; these were published in journals such as *Nevskii zritel'*, *Syn otechestva* and *Vestnik Evropy*, or in the poets' collected works. From 1824 to 1838 the blind poet I. I. Kozlov wrote some twenty literary ballads in imitation of Zhukovsky's model.

Almost each one of these imitations became the object of repeated criticism. Glagolev, after his attack on Pletnev's ballad in 1820, continues as follows: 'You will discover [in our journals] an enormous quantity of such horrible, mysterious monsters. Other [ballads] are perhaps less terrible, but just as lavishly adorned.'[3] In 1833 Bestuzhev criticized the ballad imitators in the following terms: 'And then the canine howling of their ballads, frightening only in their absurdity. . . .'[4]

In this chapter an attempt will be made to examine representative ballads by P. A. Katenin, A. I. Meshchevsky, and I. I. Kozlov: Katenin, regarded by contemporary critics as Zhukovsky's 'opponent', whose ballads were said to be based on a different set

[1] 'O romane N. Polevogo', *Sochineniya*, II (M., 1958), 592.
[2] See above, pp. 107–10.
[3] *Vestnik Evropy*, No. 11 (1820), 215.
[4] *Sochineniya*, II, 592.

of stylistic principles; Meshchesvky, recently 'discovered' and labelled as Zhukovsky's 'double', whose ballads provide an illuminating contrast with those of Zhukovsky himself; and Kozlov, Zhukovsky's most devoted 'disciple', whose ballads represent the closest imitation of the genre as created by Zhukovsky.

Ever since the literary controversy in 1816 concerning *Ol'ga* and *Lyudmila*, critics have compared Katenin's ballads with Zhukovsky's.[5] Whereas Zhukovsky's ballads are usually based on borrowed Ossianic or classical Greek legends, it is alleged that Katenin's ballads are based on original *narodnyi* themes. Whereas Zhukovsky's ballads are full of abstract images and generalized elegiac motifs, Katenin's images are said to be concrete and to encompass a depiction of the peasants' everyday life. Finally, whereas Zhukovsky's language is 'romantic' and 'poetic', the language of Katenin's ballads is described as 'popular', a quality manifested both in the vocabulary and the syntax of his dialogues, and in the flat, prosaic intonations of his consciously 'unpoetic' narrative.

Katenin's first literary ballad, *Pevets* (1814),[6] dramatically contradicts this generally accepted view of his poetry. It is not an original Russian work; it is a free translation of a ballad entitled *Der Sänger* from Goethe's *Wilhelm Meister* (Chapter 11). The German original is not set in any specific period or location; it consists almost entirely of a minstrel's speech, the simplicity of which is in contrast to the magnificence of a royal hall. The king's generous offer of a reward to the minstrel is refused; instead, the minstrel expounds the doctrine of 'art for art's sake':

> Das Lied, das aus der Kehle dringt,
> Ist Lohn, der reichlich lohnet. (5: 3–4)

Katenin, in his version, invents an Old Russian setting for the subject. At one of Vladimir's feasts in Kiev boyars and *bogatyri* sit around a *dubovyi stol*, sipping *sladkii med* from *yantarnye chashi*. Katenin transforms the minstrel into a traditional Russian bard, whose *veshchii perst* plays on *zhivye struny*. The images and language of *Pevets* are obvious borrowings from the *Slovo o polku Igoreve*: for example, the bard—*v'etsya ptitsei v nebesa*, and the prince—*izronil zlatoe slovo*. In addition to stylized folk epithets,

[5] See *IRL* VI. 52–61 and *IRP* I. 287–91.
[6] *Syn otechestva*, No. 16 (1815), 138.

literary epithets are also employed: *Grusten pir, gde net pevtsa*; *Vdokhnovennyi . . . Uslad*; and *pesni sladkie*. The poet's aesthetic views, as expounded in the last two stanzas, reveal the strong influence of Zhukovsky, particularly of his early lyric, also called *Pevets* (1811). Here Katenin replaces the Old Russian flavour with abstract romantic lyricism:

Я пою, как птица в поле,
Оживленная весной;
Я пою: чего мне боле?
Песнь от сердца—дар драгой. (6: 1–4)

The final stanzas, in both the first published version and the revised text, contain passages which closely resemble lines in Zhukovsky's *Lyudmila*.[7] The choice of Goethe as his source, the individual interpretation of his theme, and finally the language of his version demonstrate Katenin's heavy dependence on Zhukovsky as a model for his own literary ballads.

The subject of Katenin's second ballad, *Natasha* (1814),[8] has its source in the Russian literary ballads of the 1790s, and also reveals the influence of Zhukovsky's *Lyudmila*. The ballad relates the conventional story of a tearful parting between two lovers, the hero's death in war, the heroine's grief, and the spiritual union of the lovers after death. Natasha's patriotism (since it is she who urged the hero to fight) is a familiar motif from the 1790s; her humility and faith (*Vse v bozh'ei vole*) are borrowed from Zhukovsky's heroine. The language of *Natasha* consists of a mixture of

[7] Compare the first published version of *Pevets:*

Счастлив дом, где дар сей скуден;
Бог к вам щедр, Он правосуден:
Благодарны же небесам
Будьте так, как гость ваш вам. (7: 5–8)

the revised version of *Pevets:*

Дом ваш полон всем, и сами
Вы любимы небесами:
Благодарны ж будьте им,
Сколько гость ваш вам самим. (7: 5–8)

and *Lyudmila:*

Будь послушна небесам . . . (6: 12)

Смертных ропот безрассуден;
Царь всевышний правосуден. (21: 9–10)

[8] *Syn otechestva*, No. 13 (1815), 16 ff.

conventional folk elements (*zhila-byla, bela grud', krasna devitsa, syraya zemlya*) and literary expressions, reminiscent of those used by Zhukovsky in his lyrics and ballads: *serdechnyi/Milyi drug; dorogoe/ Vremya kratkoe, zlatoe; prezhnie radosti;* and *skvoz' slez unylyi*.

Although Katenin's ballad *Ubiitsa* (1815)[9] probably originated in a Grimm Brothers' fairy-tale,[10] and although it too borrowed motifs from Zhukovsky, nevertheless it represents a more original work than either of his previous ballads. *Ubiitsa* relates the story of an old peasant who adopts a poor orphan child. When the ungrateful orphan later murders the peasant, he allows the blame to fall on some passing merchants. The orphan inherits the peasant's land, and soon marries, but he knows no peace. Finally he confesses his terrible crime to his wife, who reports it to the authorities. The orphan falls ill and dies, punished by a just Creator.

The events are related as a realistic narrative in a prosaic style. Katenin uses both conventional folk elements such as *shirokii dvor, tesovaya izba*, and *belyi svet*, as well as literary devices, typical of the ballad genre, including rhetorical questions and the repetition of the epithet *strashnyi*. In general there are relatively few epithets and no elegiac melancholy. The extended dialogue between husband and wife contains unusual elements of colloquial vocabulary and syntax:

И что на месяц пялишь очи . . . (18:3)

Молчи, жена, не бабье дело . . . (19: 1)

Я с рук сбыл дурака . . . (21: 4)

Проснулся, черт, и видит: худо! (24: 1)

While there is little reference to the husband's emotional state, his crazed laugh both before and after his confession (stanzas 16 and 29), and his insomnia before, and deep sleep after,[11] reveal a measure of psychological complexity of character lacking in Zhukovsky's ballads.

[9] Ibid., No. 23 (1815), 143 ff.

[10] See R. M. Volkov, 'Russkaya ballada pervoi chetverti XIX stoletiya i ee nemetskie paralleli', *Uchenye zapiski Chernovitskogo universiteta*, XXXVII (1957), 3–48.

[11] Cf. Coleridge's *The Rime of the Ancient Mariner*, ll. 240–88.

Just as in Zhukovsky's *Ivikovy zhuravli* (1813) the cranes invoked by Ibycus to avenge his foul murder drive the culprits to give themselves away, so in Katenin's *Ubiitsa* the influence of the moon eventually forces the murderer to confess his crime to his wife. The murderer's invocation to the moon exists in two variants; the original 'popular' version was published in *Syn otechestva*:

Да полно, ты! ты нем ведь, лысый!
    Так не боюсь тебя;
Гляди сычом, скаль зубы крысой,
    Да знай лишь про себя. (28)

The more literary variant was published in the 1832 edition of Katenin's works:

Да полно, что! гляди, плешивый!
    Не побоюсь тебя;
Ты, видно, сроду молчаливый:
    Так знай же про себя.[12] (28)

The original version was attacked by Katenin's critics as being too 'crude' and 'low' to be used in an apostrophe to the moon.[13] Pushkin, writing in praise of *Ubiitsa* in 1828, expressed his approval of the original version of the murderer's invocation, because it was full of 'genuine tragic force'; he continued: '. . . . few people understood the strength and originality of *Ubiitsa*, a ballad which one can place on a par with the best works by Bürger and Southey.'[14] In its realistic narrative, its psychological complexity, and its colloquial language, Katenin's *Ubiitsa* represents a new development of the ballad genre, which was in complete contrast to the models established by Zhukovsky.

Yet another contrast with Zhukovsky's ballads is provided by Katenin's *Leshii* (1815).[15] Although it was influenced by Goethe's *Erlkönig*, and said by Bestuzhev to contain motifs borrowed from Derzhavin,[16] nevertheless it represents a further development of

[12] P. A. Katenin, *Izbrannye proizvedeniya*, *Biblioteka poeta*, *Bol'shaya seriya*, 2-oe izd. (M.-L., 1965), 666.

[13] Cf. Zhukovsky's lyric *Podrobnyi otchet o lune* (1820) in which he summarizes his own different styles for describing the moon. None of them corresponds to Katenin's.

[14] 'O poeticheskom sloge', *PSS* XI. 73.

[15] *Syn otechestva*, No. 47 (1815), 57 ff.

[16] Ibid., No. 20 (1822), 253–69.

the genre. *Leshii* relates the story of a young boy who disobeys his mother's warning and wanders off alone into the forest at night in search of the wood-goblin. He loses his way, and asks help from an old man; the boy follows the directions given, but returns to the same place—under the spell of the old man/wood-goblin. The neet morning the mother is distraught: her son has vanished.

The greatest originality of the ballad lies in the contrast between the boy's imagined vision of the wood-goblin's kingdom and the reality which he discovers in the forest. His dream is a collage of 'popular' folkloric motifs: *prekrasnyi, chudesnyi dom; zolotye teremy, chistye vody, krasnye devushki, sladkie piry*; the lord of this realm is imagined to be a *slavnyi khozain: dobryi, laskovyi, zabavnyi*. However, the actual setting proves to be quite different: *serye tuchi, gustoi mrak, temnyi les*—and this landscape is convulsed by thunder and lightning, wind and rain. The old man/wood-goblin turns out to be *ugryumyi*, possessing a *nasmeshlivyi, zloi vid*.

Although Katenin employs a number of colloquial forms such as *vplot', znat', svetik*, and, in the original version, *gushcha*,[17] the narrative is related almost entirely in unemotional, unambiguous language. Only the conclusion describing the mother's unsuccessful search reverts to substantivized adverbs, similar to those in Zhukovsky's lyrics:

С каждым днем безумье то же:
Ищет сына по лесам.
Здесь не на́йдет; дай ей Боже
С ним увидеться хоть там. (14: 9–12)

Katenin's next ballad, *Ol'ga* (1816),[18] was written as a direct challenge to Zhukovsky. Based on Bürger's *Lenore*, it was Katenin's attempt to demonstrate that Zhukovsky's *Lyudmila* was not a 'popular' ballad at all, but rather the product of Karamzin's sentimentalism.[19]

A comparison of *Ol'ga* with *Lyudmila* and *Lenore* shows how much closer Katenin's translation is to Bürger's original than was

[17] This word was criticized by Bestuzhev in his 1820 article. Katenin, in a letter to N. I. Bakhtin, defended the word ('Gushcha ves'ma russkoe i upotrebitel'noe slovo'), but later replaced it by *debri*. See *Pis'ma P. A. Katenina k N. I. Bakhtinu* (SPb., 1911), 37.

[18] *Vestnik Evropy*, No. 9 (1816), 14 ff.; *Syn otechestva*, No. 24 (1816), 186 ff.

[19] See above, Ch. V, pp. 107–10.

Zhukovsky's version.[20] Whereas the setting of *Lyudmila* is generalized, *Ol'ga*, like *Lenore*, begins with a reference to a specific time and place: the hero had gone off to fight with the army of Peter the Great at Poltava. Whereas Zhukovsky transforms his characters into sentimental heroes and heroines, Katenin follows Bürger's characterizations more closely. For example, Ol'ga's lament is preceded and followed by violent physical gestures:

Тут, залившися слезами,
В перси бьет себя руками;
Рвет, припав к сырой земле,
Черны кудри на челе. (4: 5–8)

The hero's speech is more colloquial and less poetic than in Zhukovsky's version, as for example, in the apostrophe to his horse:

Конь мой! петухи пропели;
Чур! заря чтоб не взошла;
Гор вершины забелели:
Мчись как и́з лука стрела. (27: 1–4)

Ol'ga's lament also contains some colloquial expressions (*net kak net; svetu-radosti ne stalo*). The symmetrical alternations of the mother's advice and Ol'ga's replies, both gradually increasing in length, approximate the effect which Bürger achieved.[21]

Whereas Zhukovsky extends Bürger's descriptive transition from three lines to nineteen (which includes thirteen epithets), Katenin limits himself to four lines, using folk, rather than literary, epithets:

И стемнело небо ясно,
Закатилось солнце красно,
Все к покою улеглись,
Звезды яркие зажглись. (11: 5–8)

Although Katenin's version contains no equivalent for the sound effects of Bürger's ride, the refrain in *Ol'ga* is close to the German

[20] See above, Ch. III, pp. 51–6 for a detailed comparison of Zhukovsky's *Lyudmila* and Bürger's *Lenore*.

[21] Schematically, let M = mother, O = Ol'ga, number = lines spoken: M-3, O-4, M-4, O-4, M-8, O-8, M-8, O-8. Totals: M 23; O 24. Cf. above, Ch. III, p. 53 on *Lyudmila* and *Lenore*.

original in meaning and function; it is introduced in 16: 5–6, and repeated in 19: 5–6, 23: 5–6, and 26: 5–6:

Месяц светит, ехать споро;
Я как мертвый еду скоро.

The hero's transformation into a corpse, glossed over in *Lyudmila*, is depicted by Katenin in graphic detail:

Голова, взгляд, руки, тело—
Все на милом помертвело,
И стоит уж он с косой,
Страшный остов костяной. (29: 5–8)

Finally, the moral, significantly reinterpreted by Zhukovsky, is rendered by Katenin as a close restatement of the original:

С Богом в суд нейди крамольно;
Скорбь терпи, хоть сердцу больно. (31: 5–6)

In 1831, after Zhukovsky's second translation of *Lenore* was published, Katenin decided to revise his own version. In spite of the letter to Bakhtin in which he claims that Griboedov's defence and the fact of Zhukovsky's retranslation had justified his own writing of *Ol'ga*,[22] Katenin incorporated in his revised version several suggestions made by Gnedich, and he profited from Zhukovsky's second, more literal, rendition.[23]

Katenin's last ballad, *Pevets Uslad* (1817),[24] comes as an unexpected conclusion to his series of literary ballads. The poem relates the story of the poet Uslad and his beloved Vsemila. The heroine's early death drives the hero to seek refuge in battle and then in travel; finally he returns home to *Rus'*, still grieving for his beloved. There his friends reproach him for his unseemly behaviour; Uslad tearfully replies that his happiness can consist only in union with Vsemila after his own death.

Motifs such as the faithful hero, the untimely death of the

[22] See above, Ch. V, p. 109. For example, Gnedich argued that 'Zheny, deti im v dorogu/Klichut:' (3: 5–6) was 'bad Russian'; Katenin altered the line to 'Vse navstrechu, na dorogu;/Klichut:'.

[23] See Katenin, *Izbrannye*, 667–8 for further examples.

[24] *Vestnik Evropy*, No. 2 (1818), 89. Katenin's later works *Sofokl* (1818) and *Mstislav Mstislavich* (1819) are heroic *poemy*, rather than literary ballads. The poet defined the genre of *Natasha*, *Ubiitsa*, *Leshii*, *Sofokl*, and *Mstislav Mstislavich* as lyrical *povesti*.

heroine, and the union of lovers after death, were, of course, central to the literary ballads of the 1790s. The language of *Pevets Uslad* demonstrates few of the characteristics of *Ubiitsa*, *Leshii*, and *Ol'ga*: no folk epithets, 'popular' expressions (except for *znat*' and *avos*'), or colloquial dialogue. On the contrary, literary epithets are frequent: *rodnaya strana; zemli dalekie/ I chuzhdye; krasavitsy chernookie*; and *Rus' svyataya*. The hero's reply to his friends' reproach recalls the language of Zhukovsky's elegies:

—Нет счастья мне под небесами,
Надежды нет. (7: 3–4)

—Певец Услад лишь за могилой
Быть может рад: (8: 1–2)

Thus, in his last ballad, Katenin reverts to the motifs and style of the Russian ballads of the 1790s and to the pattern of his earlier works *Pevets* and *Natasha*.

Katenin's contribution to the genre of the literary ballad is ambiguous. On the one hand, in *Pevets*, *Natasha*, and *Pevets Uslad*, the influence of the ballads of the 1790s and of Zhukovsky's models predominates,[25] on the other hand, in *Ubiitsa*, *Leshii*, and *Ol'ga*, although there are still themes and expressions borrowed from Zhukovsky, Katenin is attempting to develop the genre in his own way. The realistic narrative, psychological leitmotivs, folk epithets, and the colloquial vocabulary and syntax of these three ballads make them unlike any previous examples in the genre.

In 1816, after reading *Ol'ga*, Zhukovsky wrote to Gnedich that he thought that Katenin 'definitely has talent'.[26] Kyukhel'beker, after he turned against Zhukovsky, praised Katenin's ballads, arguing that '. . . although only experiments, [they] are . . . perhaps the only works in all of our literature which belong to

[25] The similarity between Katenin's and Zhukovsky's language is particularly striking in the range and usage of epithets. Of the total of 132 epithets in Katenin's ballads, the most frequent are: *belyi*, *bozhii*, *zlatoi*, *zloi*, *krasnyi*, *novyi*, *svyatoi* (used 4 or more times each); and *gor'kii*, *milyi*, *rodnoi*, *sladkii*, *strashnyi*, *syryi*, *temnyi*, *yasnyi* (used 3 times each). The following combinations of epithet and substantive occur: *vozdushnaya vyshina*, *lyubeznyi drug*, *dremuchii les*, *gustoi mrak*, *pechal'nyi zvon*, *yasnyi mesyats*. Most of these frequent epithets and all of these combinations are commonly used in Zhukovsky's ballads. Original epithets, such as *lysyi/pleshivyi mesyats*, are the rare exceptions.

[26] *SS* IV. 569.

Romantic Poetry.'[27] Pushkin, in a review of Katenin's *Sochineniya i perevody* (1832), wrote that the author had been underestimated by his critics and had in fact achieved a considerable degree of originality and success. He praised his introduction of 'popular' subjects into the elevated language of poetry, and expressed approval of the 'simplicity or even crudity' of his language which had so distressed contemporary readers.[28]

Zhukovsky was being generous to his 'opponent'; Kyukhel'-beker was exaggerating in order to make a polemic point; only Pushkin, with his usual critical acumen, was able to render a just evaluation.

A. I. Meshchevsky (1791–1820?) was a talented poet and *balladnik* who by now is almost completely forgotten. A close friend of Zhukovsky's during their years at Moscow University boarding school, he was later exiled for some apparently insignificant reason. Zhukovsky rallied to his defence: in late 1816 or early 1817 he wrote to A. I. Turgenev, reproaching the members of Arzamas for their lack of concern over Meshchevsky's strange fate: 'And you should remember that more important to Arzamas is Meshchevsky in Siberia; but you, my friends, are leading your jolly lives in Petersburg.'[29] Zhukovsky and Vyazemsky prepared an edition of Meshchevsky's work, consisting primarily of ballads, many of which were translated from German originals; however, they failed to obtain permission to publish it.[30]

Recently Yu. M. Lotman published a small selection of Meshchevsky's poetry, including only two ballads;[31] the texts are preceded by a critical introduction in which Lotman refers to Meshchevsky as 'Zhukovsky's double', inasmuch as he pursued to their logical conclusion those principles of the literary ballad genre which had been established by Zhukovsky.[32] Lotman argues that,

[27] *Syn otechestva*, No. 17 (1825), 71. Kyukhel'beker wrote several ballads in what he thought was Katenin's style. In fact *Les* (1818–20) and *Ruchei* (1819) were more influenced by Goethe and Zhukovsky; his later works, such as *Rogdaevy psy* (1824) and *Kudeyar* (1833), are heroic *poemy* not ballads.

[28] *PSS* XI. 220–1.

[29] *Russkii arkhiv* (1867), col. 811.

[30] The manuscript number is GPB-286;2;296.

[31] *Uchenye zapiski TGU*, CIV (1961), 277–80; and *Poety 1790–1810-kh godov, Biblioteka poeta, Bol'shaya seriya*, 2-oe izd. (L., 1971), 703–18.

[32] *Poety 1790–1810-kh godov*, 37.

whereas Zhukovsky's ballads are rich in complexity, Meshchevsky's are simpler in subject, structure, and theme. While Meshchevsky's style does bear a distinct resemblance to Zhukovsky's, the former tends to exaggerate certain devices and to introduce unnecessary complications.

The first of Meshchevsky's published ballads, *Edvin* (1815–18), a translation of Schiller's *Ritter Toggenburg*, provides an interesting contrast with Zhukovsky's rendition of the same work, published in 1818 as *Rytsar' Togenburg*. Schiller's original ballad relates the story of a knight's interview with a lady: she rejects his offer of love and agrees to care for him only as a sister would her own brother. The knight, unsatisfied, goes off to war in Palestine. He returns, still burning with desire, to learn that the lady has taken holy vows. He too forsakes the world, and settles in a hut near her convent. There he lives in anticipation of catching a glimpse of his beloved; and there, his desire still unfulfilled, he dies.

Zhukovsky's version emphasizes the lady's rejection of the knight's offer of romantic love: she characterizes that love as one of endless meetings and partings, anguish and suffering:

При разлуке, при свиданье
Сердце в тишине—
И любви твоей страданье
Непонятно мне. (1: 5–8)

Similarly, the knight's frustration is expressed in Zhukovsky's favourite verbal leitmotivs: Schiller's *stille Hoffnung* is replaced by *strastnaya múka*, and the knight's *unynie* is conveyed even in the description of his corpse:

Раз—туманно утро было—
Мертв он там сидел,
Бледен ликом, и уныло
На окно глядел. (10: 5–8)

Meshchevsky, in his translation, introduces significant changes in Schiller's subject. The rejection of romantic love is replaced by the motif of moonlight which illuminates the face of the lady, Lora:

Оттенит тебе долина
Тихий лик мой при луне. (1: 5–6)

This motif is repeated in 8: 2, and again in the final stanza, when it is Lora's death, not Edvin's, which occurs:

Вдруг свет месяца разлился . . .
Мертвой Лоры лик в огне, . . . (10: 5–6)

On the contrary, Edvin finds some serenity and spiritual comfort in his waiting.

Certain elements in Meshchevsky's style, including the repeated exclamations, interruptions, and apostrophes, are similar to Zhukovsky's. However, Meshchevsky's images are expressed in highly artificial language:

Путеводный шлем Эдвина
Веял бурей роковой! (3: 3–4)

Сон спешил страдальца вежды
Утомленны оковать— (9: 1–2)

His syntax is complicated with numerous inversions (*Sidya kel'i na kryl'tse*), participles (*slezyashchii vzor Edvina; Myshtsy, veroi okrylennoi*), and frequent separations of epithet and substantive: *mrachnyi serdtsu prigovor; proshchal'nyi broshen vzor; gromkoi yunoshu molvoi*; and *tikhii strannika privet*. Meshchevsky uses combinations of epithets and substantives such as *rodnye brega, tikhii grom, zlataya dennitsa, temny lipy*, as well as series of epithets, all characteristic of Zhukovsky's ballads:

Лик возлюбленной своей,
Тихий, ясный, умиленный—
Как заря весенних дней,— (8: 6–8)

Мертвой Лоры лик в окне,
Бледный, тихий, отразился,
Как в полночном, сладком сне! . . . (10: 6–8)

On the other hand, combinations such as *Edvin osirotelyi* and *dushevnaya nepogoda* remain somewhat obscure in their meaning.

The second of Meshchevsky's published ballads, *Lila* (1815–18), is original, although its subject resembles that of Turchaninova's prose translation *Vill'yam i Margarita* (1800)[33] and the heroine's lament contains echoes of Zhukovsky's *Lyudmila*. Lila's ghost

[33] See above, Ch. II, pp. 22–3.

enters the bedchamber of Uslad, her former lover. While he lies asleep, she relates the story of their betrothal, his betrayal, her anguish and death; she begins:

Спишь, милый, иль забыт ты сном?
Будь крест нам настороже! . . .
Со мной—на ложе гробовом!
С тобой—на брачном ложе! . . .[34] (2: 21–4)

Because Lila still loves Uslad ('Luch strasti prezhnei ne potukh'), she will forgive him.

The setting of the ballad consists of the most common Gothic motifs: *mgla*, *polnoch'*, *ten'*, *grob*, *petukh*. The syntax is even more complicated than in *Edvin*: parenthetical asides and dashes frequently interrupt the action:

Ах! некогда равнял Услад
(Лесть клятвы ненадежной!)
С лилеей—грудь и с небом—взгляд,
Ланиты—с розой нежной . . .
И с Лилой обручен —другой
И сердце дал, и руку. (2: 12–17)

Clauses are interposed between the subject and verb (*ten'* . . . *prokralas'*—1: 4–2: 3), and the accumulation of four predicates in one line results in considerable confusion:

Любить, любя—прощать учись
У презренной ⟨ты⟩ Лилы! (3: 3–4)

The vocabulary includes an occasional archaism (*ubrus*—10: 1),[35] as well as epithets characteristic of Zhukovsky's style, such as *plamennaya lyubov'*, *zolotaya luna*, *zlataya dennitsa*, and *bezmolvnaya mgla*.

Lotman's formulation, 'Meshchevsky is Zhukovsky, set straight (*vypryamlennyi*) according to the laws of canonical Zhukovsky',[36] seems to be well founded. The similarities and differences between the two poets further illuminate the stylistic principles employed by Zhukovsky in his ballads. The publication of additional ballads

[34] Cf. *Lyudmila*, 10: 1–2, 'Spit il' net moya Lyudmila?/ Pomnit druga il' zabyla?'
[35] Cf. *Edvin*, 5: 8, 'Pod ubrus posvyashchena!'
[36] *Poety 1790–1810-kh godov*, 37.

by Meshchevsky would provide additional evidence and permit more detailed conclusions.

The life history of I. I. Kozlov is, in some measure, the fulfilment of the emotional experiences expressed in Zhukovsky's lyrics. Chronic illness and subsequent blindness inspired Kozlov to become a poet; his works treat the themes of melancholy, the loss of youth, the search for love and beauty, and the cruelty of Fate—all in an extremely personal way. The *Poslanie k drugu V. A. Zhukovskomu* (1822), which Belinsky described as Kozlov's 'poetic confession',[37] shows the strong influence of Zhukovsky, as do his translations from Byron and Scott, his attempts at writing 'popular' works, and his literary ballads. Between 1824 and 1838 Kozlov wrote a number of ballads, some of which are translations from Scott and Wordsworth, from the Italian poet Tommaso Grossi, and from Mérimée. With one notable exception, these ballads are 'miniatures' which present a dramatic situation in bare outline, and as such are closer to the narrative method of the traditional genre than are Zhukovsky's ballads.

An example of Kozlov's early ballads is *Razboinik* (1825),[38] based on a song in Scott's *Rokeby* (Canto III. 16–18).[39] The setting is typical of the ballad genre: forest, river, meadows, and moonlit valley. The heroine, a beautiful maiden sequestered in a castle tower, lives in spiritual harmony with nature. The hero, a *smelyi ezdok*, comes on a *borzyi kon'* to kidnap the maiden, so that they can lead a simple, rustic life together.

The structure of the ballad consists in the alternation of the heroine's song with the hero's monologue, and is interspersed with narrative passages. The heroine's vague desires are expressed in her song:

Хочу любить я в тишине,
Не царский сан носить. (13–4)

These desires are transformed into actual intentions by the sudden arrival of her lover:

Хочу в привольной тишине
Тебя, мой друг, любить. (45–6)

[37] *PSS* V. 72.
[38] *Moskovskii telegraf*, No. 8 (1825), 276–9.
[39] The theme of *Razboinik* is similar to another of Kozlov's translations from Scott's *Marmion* (Fifth Song, 12) called *Beverlei* (1832).

The language of the ballad contains a wide assortment of conventional romantic epithets for nature: *svetlyi tok*, *tumannyi dol*, *privetnyi shum* (*vod*), *temnyi les*, *dikii krai*, *zelenyi bereg*, *dushistyi lug*, and *lesnaya glush'*.

Revnost' (1832)[40] is a somewhat later example of Kozlov's original ballad miniatures. A young woman (*prekrasnaya v slezakh*) stands alone over a fresh grave lamenting the death of her lover, whom she has murdered in order to 'fulfil her sacred duty' to her husband, Vadim. The latter suddenly emerges from his hiding-place where he has overheard the tearful lament; he murders his wife, declaring that even in death her lover must be happier than he.

The setting is typical: midnight, moonlight, and a gloomy graveyard. The heroine expresses her *tainyi strakh* in language characteristic of Zhukovsky's poetry:

> И мрачных дум тревоги неизбежной
> Невольно смущена,
> Склонясь на дерн, с тоскою безнадежной, . . . (9–11)

The appearance of the jealous husband is highly melodramatic: he is described as *blednee mertvetsov*, although he is totally real: *ne prizrak*. The whole ballad—setting, heroine's lament, and Vadim's revenge—occur within thirty-two lines of concise dramatic narrative. Although the characters and situation are analogous to those in Zhukovsky's ballads, the dimensions and dynamism of Kozlov's *Revnost'* are a reasonably successful attempt to imitate the narrative unit and method of the traditional ballad.

Another of Kozlov's later ballads, *Taina* (1836),[41] is a study in the creation of atmosphere. A shield and sword hang on an oak tree which stands near a fresh grave; one night a young girl and a monk come to mourn the unidentified hero. The monk sings a dirge; the girl pronounces a lament and cuts off her golden tresses with the sword.

Kozlov presents only the barest outline of the story, without any details of setting or characterization to detract from the mysteriousness. The narrator also admits his ignorance:

> . . . никто, никто не знает,
> Кто погребен в лесу во тьме ночной? (7–8)

[40] *Russkii almanakh* (1832–3), 221–2; entitled *Revnivyi*. The possibility of Pushkin's influence (*Tsygany*) on this ballad should not be overlooked.

[41] *Biblioteka dlya chteniya* (1836), 169–70.

Nor does the monk understand: 'No kto on byl, chernets ne ponimal.' Only the pale heroine (*blednei svoei odezhdy beloi*) knows the secret, but she reveals nothing to the reader. When silence is restored in the forest, no one is any the wiser: 'Torzhestvennyi odin ostalsya strakh.' The language of this work is unexceptional; the ballad exists only in order to establish the mood of *strakh* and *uzhas*—emotions which are central to the atmosphere of Zhukovsky's ballads.

In contrast to Kozlov's miniatures is the much longer work *Vengerskii les* (1826–7).[42] Belinsky, whose general attitude towards the genre had changed,[43] wrote in 1840: 'As for the ballad [*Vengerskii les*]—besides some good verses, it has no significance, since it belongs to that false kind of poetry which depicts imaginary reality, which dreams up Veledas, Izveds, Ostans, Svezhans who never existed, and creates a fanciful Germanic ballad out of a Slavonic myth.'[44]

The plot is complicated. The first part describes a young couple's (Ostan and Veleda) escape from Kiev to the Hungarian forest. Their brief period of happiness together is destroyed by a mysterious vision seen by Ostan. In the second part, the frightened hero bids farewell to the forest, and together with Veleda he encounters a stranger wrapped in a shroud; this turns out to be the corpse of Veleda's brother, whom Ostan had murdered. Ostan vanishes dramatically, Veleda dies of grief, and tranquillity returns to the forest.

The setting of the ballad is conventional (*dremuchii les*, *bezvestnaya tish'*, *dikii krai*); the heroine, a beautiful maiden with *rusye kudry* and *golubye ochi*, has forsaken her comfortable life to escape with the hero, a *vityaz'*, who has sacrified his own military career.

Он с ней, пылающей душой,
К прекрасному стремится. (7: 7–8)

After his vision in the forest Ostan becomes *zadumchivyi* and *ugryumyi*, oppressed by his guilt and a sense of foreboding.

The structure of *Vengerskii les* (alternating speeches), the themes (ideal love and cruel Fate), and the language are derived principally from Zhukovsky's ballads, as are various verbal leitmotivs,

[42] *Nevskii almanakh* (1827), 89–97; (1828), 4–14.
[43] See above, Ch. V, p. 120.
[44] *PSS* V. 72.

including *tainyi strakh*, *toska*, and *chto-to mrachno*. Zhukovsky's favourite epithets occur frequently, as in this descriptive passage:

Когда ж повсюду тишина
И мертвое молчанье,
И полуночная луна
Льет томное сиянье,
Из тесной кельи гробовой
Тень бледная выходит . . . (32: 1–6)

In general it is the structure of Kozlov's ballads which displays the most originality. For example, in *Son nevesty* (1824) the story is related within a dream; *Nochnoi ezdok* (1828) and *Ozero mertvoi krasavitsy* (1832) are lyrical monologues pronounced by the hero and heroine respectively; *Vstrecha* (1838) is in the form of a series of questions and answers; and in several other ballads the refrain is effectively employed as a structural device.

The subjects of Kozlov's ballads are far less original than the structure and strongly resemble the general pattern of Russian ballads in the 1790s: the heroine is usually a representative of a higher social order than the hero; their mutual love is impeded by some obstacle, usually by their parents; the death of one lover is followed by the death of the other, and the lovers are united after death.

The least original aspect of Kozlov's work, however, is his style. His epithets, in particular, are derived almost exclusively from Zhukovsky's vocabulary.[45] Although epithets occur more frequently in Kozlov's descriptive passages than in Zhukovsky's, their range is the same as they are similarly employed. The difference in the effectiveness of their epithets is due to the historical evolution of literary style. When Zhukovsky composed his most important ballads, his use of epithets was innovative and original; when Kozlov started writing in the same style twenty years later, it was conventional and unoriginal.

Immediately after Kozlov's death in 1840, Zhukovsky pub-

[45] Of a sample of 122 epithets selected from Kozlov's ballads, the most frequent are: *belyi*, *grobovoi*, *milyi*, *nochnoi*, *svyatoi*, *tainyi*, *temnyi* (used 8 or more times each); *bednyi*, *groznyi*, *krovavyi*, *mladoi*, *mrachnyi*, *podzemnyi*, *prekrasnyi*, *rodnoi*, *svetlyi*, *strashnyi*, *tikhii*, *tomnyi*, *uzhasnyi*, *unylyi*, *chudnyi* (used 4–6 times each). Epithets formed with the prefixes *bez-* and *ne-* are also characteristic: *bezmolvnyi*, *nedvizhnyi*, *neotrazimyi*, *nepostizhimyi*. All these epithets are among those used most frequently by Zhukovsky.

lished a collection of his poetry, prefaced by a brief biography of the man whom 'misfortune transformed into a poet', and by a critical introduction describing Kozlov's poems as 'flowers which bloomed on the field of anguish'.[46] Belinsky's article on Kozlov was written as a reply to Zhukovsky's preface.[47] He prefers the shorter lyrics and ballads, criticizing the longer poems such as *Vengerskii les* and *Chernets*. In general Belinsky was much less enthusiastic about Kozlov's achievement than was Zhukovsky, who clearly overestimated his originality.[48]

[46] *PSS* X. 72–3.

[47] *PSS* V. 72.

[48] Belinsky himself wrote an imitation of a literary ballad. *Russkaya byl'*, published in *Listok* (1831), is his sole surviving poetic work. In a letter to M. M. Popov in 1830, he confided: "While still [a pupil] in the second class at the gymnasium, I wrote verses and considered myself a dangerous rival of Zhukovsky; but times have changed. . . ." See *PSS*, I, 507–9, 563–4.

VII

PUSHKIN'S LITERARY BALLADS

Не понимаю, что у тебя за охота пародировать Жуковского.

—Пушкин[1]

With the publication of *Lyudmila* (1808) and *Svetlana* (1813), Zhukovsky became the most influential poet on the Russian literary scene. Derzhavin, late in his own career, symbolically bequeathed to him his poetic lyre:

> Тебе в наследие, Жуковский,
> Я ветху лиру отдаю;
> А я над бездной гроба скользкой
> Уж преклоня чело стою.[2]

It was only natural that talented young poets should try to imitate Zhukovsky's models. Pushkin, who was to become his most successful *uchenik*, began his literary career by choosing the same genres, treating similar themes, and imitating the style of Zhukovsky's poetry.

Pushkin's earliest experiment with the literary ballad took place during his years at the Lycée. Evidence for this has been provided by V. P. Gaevsky in an article on the poet's early works: '[Pushkin] wrote, in competition with Illichevsky, a chivalric ballad, in imitation of Zhukovsky's ballads, but this experiment has not survived'.[3] Gaevsky suggests that this first ballad was written during the year 1812.

Two years later Pushkin composed a cycle of Ossianic poems which combined heroic motifs with love themes, and which were strongly influenced by Zhukovsky's lyrics and ballads. The first,

[1] *PSS* XIII. 248 (Letter to Kyukhel'beker, December 1825).

[2] G. R. Derzhavin, *Stikhotvoreniya, Biblioteka poeta, Bol'shaya seriya*, 2-oe izd. (L., 1957), 61.

[3] 'Pushkin v litsee i litseiskie ego stikhotvoreniya', *Sovremennik*, XCVII, No. 7 (1863), 134.

Kol'na, is a free rendition of an excerpt from Ossian; it closely follows Kostrov's prose translation.[4] *Evlega*, the next, is a free translation of the fourth song in Parny's long Ossianic poem, *Isnel et Asléga*. *Garal' i Gal'vina*, in the same series, belongs to Pushkin's *dubia*. By far the most interesting of these early experiments is *Osgar*, Pushkin's only original work based on an Ossianic theme; it reveals the extent of Zhukovsky's influence on the young poet.

In the poem an old bard stops a traveller in a graveyard so that he can relate to him tales of past heroes, particularly that of Osgar, a bold warrior who was in love with the beautiful Mal'vina. But Mal'vina was unfaithful, so Osgar murdered her new lover and wandered about the earth in despair. Years later his ghost returned to watch over Mal'vina's grave.

The setting of the poem and the description of the characters contain all those elements characteristic of Zhukovsky's ballads: graveyard, moonlight, midnight, a steep cliff, and a dense forest. The old bard is referred to as a *zadumchivyi pevets* and a *starets vdokhnovennyi*. Osgar is young (*vo tsvete nezhnykh let*) and *milyi*; Mal'vina is young and beautiful.

Zhukovsky-type epithets predominate, particularly in the description of the setting: *t'ma gustaya*, *dremuchii bor*, *groznye skaly*, *tusklyi luch*, *bezdna morskaya*. Epithets with heavy emotional overtones are frequent: *bereg ugryumyi*; *mrachnaya iva*; *zimy pora unylaya*; *mrachnaya*, *bezmolvnaya toska*; *sladkoe ocharovanie*; *unylaya ten'*. The atmosphere is created principally by the repetition of words conveying silence and mystery:

> И тихо за порог выходит он в молчанье,
> Окован мрачною, безмолвною тоской— (8: 5–6)
>
> Побегли вспять враги—и тихий мир герою!
> И тихо все вокруг могильного холма! (11: 1–2)

The syntax of the poem is characterized by rhetorical questions, exclamatory intonation, frequent interruptions and interjections—all typical of Zhukovsky's language. It should be noted that Zhukovsky's most Ossianic ballad, *Eolova arfa*, was written in the same year as Pushkin's *Osgar*; striking similarities between the phraseology of the two works have been recorded.[5] *Osgar* is

[4] See above, Ch. I, p. 10.

[5] Iezuitova, 'Iz istorii', 271.

clearly Pushkin's most imitative experiment and employs the subject, characters, setting, and style of Zhukovsky's early ballads and balladic lyrics.

From 1814 to 1820 Pushkin wrote several works which in one way or another demonstrate the influence of Zhukovsky's poetry. In *K Zhukovskomu* (1816) Pushkin reviews the most recent developments in Russian poetry, including Zhukovsky's substantial contribution; in *K portretu Zhukovskogo* (1818) he praises Zhukovsky's verse for its *plenitel'naya sladost'*, *bezmolvnaya pechal'*, and *rezvaya . . . radost'*; in *Zhukovskomu* (1818) he characterizes the (balladic) world of Zhukovsky's poetry as one where:

. . . сменяются виденья
Перед тобой в волшебной мгле. (5–6)

In the same *poslanie* Pushkin reinterprets the title of Zhukovsky's periodical, *Für wenige—Dlya nemnogikh*, which was originally intended to refer literally to the small audience to whom the poems were addressed, but which is characteristically applied by Pushkin to the figurative 'few' who could understand and appreciate real poetry.

Pushkin's *Kazak* (1814), sub-titled *Podrazhanie malorossiiskomu* and probably based on the Ukrainian folk-song *Ekhav kazak za Dunai*, shows evidence of Zhukovsky's influence in its heroine, setting, and dialogue. It is only with the ironic reversal in the final stanza that Pushkin destroys the romantic idyll of the lovers' elopement:

Поскакали, полетели.
Дружку друг любил;
Был ей верен две недели,
В третью изменил. (15)

Pushkin's lyric *Srazhennyi rytsar'* (1815), although lacking a real subject, nevertheless manages to capture the mysterious atmosphere of Zhukovsky's ballads in its language, rich in enigmatic hints and suggestions. *Tam u leska* (1819) is a balladic lyric which relates a love story in typical Zhukovsky style[6] except that the poet stands apart from the narrator. Finally in the balladic *Chernaya shal'* (1820), sub-titled *Moldavskaya pesnya* although no source has yet been discovered, Pushkin's narrator emerges as a genuine

[6] Cf. Zhukovsky's ballad *El'vina i Edvin* (1814).

character; furthermore, the device of the refrain, repeated in the last stanza, acquires tragic significance:

> Гляжу, как безумный, на черную шаль,
> И хладную душу терзает печаль. (16)

It has been argued that this work is a parody of Zhukovsky's ballads—an interpretation which seems unjustified; nor is there any indication of parody either in the manuscript copy or in the variant redactions of the work.[8]

In a letter to Kyukhel'beker in December 1825 Pushkin stated: 'I don't understand what makes you parody Zhukovsky.'[9] In spite of his alleged incomprehension, after the series of Ossianic works in 1814, and both during and after the various poems written between 1814 and 1820 which clearly reflect Zhukovsky's influence, Pushkin began to parody precisely those elements of Zhukovsky's style which he had so faithfully imitated. In an article written later in his career, Pushkin observed of parody in general: 'This sort of joke requires rare versatility of style: the good parodist is master of all styles'.[10] Pushkin was to demonstrate in his parodies of Zhukovsky's literary ballads that he possessed that 'rare versatility' and that he was indeed the undisputed 'master of all styles'.

Evidence of Pushkin's first experiment in parody has been provided by Gaevsky:

> Attracted by the success of the talented and witty poem written by his uncle, V. L. Pushkin, called *Opasnyi sosed*,[11] which was circulating in manuscript and being avidly read and reread, the nephew [Pushkin] adopted the same genre and . . . wrote *Ten' Barkova*, a ballad, known in several copies. At first he passed it off as a work by Prince Vyazemsky, but seeing that it was enjoying great success, he acknowledged that he wrote it.[12]

Composed while Pushkin was working on his unfinished *poema Monakh*, and said by Gaevsky to be an imitation of Barkov's porno-

[7] See B. P. Gorodetsky, *Lirika Pushkina* (M.-L., 1962), 265; and G. F. Bogach, *Pushkin i moldavskii fol'klor* (Kishinev, 1963), 62–5.

[8] See *PSS* II. 631–4.

[9] *PSS* XIII. 248.

[10] 'Angliya est' otechestvo karikatury (1830)', *PSS* XI. 118.

[11] V. L. Pushkin's poem describes the diverse clientele at a local brothel; see *Poety 1790–1810-kh godov*, 668–72.

[12] 'Pushkin v litsee', 155–7.

graphic works, *Ten' Barkova* is in fact a witty pornographic parody of Zhukovsky's ballad *Gromoboi* (1810). Although the complete text has never been published, excerpts have appeared in various editions of Pushkin's collected works. In 1929 N. O. Lerner published the largest section to date (70 lines). In his introduction to *Ten' Barkova* Lerner dispels any doubts concerning Pushkin's authorship and establishes the date of the work as no later than 1814.[13] During the 1930s M. A. Tsyavlovsky prepared the text of the poem for a special supplement to Volume I of the Academy of Sciences' edition of Pushkin's complete collected works (1936–59); in his commentary he compared the texts of *Ten' Barkova* and *Gromoboi* in order to show how closely Pushkin parodied Zhukovsky's religious passages. Tsyavlovsky's supplement and commentary have never been published.[14] All subsequent attempts to publish Pushkin's poem have failed, and neither the complete text nor the commentary is available for scholarly consultation.

If the various published excerpts are compiled, it is possible to form a general impression of *Ten' Barkova.* On a certain winter evening a defrocked priest, a poet, and several other unsavoury characters gather in a Petersburg brothel. The cleric is by far the most high-spirited, and earns himself the title of 'Zealous priest of Priapus'; the poet appears to be impotent, but the ghost of Barkov materializes and offers to rescue him. If the poet will agree to sing Barkov's praises, his potency will be restored:

Возьми задорный мой гудок,
  Играй как не попало!
Вот звонки струны, вот смычок,—
  Ума в тебе немало.

The young poet eagerly accepts the offer and at once enjoys his reward:

—Барков! доволен будешь мной!—
  Провозгласил детина.
И вмиг исчез призрак ночной,
  И мягкая перина
Под милой . . .
Не раз потом измялась . . .

[13] *Rasskazy o Pushkine* (L., 1929), 47–56.
[14] See his *Stat'i o Pushkine* (M., 1962), 418.

A general similarity between Zhukovsky's *Gromoboi* and Pushkin's *Ten' Barkova* is unmistakable. Zhukovsky's disenchanted hero enters into a Faustian bargain with the evil Asmodei: if he signs over his soul to the devil, he will be rewarded with honours and riches. Pushkin's impotent poet enters into an agreement with the talented, though underrated Barkov: if he praises Barkov's poems, he will regain his potency. Unfortunately, without access to the full text of Pushkin's parody or to Tsyavlovsky's commentary, no further comparison is possible.

While Pushkin's first experiment in parody was based on Zhukovsky's *Gromoboi*, his next was based on Zhukovsky's *Vadim*.[15] In September 1815 the two poets met in Tsarskoe Selo and became lifelong friends. From 1814 to 1817 Zhukovsky worked on the sequel to his ballad *Gromoboi* which he completed in 1817; both parts (*Gromoboi* and *Vadim*) were published that year. From 1817 to 1820 Pushkin worked on his poem *Ruslan i Lyudmila*, which was published in 1820. Zhukovsky read the work and sent his portrait to Pushkin with the now famous inscription acknowledging his own defeat.[16] Since its publication, critics have tended to read *Ruslan*, particularly the fourth canto, as a parody of Zhukovsky's *Vadim*. Pushkin later acknowledged this interpretation: 'They accused my poem of immorality . . . and [said it was] a parody of *Dvenadtsat' spyashchikh dev*; for this second charge, I should have been soundly rebuked for a lack of aesthetic feeling. It was unforgivable (especially at my age) to parody a virginal, poetic creation in order to delight the crowd.'[17]

The fourth canto of *Ruslan* begins with an invocation to Zhukovsky which first characterizes and praises his poetic talent and then begs forgiveness in advance for what is to follow (17–27). Pushkin continues with a succinct summary of *Gromoboi* (28–37), followed by a general description of Zhukovsky's ballads, written in imitation of Zhukovsky's own style:

И нас пленили, ужаснули
Картины тайных сих ночей,
Сии чудесные виденья,

[15] There exists a short poem, *Ballada* ('Chto, ty devitsa, grustna') (1819), a joint effort at comic verse on the subject of writing ballads. The first five words were written by Zhukovsky, the remainder by Pushkin.

[16] See above, p. 118.

[17] 'Oproverzhenie na kritiki (1830)', *PSS* XI. 144–5.

Сей мрачный бес, сей божий гнев,
Живые грешника мученья
И прелесть непорочных дев.[18]

(38–43)

Then comes the genuine parody. Pushkin's Ratmir, in pursuit of Lyudmila, temporarily succumbs to temptation and accepts precisely those physical pleasures which Zhukovsky's Vadim had rejected. On the other hand, the hero Ruslan proves to be the faithful lover, who does not succumb to temptation, but rather overcomes insuperable obstacles to achieve his goal. However, this goal is not the abstract, mystical illumination towards which Vadim aspired; on the contrary, it is the very beautiful and very physical heroine, Lyudmila. Pushkin has turned Zhukovsky's theme upside down. All the hero's sacrifices and torments are aimed not at achieving some sort of spiritual fulfilment, but at discovering personal contentment in earthly love.

In his recent study of Pushkin, J. O. Bayley, referring to *Stantsionnyi smotritel'*, wrote: 'Like all Pushkin's parodies it does not deride or belittle the source, but gives it a further dimension of humanity.'[19] Such is the essence of Pushkin's parody of Zhukovsky in *Ruslan i Lyudmila*. The spiritual Vadim has been reincarnated in the physical Ruslan, and the former's abstract ideal has been replaced by the latter's human emotion. This is parody in its most creative sense.[20]

Another, though perhaps less obvious, example of Pushkin's parody of Zhukovsky's ballads occurs in Chapter V of *Evgenii Onegin*. Tat'yana's dream has by now acquired a lengthy critical bibliography;[21] two entries have particular relevance for this discussion. M. P. Samarin, in a little-known article entitled 'Iz marginalii k *Evgeniyu Oneginu*',[22] studies the relationship of the dream to Pushkin's ballad *Zhenikh*. Basing his statements on

[18] (My underlining.) Pushkin's description of the castle and the maiden's song (68–95) parody Zhukovsky's epithets in the conclusion to *Gromoboi* (68–74).

[19] *Pushkin: A Comparative Commentary* (Cambridge, 1971), 311.

[20] See W. Arndt's introduction to his translation of *Ruslan and Liudmila* (Ann Arbor, Mich., 1974), ix–xxi.

[21] See R. A. Gregg, 'Tat'yana's Two Dreams', *SEER* XLVIII, No. 113 (1970), 492–505, for a select bibliography.

[22] *Naukovi zapiski naukovo-doslidchoi katedri istorii ukrains'koi kul'turi*, No. 6 (1927), 307–14.

manuscript evidence, Samarin notes, firstly, that Pushkin was working on chapters IV and V of *Onegin* and on *Zhenikh* simultaneously; and, secondly, that in a rough draft of *Zhenikh* the heroine was called Tat'yana, while the heroine of *Onegin* was originally called Natasha. In his analysis of the texts, Samarin reveals some intriguing similarities between the two: the settings of the dream and the ballad are almost identical (forest, night, little hut); specific details in the narration are common to both works (*shaika*, door, long knife); some of the phraseology coincides (cf. *EO*, V: 17, 'Lyudskaya molv' i konskii top', and *Zhenikh*, 18: 1, 'Vdrug slyshu krik i konskii top'); and, finally, Natasha's story in *Zhenikh* is related as if it too were a dream. Thus it is possible to identify balladic motifs and expressions in Tat'yana's dream.

R. E. Matlaw, in an article entitled 'The Dream in *Yevgeniy Onegin*',[23] considers the relationship of Tat'yana's dream to Zhukovsky's ballad *Svetlana*. He argues that *Svetlana* was one of Pushkin's sources for material on Russian folklore, and finds some resemblance in vocabulary between the two (particularly in descriptions of the snowy setting, the chase, and the heroine's fears). Matlaw concludes that the romantic diction of the dream constitutes either a parody of Zhukovsky's language, an example of Tat'yana's own inventive exaggeration, or evidence of Pushkin's ironic attitude towards romantic heroines.

The epigraph to chapter V and references to Zhukovsky's *Svetlana* in earlier chapters leave little doubt as to the presence of parody. In chapter III: 5 Lensky compares Tat'yana to Svetlana, using Zhukovsky's epithets *molchaliva i grustna*. In chapter V: 10 the narrator intervenes to recall the fortune-telling scene in *Svetlana* and to express his fears on behalf of Tat'yana. The epigraph to chapter V is borrowed from Zhukovsky's epilogue to the ballad:

> О, не знай сих страшных снов
> Ты, моя Светлана. . . . (20: 1–2)

The point is made by Matlaw that this epigraph is meant to be ironic: Svetlana's dream turns out to be false, and its melodramatic horrors are replaced by the joys of marriage. While Tat'yana's dream also proves to be false in that she does not marry Onegin, in a much deeper sense her dream comes true: Lensky is killed and

[23] *SEER* XXXVII, No. 89 (1959), 487–504.

she is married off to someone else. Thus Tat'yana's dream is a subtle parody of Zhukovsky's *Svetlana* in which Pushkin ironically reverses the whole function of the dream itself. Svetlana's dream is unreal and forgotten; Tat'yana's dream is real and fulfilled.

Not all of Pushkin's parodies of Zhukovsky's ballads were written in verse. In 1830 Pushkin turned once again to *Svetlana* for an epigraph to one of his *Povesti Belkina*, *Metel'*. He borrowed twelve lines from the ninth and tenth stanzas of the ballad, which depict the snowy setting of Svetlana's ride, the little church by the roadside, and the ominous black raven.

Bayley interprets *Metel'* as an attack on 'the contemporary vogue for tales of romantic elopements and demon bridegrooms' and he notes 'parallels with Bürger's *Lenore* that are hinted at in the nightmare of the heroine Masha'.[24] Bayley's observations can be extended: it is possible to interpret *Metel'* as a parody of the subject and setting of a conventional literary ballad. The poor hero and pale heroine come from different social classes; the obstacle to their love is present in the heroine's parents; an elopement is planned in an atmosphere of mystery and is followed by a midnight ride through a snowy landscape. Two motifs occur in Mar'ya's dream: her father hurls her into a bottomless pit (cf. Lyudmila's demise in a grave), and her lover appears near death (cf. the disembodiment of Lyudmila's lover). But, unlike Tat'yana's dream, Mar'ya's is not completely fulfilled. Her lover fails to appear at the church; he departs in disgrace and soon afterwards is killed in battle. The heroine is married off to a passing stranger who also disappears.[25] Only by an unlikely coincidence are the heroine and the stranger-husband reunited years later, in a parody of the romantic disguise/recognition motif which is so characteristic of Zhukovsky's ballads. *Metel'* ends with the words:

Бурмин побледнел . . . и бросился к ее ногам.

Zhukovsky's ballad *Pustynnik* (1812) includes a tearful reunion between former lovers, described in almost the same words:

—Мальвина!—старец восклицает,
И пал к ее ногам. (36: 1–2)

[24] *Pushkin*, 311–12.

[25] Gregg, in 'Tat'yana's Two Dreams', argues that Tat'yana must have known perfectly well the fate of eligible maidens who do not marry the man they love—they marry someone else. Thus Tat'yana marries the general. Similarly in *Metel'*, Mar'ya marries the stranger.

Metel' ends happily. The heroine fails to recover her original lover; instead she is provided with an acceptable substitute. Once again Pushkin has ironically reversed the ballad situation.

Another of the *Povesti Belkina* contains elements of ballad parody. In *Grobovshchik* all the various miraculous and mysterious motifs of the literary ballads are present, once again in the form of a dream. The hero's 'invitation' extended to his former clients to attend a house-warming party is vividly enacted in his imagination. While the hero is terrified, the comic tone of the narrator's description of the skulls, skeletons, and corpses transforms the Gothic paraphernalia of a literary ballad into the prosaic details of the old grave-digger's dream.

Pushkin returned to verse parody once more in his cycle *Pesni zapadnykh slavyan* (1834). *Vurdalak*, one of the songs translated from Mérimée's literary hoax, *La Guzla* (1827), is an amusing parody of the fear which ballads were supposed to arouse.[26] The hero Vanya, wandering through a graveyard late one night, is frightened by a horrible noise which he takes to be a vampire; it turns out to be a dog chewing an old bone. Vanya's irrational terror is the object of amusement: he is described as *ot strakha blednyi*, and the tension is sustained in balladic language:

Бедный Ваня еле дышит,
Спотыкаясь, чуть бредет
По могилам; вдруг он слышит,
Кто-то кость, ворча, грызет.[27] (2)

Although Pushkin's parodies date from 1814 (*Ten' Barkova*) to 1834 (*Vurdalak*), the works in which Zhukovsky's motifs and style were subjected to the most significant reinterpretation were written between 1817 and 1825. By 1825 Pushkin had freed himself from the narrow conventions of the Russian ballad. He started using the genre not only for imitations or for parodies but also to create original literary ballads.

Pushkin's first creative experiment in the ballad genre was *Rusalka*, written in 1819 but, because of problems with the censor, not published until 1826. This ballad has attracted little attention

[26] See above, Ch. III, p. 42.

[27] (My underlining.) Cf. *Svetlana*, 6: 2, *Chut' Svetlana dyshit*, and *Zhenikh*, 1: 8 *Drozhit i ele dyshit*.

from literary critics. Tomashevsky dismisses it as Pushkin's 'Western European ballad',[28] while Iezuitova merely calls attention to its 'anti-clerical theme'.[29] No one has noted or explained the relationship of Pushkin's *Rusalka* to Zhukovsky's ballad *Rybak* (1818).

Rusalka tells the story of a monk whose evening prayers are interrupted when a mermaid suddenly appears and beckons to him. Her reappearance on the following night torments the monk and keeps him from his devotions. On the third night the monk disappears mysteriously; his corpse is discovered the next day by some children.

The resemblance to Zhukovsky's *Rybak* is unmistakable: the ballad setting and atmosphere; the mermaid's summons, the hero's submission; and the power of nature-magic over human beings. But each of these motifs, adapted by Zhukovsky from Goethe's original, was substantially reworked by Pushkin in *Rusalka.*

While Zhukovsky's setting for *Rybak* is abstract and merely implied, Pushkin emphasizes the immediate connection between nature and supernature. Each appearance of the mermaid is preceded by a mysterious transformation of the landscape, brought about by shadows, darkness, and moonlight (stanzas 2, 5, 7). The explanation of the mystery is found in the phrase *ocharovannye brega* (7: 2): the landscape may appear to be 'natural', but in fact it is under the control of the supernatural.

Whereas Zhukovsky's mermaid is a pure and idealized *krasavitsa*, Pushkin's legendary *rusalka*[30] represents a physical temptation in human form. She appears naked and alluring, flirtatious and playful. Some of the epithets which are used to describe her are borrowed from Zhukovsky: '. . . *legka, kak ten' nochnaya,/ Bela, kak rannii sneg kholmov*' (3: 5–6); *vlazhnye vlasy* (cf. *Rybak: vlazhnaya glava*); and *chudnaya deva*, . . . *prelestna* . . . *bledna*. However, the description of the mermaid in stanza 6 is strikingly original in its almost exclusive use of verbs:

Глядит, кивает головою,
Целует издали шутя,

[28] Pushkin, II (M.-L., 1961), 375.

[29] 'Iz istorii', 425.

[30] Vasmer in *Etymologicheskii slovar' russkogo yazyka*, III (M., 1971), 520, traces of origin of *rusalka* to OR *rusaliya*—the pagan holiday of springtime, later the resurrection of the holy fathers before Trinity; the OR is borrowed from Middle Greek ῥουσάλια, Trinity, or Latin *rosālia*, the holiday of roses.

Играет, плешется волною,
Хохочет, плачет, как дитя,
Зовет монаха, нежно стонет . . .

Zhukovsky's fisherman is a passive and uninvolved observer. Pushkin's monk is chosen not for 'anti-clerical' reasons but because the poet wants to demonstrate the power of nature-magic over someone who is leading a spiritually disciplined, ascetic life. Pushkin's real interest lies in the gradual development of the hero's obsession: the monk is first described as *staryi* and *svyatoi*; on the second night the vision of the mermaid has made him *ugryumyi*; and by the third night the *otshel'nik strastnyi* is near distraction.

The final image of the monk's corpse is beautifully understated and completely unemotional. The manuscript version reads:

И только бороду седую
Русалки дергали в воде.[31]

In the published text, this was altered to:

И только бороду седую
Мальчишки видели в воде. (7: 7–8)

The realistic physical image of the beard visible in the water is very striking. Bayley considers the bathos of this climax an example of Pushkin's complete non-involvement:[32] the mermaid does not appear on the third night, thus frustrating the reader's expectations and deviating from the pattern of Zhukovsky's *Rybak*. The vision or hallucination of the monk is replaced by the factual observation of outsiders. The elimination of the *rusalki* from the manuscript and the substitution of the *mal'chishki* support Bayley's view. Pushkin is clearly trying to achieve the distance between narrator and subject which was the basic characteristic of the narrative method in traditional folk ballads.

The various manuscript versions of *Rusalka* contain additional evidence of Zhukovsky's influence, much of which was eliminated in the final copy.[33] Pushkin's first description of the setting uses the favourite Zhukovsky epithet *tikhii* (*Sidit u tikhikh beregov*); the mermaid is referred to as *krasavitsa nagaya* (cf. *Rybak*, 1: 8), which is altered to *zhenshchina nagaya*; and the intonations and

[31] *PSS* II. 573.
[32] *Pushkin*, 56.
[33] *PSS* II. 569–73.

interruptions characteristic of Zhukovsky's syntax are much more apparent in the early versions.

Rusalka is Pushkin's own version of *Rybak*, written not as a parody of Zhukovsky but as a creative reinterpretation of his theme. Although some of Pushkin's description still shows the influence of Zhukovsky's style, nevertheless the dominant supernatural element, the sensuous mermaid, the obsessed monk, the objective narrator, and the vivid realism foreshadow Pushkin's original contribution to the ballad genre. Pushkin remained silent during the polemics which enveloped *Rybak* in 1820.[34] *Rusalka* was his own form of poetic participation in the debate.

In 1822 Pushkin wrote the *Pesn' o veshchem Olege*, which has sometimes been included in discussions of his literary ballads,[35] although it really belongs to the tradition of Russian historical *poemy*, such as Katenin's *Mstislav* (1819), Ryleev's *Dumy* (1821–3), Kyukhel'beker's *Svyatopolk* (1824), and Yazykov's *Oleg* (1827). Pushkin borrowed the subject of the *Pesn'* from two sources. Karamzin's *Istoriya Gosudarstva Rossiiskogo*, which contained the Primary Chronicle's concise account of Oleg's career; and the so-called L'vov Chronicle,[36] an edition of which was in Pushkin's library, and which included some dialogues later adapted by the poet.[37]

In his *Pesn'* Pushkin attempted to create an accurate historical picture of life in ninth- and tenth-century *Rus'* by including numerous details relating to the heroic *byt* (military campaigns, funeral feasts, and so on). The language of the poem is not stylized; it is a conscious mixture of elements borrowed from folklore (*temnyi les*, *vernyi kon'*), the chronicle sources (*veshchii Oleg*), and the contemporary literary language (*vdokhnovennyi kudesnik*, *pokornyi Perunu*).[38] Pushkin's theme, the inevitability of Fate, is indeed similar to that found in literary ballads.

Zhenikh, written in 1824–5, is one of Pushkin's most original

[34] See above, Ch. V, pp. 113–15.

[35] See Gukovsky, *Pushkin i russkie romantiki*, 331 ff.; and Tudorovskaya, 'Stanovlenie zhanra narodnoi ballady', 67–83.

[36] *Letopisets russkoi ot prishestviya Rurika do konchiny tsarya Ioanna Vasil'evicha* (SPb., 1792).

[37] See K. A. Nemirovskaya, '*Pesn' o veshchem Olege* i letopisnoe skazanie', *Uchenye zapiski LGPI im. Gertsena*, LXXXVI (1949), 13–56.

[38] See O. V. Tvorogov, 'Leksika *Pesni o veshchem Olege*', *Uchenye zapiski LGPI im. Gertsena*, CLXIX (1959), 229–53.

literary ballads, although both its genre and its sources are in dispute. When it was first published in *Moskovskii vestnik* in 1827, its genre was defined by the sub-title *prostonarodnaya skazka*. The fact that this description was removed when the work was included in the 1829 edition of Pushkin's poetry shows the poet's own vacillation concerning its true genre. *Zhenikh* is neither a *skazka* in the traditional sense nor is it a conventional literary ballad. Instead, Pushkin combines the subject and narrative method of a *skazka* with the form and narrative attitude of a ballad to create an original work of art.

Belinsky, in his series of arictles on Pushkin, considers *Zhenikh* a genuine, *narodnyi* Russian work: 'This ballad, in terms of both its form and its content, is permeated with Russian spirit; one can say about it a thousand times more than about *Ruslan i Lyudmila: Zdes' russkii dukh, zdes' Rus'yu pakhnet*.'[39]

A letter written by Pushkin from Mikhailovskoe in November 1824 to his brother is often cited as authoritative evidence of the *narodnyi* sources of *Zhenikh:* '. . . in the evenings I listen to *skazki*—and compensate for the deficiency in my damned upbringing. How lovely these *skazki* are! Each one is a *poema*!'[40] N. F. Sumtsov undertook a detailed comparison of *Zhenikh* with twenty versions of the Russian *skazka* based on exactly the same subject.[41] He concludes that Pushkin's work, although it contains motifs similar to those in the *skazki* (e.g. the matchmaker's offer, the father's acceptance, the youth in the troika, the girl at the gate), differs from each one in some particular way; thus he eliminates the variants as immediate sources for *Zhenikh*. N. M. Dolgova has studied the songs recorded by Pushkin which were later included in Kireevsky's collection (1868) and discovered that some of the wedding songs have elements in common with *Zhenikh*.[42]

In addition to these Russian folk sources, foreign sources have also been cited for the ballad. M. K. Azadovsky has suggested that *Zhenikh* may have been influenced by the Grimm Brothers.[43] The

[39] *PSS* VII. 433–4.

[40] Ibid. XIII. 121.

[41] 'Issledovaniya o poezii A. S. Pushkina', in *Khar'kovskii universitetskii sbornik v pamyat' A. S. Pushkina* (Khar'kov, 1900), 276–86.

[42] 'K voprosu ob istochnikakh ballady A. S. Pushkina *Zhenikh*', *Uchenye zapiski Gor'kovskogo gosudarstvennogo universiteta*, XLVIII (1958), 27–36.

[43] 'Istochniki skazok Pushkina', *Vremennik Pushkinskoi komissii*, I (1936), 134–63.

most convincing argument was presented by A. M. Kukulevich and L. M. Lotman, based on an analysis of *Der Räuberbräutigam* from the Grimm Brothers' *Kinder- und Hausmärchen* (1812–13). They compared the content of the German story with *Zhenikh* and came to the conclusion that the former contains all the major motifs of Pushkin's poem, including the wedding feast and dream interpretation, some of which are absent from the Russian *skazki*. They also compared the language of the two works, and found several curious parallels in phraseology.[44]

The problem is to explain how Pushkin could have known the German source, since it was not included in the available French translation of the Grimm Brothers. It is supposed that either Pushkin read it in German or Zhukovsky served as the intermediary. Tomashevsky in his major study of Pushkin fully accepts the conclusions reached by Kukulevich and Lotman.[45] It is most likely that Pushkin began with the Grimm Brothers' story, and then added motifs borrowed from Russian *skazki* and songs in order to create a truly *narodnyi* Russian ballad.

Pushkin was certainly influenced by other literary ballads, particularly by Bürger's *Lenore*, from which the stanza and metre of *Zhenikh* were borrowed, and by the several versions of *Lenore* written by Zhukovsky and Katenin. The rough draft of Pushkin's *Zhenikh*, which is twice as long as the final version, shows how important these influences were. The following passages in the manuscript, which were either eliminated or greatly reduced, reveal the similarities between the original version of *Zhenikh* and Zhukovsky's ballads:[16]

И кинулась рыдая мать
В слезах Наташу обнимать . . .[47]

Стоит бледна как полотно
  Открыв недвижно очи
И все глядит она в окно
  В печальный сумрак ночи.[48]

[44] 'Iz tvorcheskoi istorii ballady Pushkina *Zhenikh*', ibid. VI (1941), 72–91.
[45] *Pushkin* II. 103.
[46] *PSS* II. 957–64.
[47] Cf. *Lyudmila*, 4 (the scene between mother and daughter).
[48] Cf. *Lyudmila*, 8: 9 'V svetlyi sumrak oblechenny'.

Наташа снова задрожит
И взоры снова устремит[49]
То в окны то к порогу
Молясь тихонько Богу.

The scene between mother and daughter, the heroine's temperamental nature, and her religious devotion are motifs familiar from Zhukovsky's *Lyudmila* and *Svetlana*. Even the final version of *Zhenikh* shows traces of Zhukovsky's influence in its pervasive atmosphere of *strakh* and mystery, and in the frequent use of the adverbs *vdrug* and *vot*. And the last stanza of Pushkin's ballad is similar in both language and theme to the final stanza of Zhukovsky's *Ivikovy zhuravli*.

Katenin, in a letter written to Bakhtin in November 1827, complained: 'Pushkin's *Natasha* [i.e. *Zhenikh*] is sewn together out of scraps, *Svetlana* and *Ubiitsa* have been shamelessly pillaged.'[50] And, indeed, *Zhenikh* also shows some influence of Katenin's ballad *Natasha*.[51] Furthermore, there are striking similarities in names, motifs, and phrases between *Zhenikh* and chapter V of *Evgenii Onegin*, which were being written simultaneously.[52] Yet in spite of this wide variety of foreign and Russian sources and influences, *Zhenikh* remains one of Pushkin's most original works.

The ballad begins *in medias res:* Natasha, a merchant's daughter, returns home after an absence of three days and resumes her normal life without a word of explanation to her parents. One day a troika goes by, and she recognizes the driver but remains silent. The driver, attracted by Natasha, sends a matchmaker to her father to arrange a wedding. At the wedding feast Natasha recounts her mysterious 'dream', and in so doing exposes her bridegroom as a robber and a murderer.

The brevity of *Zhenikh* and the maintenance of the enigma until the understated conclusion contribute to the heightened dramatic tension. Horror is inherent in the situation itself and does not need to be made explicit by frequent use of Zhukovsky-type epithets such as *uzhasnyi* and *strashnyi*. Natasha's practical heroism, shown

[49] The variants of this line include two Zhukovsky epithets: *I vzor nedvizhnyi/uzhasnyi* ⟨?⟩ *ustremit*.

[50] *Pis'ma P. A. Katenina k K. N. Bakhtinu*, 100–1. Katenin mistakenly used the heroine's name as the title.

[51] Cf. *Zhenikh*, 13: 7, 'Ne p'et, ne est, ne sluzhit'; *Natasha*, 12: 5, 'Ne pila tri dnya, ne ela'.

[52] See above, p. 145.

in her invention and execution of a plan to expose the villain, is in marked contrast to the humble submission to Fate of Zhukovsky's heroines and heroes.

The language of the ballad combines both popular and literary elements. Repetition of individual words and motifs, sometimes ternary or augmented, is functional rather than ornamental, and therefore is similar to repetition in traditional folk ballads.[53] R. M. Volkov has traced the numerous parallels between Pushkin's language in *Zhenikh* and Russian popular songs, sayings, riddles, and *chastushki*, many of which were later recorded in Dal''s dictionary.[54]

Pushkin uses folkloric features such as diminutives, affectionate suffixes, and noun-epithets (*dusha-devitsa, devitsa-krasa*), as well as literary devices, including rich synonym groups, to describe Natasha and her bridegroom, in addition to the noun catalogue:

Крик, хохот, песни, шум и звон,
Разгульное похмелье . . .[55] (20: 1–2)

Epithets are comparatively rare in *Zhenikh*. Pushkin uses some folk epithets (*tesovye vorota, likhaya troika, perstni zolotye, ditya rodnoe*) and describes Natasha in folkloric terms (*rumyana* and *vesela*). The matchmaker also employs a series of folk epithets to characterize the suitor:

И статный, и проворный,
Не вздорный, не зазорный. (6 : 7–8)

Literary epithets are used side by side with folkloric expressions: *bednaya nevesta*, the conventional expression of the narrator's sympathy for his heroine, and *svyataya volya*—both are borrowed from Zhukovsky's repertoire.

The originality of Pushkin's style lies principally in his use of verbs. The frequency and importance of the predicate in the language of traditional folk ballads has been discussed earlier.[56] Pushkin employs verbs in *Zhenikh* in a variety of ways: repetition for retardation (*tuzhit'* in 2: 1 and *poglyadet'* in 4: 1), or to establish a leitmotiv (*tuzhit'* in 2: 1, 13: 8, 22: 3); antonyms (*pristupat'*

[53] See above, Ch. I, p. 5 on *Brat'ya razboiniki i sestra.*
[54] 'Narodnye istoki tvorchestva A. S. Pushkina', *Uchenye zapiski Chernovitskogo gosudarstvennogo universiteta*, XLIV, No. 13 (1960), 3–46.
[55] Cf. *Evgenii Onegin*, V: 17: 7, 'Lai, khokhot, pen'e, svist i khlop'; and V: 25: 12, 'Shum, khokhot, davka u poroga'.
[56] See above, Ch. I, p. 4.

in 1: 6, 2: 2 and *otstupat'sya* in 2: 3); tautologies (*vek . . . vekovat'* in 9: 5 and *divu divovat'sya* in 17: 8); and homonyms (*slezy tochit* in 21: 2 and *nozh . . . tochit* in 21: 4). He tends to load the final couplets of his stanzas with as many as four verbs (stanzas 1, 3, 12, 13); verbs establish a parallel between the victim in the robber's hut (*Ne p'et, ne est, ne sluzhit* in 13: 7) and Natasha at the wedding feast (*Sidit, molchit, ni est, ni p'et* in 21: 1); and ellipsis of the verb in dialogue is used for acceleration (*Otets ei* in 5: 3, 14: 6). Natasha's dream contains a representative selection of folk and literary devices, of verbs and epithets:

И вдруг, как будто наяву,
  Изба передо мною.
Я к ней, стучу—молчат. Зову—
  Ответа нет; с мольбою
Дверь отворила я. Вхожу—
В избе свеча горит; гляжу—
  Везде сребро да злато,
  Все светло и богато. (16)

The Grimm Brothers' story, Russian *skazki* and songs, Bürger's *Lenore*, Zhukovsky's *Lyudmila* and *Svetlana*, and Katenin's *Natasha*—these are the works which comprise the background of *Zhenikh*. Pushkin synthesized his sources and adapted his models to produce what is certainly one of the best-known Russian literary ballads, one which has been included along with Goethe's *Erlkönig* and Keats's *La Belle Dame Sans Merci* among the greatest examples of the ballad genre in European literature.[57]

In an article on the subject of *narodnost'* Pushkin wrote: 'Climate, the system of government, and faith give to each people its particular physiognomy which is more or less reflected in the mirror of their poetry. There is a pattern of thought and feeling, a multitude of customs, beliefs, and habits which belong to each people exclusively.'[58] In other words, local colour could not be imposed on a text by the artificial introduction of an occasional Slavonic name or an Old Russian word; rather, poetry was supposed to reflect naturally the uniqueness of that culture which produced it. In *Zhenikh* Pushkin included various motifs and expressions derived from popular Russian sources. In his remain-

[57] Bayley, *Pushkin*, 57.
[58] 'O narodnosti v literature (1825–26)'. *PSS* XI. 40.

ing ballads he continued to characterize in poetry the 'customs, beliefs, and habits' of his own *narod*.

One popular motif, which was eliminated from the final version of *Zhenikh*, namely the *domovoi*,[59] was used as the basis of Pushkin's unfinished ballad 'Vsem krasny boyarskie konyushni' (1827). The work is in two parts: in the first, an old groom complains of the disturbances caused by the presence of the *domovoi* in his boyar's stables; every morning he finds one horse overheated from having been ridden all night. In the second part the narrator presents the reason for the occurrence in folkloric style; it is not a *domovoi*, but only the young groom who rides out alone each night to visit his beloved. The *domovoi* motif and the folkloric style (e.g. *krasna devka, borzyi kon'*; *potikhon'ko, polegon'ko*; and terminal verbs) were to reappear in Pushkin's later ballads.

Utoplennik (1828), Pushkin's next ballad, is based on another popular belief, namely that the soul of a murderer can never enjoy spiritual peace. When the work was first published in *Moskovskii zhurnal* in 1829, it was sub-titled *prostonarodnaya pesnya;* later that year, when it was included in an edition of Pushkin's poetry, it was called a *prostonarodnaya skazka*, the same sub-title which had been removed from *Zhenikh* in the 1829 edition. Neither a *pesnya* nor a *skazka*, *Utoplennik* is certainly the most *prostonarodnyi* of Pushkin's literary ballads.

In an article on poetic style in 1828 Pushkin wrote: 'There comes a time in mature literatures when intellects, bored with monotonous works of art and with the limited range of conventional language, turn to novel popular conceptions and to unfamiliar popular speech, which had previously been despised.'[60] *Utoplennik* is the poetical realization of this theoretical statement. In it the 'popular conception' is carried over without authorial comment into a literary form and it is expressed in 'the real language of men'.[61] The children who first discover the corpse use colloquial diction and popular speech rhythms. The father's crude words addressed to his children and to the corpse convey both his non-reflective spontaneity and his superstitious terror. On the other

[59] See *PSS* II. 960, *Il' shutit shutki domovoi*.

[60] 'O poeticheskom sloge (1828)', *PSS* XI. 73.

[61] In the same article Pushkin refers to Wordsworth and Coleridge, whose 'deep feelings and poetic thoughts' were expressed in the language of the common man.

hand, the narrator, in his description of the corpse and in his digression on its possible identity (2: 6–3: 8), employs rhetorical questions and literary epithets: *trup uzhasnyi* is a typical Zhukovsky phrase (cf. *slukh uzhasnyi* in 10: 1); *neschastnyi goremyka* combines a literary epithet with a colloquial substantive (cf. *muzhik neschastnyi* in 10: 3); *khmel'nyi molodets* is a folkloric expression: and both *nedogadlivyi kupets* (3: 8) and *lenivaya ruka* (7: 7) are good examples of Pushkin's original, individualizing epithets.

The corpse's reappearance is described in vivid physical images: the dripping beard, immobile gaze, and naked body.[62] The effective repetition of the refrain (9: 7–8):

И до утра все стучались
Под окном и у ворот

in slightly altered form (10: 7–8):

И утопленник стучится
Под окном и у ворот

contains the only use of the title-word in the ballad, insists on the connection between nature and supernature (the storm always precedes the appearance of the corpse), and reinforces the reality of the occurrence by its repetition of the time and place.

It is Pushkin's placing of this 'popular conception' and his use of popular speech within the framework of sophisticated narration without any interference or interpretation on the part of the author that constitute the originality of *Utoplennik*.

In 1828 Pushkin wrote a short ballad which begins 'Voron k vorunu letit'; in manuscript copies it is called either *Dva vorona* or simply *Shotlandskaya pesnya*.[63] The ballad is based on *The Twa Corbies*, included in the section 'Romantic Ballads' in Scott's *Minstrelsy of the Scottish Border*.[64] A French translation of the *Minstrelsy* by N. L. Artaud,[65] which included a prose version of *Les deux corbeaux*, is known to have been in Pushkin's library.

[62] Cf. *Rusalka*, 7: 7–8, 'I tol'ko borodu seduyu/Mal'chishki videli v vode.'

[63] *PSS* III. 674.

[64] Scott notes the parallel between *The Twa Corbies* and an ancient English dirge, *The Three Ravens*, included in Joseph Ritson's *Ancient Songs* (1792). Scott presents the texts of both 'in order to enable the curious reader to contrast these two singular poems, and to form a judgment which may be original'.

[65] *Chants populaires des frontières méridionales de l'Écosse* (Paris, 1826). See P. Struve, 'Walter Scott and Russia', *SEER* XI, No. 32 (1933), 397–410.

Pushkin translated only the first three stanzas of the ballad, which he enlarged to four, and omitted the last two.[66] He thus reduced the story to its basic components: two ravens discuss the source of their next meal; one knows of a *bogatyr'* who lies slain in the field. Only his falcon, his mare, and his wife know why and by whom the *bogatyr'* was slain; but his falcon has flown away, an enemy has taken the mare, and his wife has found a new lover.

Folk elements are closely combined in the language of the ballad: the dominant verbs in the simple syntactic units; the haunting repetition of the folk motif *voron*; and the carefully selected folk epithets (*chistoe pole*, *kobylka voronaya*, *khozaika molodaya*). However, the most interesting changes introduced by Pushkin in his version are, firstly, the intensification of what Balashov calls the *zagadochnost'* or *nedoskazannost'* of a ballad[67] and, secondly, the emphasis on the theme of infidelity.

In Scott's version and in the French translation one raven states laconically:

> And nae body kens that he lies there,
> But his hawk, his hound, and lady fair. (2: 3–4)

. . . et personne ne sait qu'il gît en ce lieu, excepté son épervier, son chien et sa dame. (Struve, 'Walter Scott', 401.)

Pushkin's third stanza attempts to probe the mystery:

> Кем убит и отчего,
> Знает сокол лишь его,
> Да кобылка вороная,
> Да хозайка молодая.

The enigma implicit in the folk ballad is made more explicit in the literary ballad: the reader is teased into thinking that there may be an explanation (*kem* and *otchego*). But although the question is posed, no answer is provided: the mystery is heightened.

[66] The manuscript contains some evidence that Pushkin attempted to translate the last two stanzas; see *PSS* III. 674.

[67] See above, p. 4.

In Scott's version and in the French translation the lady's infidelity is simply one of the consequences of the knight's death:

His hound is to the hunting gane,
His hawk to fetch the wild-fowl hame,
His lady's ta'en another mate,
So we may make our dinner sweet. (3)

Son chien est allé à la chasse; son épervier lie pour autre maître les oiseaux sauvages; sa dame a pris un autre serviteur; ainsi, nous pourrons faire un bon dîner. (Struve, 'Walter Scott', 401.)

This stanza is followed by a gruesome description of the ravens' imminent feast and a preview of the knight's skeleton, soon to be exposed to the winds.

Pushkin alters this stanza substantially, and his version ends ironically:

Сокол в рощу улетел,
На кобылку недруг сел,
А хозайка ждет милóго,
Не убитого, живого. (4)

The emphasis is clearly on the wife's infidelity, on her betrayal of the slain *bogatyr'*. She knows both 'by whom' and 'how' he was killed, and she has chosen a new *milói*.[68] Unlike the sentimental heroines of the love-ballads of the 1790s who faithfully embrace the corpses of their slain lovers and then expire, expecting to be united with them in death, Pushkin's heroine would seem to be a descendant of Dmitriev's hero in *Karikatura* (1792).[69] Upon hearing that his wife had vanished, the husband reacts 'heroically':

Несчастный муж поплакал,
Женился на другой. (25: 3–4)

While Dmitriev's ballad was intended as a parody, Pushkin's is a successful imitation of the unemotional realism inherent in the traditional folk ballads.

One year after writing 'Voron' Pushkin composed an enigmatic

[68] Perhaps she is even implicated in the foul deed!
[69] See above, Ch. II, pp. 33–5.

ballad which begins 'Zhil na svete rytsar' bednyi' (1829); it was later included, though in somewhat abbreviated form, in his dramatic work *Stseny iz rytsarskykh vremen*. The ballad relates the tale of a knight who has witnessed a mysterious vision which he is unable to fathom. Since that experience he shuns all women, prays exclusively to the Virgin Mary, and fights infidels on her behalf. At his death the devil comes to claim the knight's soul, arguing that he prayed only to Mary and not to God, and that he failed to observe the obligatory religious fasts; but Mary intercedes, and admits the knight to paradise.

It has been suggested that in Pushkin's 'Zhil na svete' the knight, a stock figure of the pseudo-medieval ballad, is related to his true medieval context, that is, mystical devotion to Our Lady; thus the ballad is seen as a vulgarization of the chivalric cult of the Virgin.[70] This explanation is plausible, but it overlooks the fact that this vulgarization is achieved by presenting the knight as a romantic lover and by demonstrating that his religious devotion to the Virgin is a perversion of normal human affection.

The epithets of the first stanza (*bednyi*, *molchalivyi*, *prostoi*, *sumrachnyi*, *blednyi*, *smelyi*, *pryamoi*) are the conventional epithets used to describe the hero in romantic literary ballads. The knight's mystical experience is presented as an emotional one, not as an intellectual one (stanza 2), and his vision results in his being unable to look at or speak to any earthly woman. Consequently his chaste nights are spent in prayer before the Virgin's image: '. . . skorbny ochi/ Tikho slezy l'ya rekoi' (7: 3–4). To the end of his life the knight remains faithful to his jealous mistress: 'Vse vlyublennyi, vse pechal'nyi' (11: 3). The ironic observation, 'Strannyi byl on chelovek' (6: 4), is the narrator's understated evaluation of the knight's character. Whereas Zhukovsky described a knight's spiritual love for his idealized lady in *Rytsar' Togenburg* (1818),[71] in 'Zhil na svete' Pushkin interprets the love of *the* most ideal Lady ironically.

Pushkin's last original ballad, *Besy* (1830), is more concerned with creating atmosphere than with relating a story. The visual imagery of white on white (clouds, snow, moonlight), the repetition of verbs (*mchatsya*, *v'yutsya*, *edu*), nouns (*tuchi*, *v'yuga*), and epi-

[70] Bayley, *Pushkin*, 62.

[71] See above, Ch. VI, p. 131.

thets (*mutno nebo, noch' mutna; strashno, strashno ponevole*),[72] the parallelism within stanzas, the refrain, the breathless speed of the verse, and the intricate sound patterns—all these combine to produce the hypnotic effect of an incantation.

The driver's speech combines colloquial diction and syntax with literary expressions (3: 5–8). He explains away the eeriness of the situation by introducing the motif of the demon (*bes*—singular), and describes its activities as pranks (*shalost'*), which in an early manuscript version was either the title or sub-title of the ballad.[73] After the driver's simple explanation, the refrain re-establishes the opening mood. This is followed by an ominous silence: the horses sense the presence of the supernatural. The narrator then tries to explain away the occurrence, employing a variety of folkloric motifs:

Закружились бесы разны, . . .
. . . .
Домового ли хоронят,
Ведьму ль замуж выдают? (6: 3, 7–8)

The manuscript version included additional folkloric motifs:

Что за звуки! . . . аль бесенок
В люльке охает, больной;
Аль мяукает котенок
К ведьме ластится лихой—
Али мертвых черти гонят—
Не русалки ль там поют?
Домового ли хоронят
Ведьму ль замуж отдают . . .[74]

The opening mood is once again established by the refrain; this is followed by the unexpected conclusion:

Мчатся бесы рой за роем
В беспредельной вышине,
Визгом жалобным и воем
Надрывая сердце мне. . . . (7: 4–8)

[72] The manuscript variant for this latter phrase echoes Zhukovsky: *Chto-to strashno ponevole*—the vague *chto-to* is Zhukovsky's; the *ponevole*, expressing the unintentional fear, is Pushkin's.

[73] *PSS* III. 834.

[74] Ibid. 837.

The repetition of the verb *mchatsya* with *besy* (plural) instead of with *tuchi*, the climax of sound effects reached in the phrase *roi za roem/ . . . voem*, the vague, Zhukovsky-like combination *bespredel'naya vyshina* all characterize the external demons. Then, in the last line, these external demons are suddenly related to the poet's internal emotional state. The parallel between nature and psychology, which had been employed in Russian literary ballads since the 1790s, is here completely reinterpreted by Pushkin. The ballad *Besy* has been transformed into a profound personal lyric.

Pushkin's last contributions to the ballad genre are translations of two Polish ballads by Adam Mickiewicz and were written during the autumn of 1833 at Boldino.[75] The first is a free translation of *Czaty, Ballada ukraińska* (1827), which Pushkin calls *Voevoda, Podrazhanie Mitskevichu* or *Pol'skaya ballada.* Pushkin alters the metre of the original and changes some details of the plot. In a study of Pushkin's manuscript version of this ballad, Ya. L. Levkovich documented the poet's conscious elimination of Russian details and his introduction of elements of Polish local colour.[76] For example, he alters *svetlitsa* to *spal'nya*, *pukhovik* to *krovat'* (Pol. *łoże*), *kazachka* to *khlopets* (Pol. *kozak*), and introduces the Polish titles *pan* and *panna*[77] instead of *muzh* and *moloditsa* or *zhena.* Levkovich also noted the similarity in vocabulary and intonation between the boy's reply to his master in *Voevoda:*

Ветер, что ли, плачут очи,
Дрожь берет; в руках нет мочи. (9: 4–5)

and the driver's reply to the narrator in *Besy:*

. . . Нет мочи:
Коням, барин, тяжело;
Вьюга мне слипает очи; (2: 1–3)

The second ballad Pushkin translated from Mickiewicz is called *Budrys i ego synov'ya*; it is a fairly literal rendition of *Trzech Budrysów, Ballada litewska* (1827). Some minor alterations are

[75] In the same year Pushkin wrote *Gusar*, a short narrative poem in colloquial style, which has a few characteristics of the ballad genre. See V. Danilov, 'Istochnik stikhotvoreniya Pushkina *Gusar*', *Russkii filologicheskii vestnik*, LXIV, No. 3–4 (1910), 243–52.

[76] 'Perevody Pushkina iz Mitskevicha', in *Pushkin. Issledovaniya i materialy*, VII (L., 1974), 164.

[77] *Panna* is an error, since it indicates an unmarried woman.

introduced by Pushkin in the details used to convey the local colour of each of the three countries to which one of Budrys's sons is dispatched. For example, Mickiewicz describes the faces of Polish girls as *Lice bielsze od mleka*, which Pushkin changes to *bela, chto smetana*.[78] But in general, the simplicity of the narrative, the ternary structure, and the effective use of repetition in the Polish original are accurately conveyed by Pushkin in his translation.

Bayley's study of Pushkin includes the following observation: 'All the ballads give the impression of being models, demonstrations without further comment of how the thing should be done.'[79] While Pushkin's Ossianic poems and early balladic lyrics closely imitate the subject, setting, characters, and style of Zhukovsky's ballads,[80] and his parodies treat in an ironic manner those same elements which he earlier imitated, each of his original ballads does stand in some sense as a 'model': *Rusalka* is an individual reinterpretation of the nature-magic theme; *Zhenikh*, an original *narodnyi* ballad, combines a German source with Russian folk motifs; *Utoplennik* places a popular motif and colloquial speech within the framework of sophisticated narration; *Voron* imitates the simplicity and unemotional realism of the traditional genre; and *Besy* is an example of the evocation of atmosphere and a transformation of a ballad into a personal lyric.

Bayley compares Pushkin's ballads to those written by Goethe and Keats for the following reasons: '. . . [their works] avoid the romantic ballad's tendency to show off its ancient lore, to put wild and passionate sentiments in stilted eighteenth-century dialogue,

[78] M. Gorlin in 'Les Ballades d'Adam Mickiewicz et Puškin', *Revue des Études slaves*, XIX (1939), 235 ff., accounts for the minor differences between Mickiewicz's and Pushkin's description of Russia by arguing that the details of Pushkin's version correspond to those in one of Mickiewicz's manuscripts, which Pushkin must either have read himself or have heard read aloud.

[79] *Pushkin*, 62.

[80] The results of a survey of 175 epithets from ten of Pushkin's ballads (768 lines) are as follows: of the total number, 147 epithets are used only once each; 18 are used twice each; 5 are used 3 times each (*veselyi, krutoi, mutnyi, pustoi, svetlyi*); and 6 are used from 4–6 times each (*belyi, vernyi, molodoi, svyatoi, staryi, chernyi*). In contrast to Zhukovsky's frequent repetition of a limited range of epithets, Pushkin tends not to repeat himself in his ballads. The epithet came to play a far less important role in Pushkin's poetry as his style matured; it was gradually replaced by the verb as the most original means of description.

or to revel in the picturesque, the horrid or pathetic.'[81] There is another reason: Pushkin succeeded, where Zhukovsky had failed, in consciously employing the form of the literary ballad to its best possible advantage. Writing without any immediate models of traditional Russian folk ballads, Pushkin, in his literary ballads, approached the compressed narrative unit, the dramatic narrative method, and the impersonal narrative attitude characteristic of the folk genre; furthermore, he succeeded in creating the intangible sense of the ballad 'world'—all within the realm of *Kunstpoesie*.

[81] *Pushkin*, 57.

VIII

LERMONTOV'S LITERARY BALLADS

Прошу вас, также, милая бабушка, купите мне полное собрание сочинение Жуковского последнего издания и пришлите также сюда тотчас.

—Лермонтов[1]

IN 1838 Lermontov became acquainted with Zhukovsky in St. Petersburg and the two poets continued to meet until Lermontov's departure for the Caucasus in April 1841. Zhukovsky's influence on his poetry is evident from the very beginning of Lermontov's literary career, both in his experiments in the ballad genre and in his application of balladic techniques in his lyric poetry. As Pushkin had progressed from imitation to parody of Zhukovsky's ballads, so too did Lermontov. From 1830 Lermontov began to parody precisely those elements of Zhukovsky's style which he had previously imitated. But in his ballad cycle of 1832, and particularly in those works written between 1837 and 1841, Lermontov transformed the ballad genre into a form capable of expressing his own deeply personal inspiration.

Lermontov's earliest experiments with the literary ballad were based on German and English sources. Both his choice of models for imitation and the style of these experiments reflect the strong influence of Zhukovsky's ballads. The first of these works, *Ballada* ('Nad morem krasavitsa-deva sidit') (1829), is Lermontov's reworking of Schiller's ballad *Der Taucher*, which Zhukovsky also began translating in 1825 (and published under the title *Kubok* in 1831). In Lermontov's version a mermaid asks a young man to brave the depths of the sea in order to retrieve her necklace and, by so doing, to demonstrate his love for her. The youth accomplishes this task, but when she sends him down again to fetch her some coral, he does not return.

[1] *Sochineniya v shesti tomakh*, VI (M.–L., 1957), 462 (Letter to E. A. Arsen'eva, June 1841).

Lermontov's characters and setting are described in language characteristic of Zhukovsky's ballads: the heroine is a *krasavitsa-deva*; the hero is referred to as *drug*, *yunosha*, and *mladoi udalets*; and the sea is variously depicted as *puchina*, *pennaya bezdna*, *grot*, and *chernoe dno*; the manuscript variants for the last phrase include the typical Zhukovsky combinations *mrachnoe dno* and *uzhasnoe dno*.[2] The numerous exclamations (*O schast'e! on zhiv*) and the repeated interruptions in the narrative are also characteristic of Zhukovsky's syntax; however, it is in the frequency and range of its epithets that Lermontov's style reveals the most notable influence of Zhukovsky's vocabulary, in expressions such as *no mrachen kak byl* (early variant: *on vykhodit pechalen i mrachen kak byl*);[3] *vlazhnye kudri*; *pechal'nyi vzor*; and *dusha beznadezhnaya*.

In 1829 Lermontov also translated Schiller's *Der Handschuh: Eine Erzählung* as *Perchatka*; Zhukovsky translated it under the same title in 1831. The subject is similar to that of *Ballada*, although its resolution is different: an aristocratic lady allows her glove to fall among the wild beasts in an arena in order to test her knight's affection. He retrieves the glove, but tosses it in her face in protest at her caprice.

The language of Lermontov's version and its emphasis on the theme of Fate paradoxically render it more Zhukovsky-like than Zhukovsky's own, relatively literal, translation:

Schiller: Da fällt von des Altans Rand
Ein Handschuh von schoner Hand
Zwischen den Tiger und den Leun
Mitten hinein. (44–7)

Lermontov: Сверху тогда упади
Перчатка с прекрасной руки
Судьбы случайной игрою
Между враждебной четою. (30–3)

Zhukovsky: Вдруг женская с балкона сорвалась
Перчатка . . . все глядят за ней . . .
Она упала меж зверей. (38–40)

[2] Ibid. I. 327.

[3] Ibid.

[4] See A. M. Garkavi, 'Zametki o M. Yu. Lermontove: Lermontov i Zhukovsky (Iz istorii russkoi ballady)', *Uchenye zapiski Kaliningradskogo pedagogicheskogo instituta*, VI (1959), 274–85.

Lermontov's short fragment 'V starinny gody zhili-byli' (1830) may possibly be a translation of an unidentified German source.[4] The single stanza which describes two knights who returned from the crusades in Palestine echoes the theme and style of Zhukovsky's translation of Schiller's *Ritter Toggenburg* in 1818,[5] and also resembles his later translations of Uhland's ballads.[6]

The ballad *Gost'* ('Klarisu yunosha lyubil'), sub-titled *Byl'* and written in the early 1830s, represents the culmination of the German influence on Lermontov's literary ballads.[7] It describes the love affair between Klarisa and Kalmar, whose marriage plans were disrupted when war broke out; Kalmar, after hearing Klarisa's pledge of eternal faithfulness, goes off to fight. However, when springtime arrives, Klarisa decides to marry someone else. At the wedding feast, a silent guest in military dress at last reveals himself to be none other than the corpse of Kalmar, and there he reclaims his Klarisa.

Basically a reworking of Bürger's *Lenore*, Lermontov's *Gost'* also combines motifs inherited from the Russian ballads of the 1790s (war as the obstacle to love; death of the hero; and subsequent union with the heroine) and from Zhukovsky's literary ballads. Kalmar, *tomim toskoi*, expresses a favourite Zhukovsky theme in unmistakably Zhukovsky language:

Пускай холодной смерти сон,
О дева красоты,
Нас осеняет под землей,
Коль не венцы любви святой! (3: 3–6)

Even Kalmar's corpse resembles those of Zhukovsky's heroes (*pryam i nedvizhim*), while the atmosphere of *strakh*, created in part by *kakoi-to strannyi zvuk*, is also characteristic of Zhukovsky's ballads.

While Schiller and Bürger, both in the German originals and in Zhukovsky's free renditions, served as one source of Lermontov's early ballads, English literary ballads provided the poet with another source of inspiration. In 1829 Lermontov wrote *Dva*

[5] See above, Ch. VI, p. 168.

[6] See, for example, *Staryi rytsar'* (1832), a translation of Uhland's *Graf Eberhards Weissdorn*.

[7] See also *Ballada* ('Gvad'yana bezhit'), included in Lermontov's early verse play *Ispantsy* (1830).

sokola, a reworking of *The Twa Corbies*, based either on Pushkin's version of 1828,[8] or on Scott's text.[9]

Lermontov's version was not intended as an imitation of the traditional genre; it is in the form of an extended lyrical dialogue between two misanthropic falcons, each expounding why he has come to hate the world and its inhabitants; the first is disenchanted with rampant hard-heartedness; the second, with common deceitfulness, particularly as embodied in women:

> Но измена девы страстной
> Нож для сердца вековой! . . . (31–2)

Even more than Pushkin, Lermontov emphasizes the theme of infidelity, which is here made explicit in Zhukovsky-type language.

In 1830 Lermontov composed two works based on Byronic subjects. *Chelnok* presents a balladic situation: a small boat, manned by two oarsmen, is buffeted about by a storm; a mysterious *chto-to*, wrapped up in white canvas, lies in the bottom of the boat. This victim of some unexplained crime is described in epithets borrowed from Zhukovsky's ballads:

> И бледный, как жертва гробов;
> Взор мрачен и дик, . . . (2: 4–5)

The enigma is left unresolved; instead, there follows a lyrical reflection on the poet's own expectation of happiness in life and the comforting proximity of peace in death.

The second work, *Ballada* ('Beregis'! Beregis'! . . .'), is an unfinished and inaccurate translation of the ballad inserted between stanzas 40 and 41 of the sixteenth canto of Byron's *Don Juan*. It describes an extraordinary 'black friar' who refused to be driven from the house of a local nobleman when the Moors overran Spain. Once again, Lermontov's style, particularly his choice of epithets, reflects the influence of Zhukovsky's ballads: *chernyi monakh*, *mrak nochnoi*, *rodimyi dol*, and *blednaya luna*.

Another ballad entitled *Gost'* ('Kak proshlets inoplemennyi') and written in 1830 represents the culmination of the English influence on Lermontov's ballads. It is a reworking of the theme

[8] See above, pp. 158–60.

[9] See D. P. Yakubovich, 'Lermontov i Val'ter Skott', *Izvestiya AN SSSR, Otd. obshchestvennykh nauk*, No. 3 (1935), 243–72.

used by Zhukovsky in his ballad *Pustynnik* (1812), which in turn is a translation of Goldsmith's *The Hermit*. Lermontov's guest, a *bednyi monakh*, arrives at an unfamiliar house late one night and is given shelter. He recognizes the lady of the house as his former beloved, and hurls himself at her feet. Then the guest retires to his chamber to sob away the night; in the morning the hosts discover his corpse.

The scene of the lovers' recognition in *Gost'* is almost identical in situation and language to that in Zhukovsky's ballad:

> Он хозайку вдруг узнал,
> Он дрожит—и вот забылся
> И к ногам ее упал.[10] (3: 6–8)

Furthermore, one of Zhukovsky's favourite epithets, *pechal'nyi*, is applied both to the features of the monk:

> Свечки луч печально льется
> На печальные черты (3: 3–4)

and to the cloak which covers those same features, now lifeless:

> И бесчувственное тело
> Плащ печальный покрывал! . . . (5: 7–8)

Scott, Ossian, Byron, and Goldsmith—in their original language and in Zhukovsky's versions—provided Lermontov with models of English literary ballads. While under their influence (1830–2) Lermontov also attempted to employ the stylistic devices of the ballad genre in traditional lyric forms, for example in *Pesn' barda*, *Mogila boitsa* (sub-titled *Duma*), and *Russkaya pesnya* ('Klokami belyi sneg valitsya').

The most interesting of these experiments, *Ballada* ('V izbushke pozdneyu poroyu'), is in the form of a mother's song addressed to her infant. She recounts her husband's heroism in leading the Russians against the Tartars. Suddenly the husband returns, mortally wounded; he reports the Russians' defeat and expires. The mother urges her child to avenge his father's death in a speech which concludes with a fair measure of bathos:

> И он упал—и умирает
> Кровавой смертию бойца.

[10] Cf. *Pustynnik*, 36: 2, 'I pal k ee nogam'; see above, Ch. VII, p. 147 on Pushkin's parody of this motif.

Жена ребенка поднимает
Над бледной головой отца:
"Смотри, как умирают люди,
И мстить учись у женской груди! . . ." (6)

After a period of considerable experimentation with German and English sources and skilful imitation of Zhukovsky's literary ballads, Lermontov wrote a series of parodies on the ballad genre and on its foremost practitioners. The first of these, *Nezabudka* (1830), sub-titled *Skazka*, is a witty parody of Schiller's *Der Taucher*, which had previously served as the model for Lermontov's own *Ballada* ('Nad morem'). *Nezabudka* begins with a comparison of human affections, past and present, and concludes that formerly love and fidelity were stronger emotions than now. An example follows: two lovers are sitting near a brook; the heroine asks the unsuspecting hero to pick a blue flower for her in order to prove his love. He succeeds, but on his way back the ground gives way under him. As he bids his last farewell to his beloved, he tosses her the flower and begs her not to forget him: hence, the name of the flower—*nezabudka*.

Schiller's tragic subject, the test of affection occasioned by a lady's caprice which results in her lover's death, is here cast in a comic vein. The descriptions of the hero (*rytsar' blagorodnyi; moi milyi*), the heroine (*lyubeznaya; deva*), and the idyllic setting (*Pod ten'yu lipovykh vetvei; Svod nad nami yasnyi*) echo phrases from Zhukovsky's ballads. At the climax Lermontov combines elevated abstract substantives with the most frequent epithets of Zhukovsky's vocabulary in delicious bathos:

Уж близко цель его стремленья,
Как вдруг под ним (ужасный вид)
Земля неверная дрожит,
Он вязнет, нет ему спасенья! (38–41)

Other epithets in *Nezabudka* would seem to parody Lermontov's own language in his earlier *Ballada* ('Nad morem'): for example, *pechal'nyi vzor* and *dusha beznadezhnaya* of the former work are superseded by *tsvetok pechal'nyi* and *ruka beznadezhnaya* in the parody.

Ballada ('Iz vorot vyezhayut'), written in 1832, turns the first two lines of a German folk-song, *Die drei Ritter*, into a parody of

Zhukovsky's chivalric ballads. Three knights ride off into battle, leaving their three loves behind; the knights are slain and the women grieve; then three *new* knights come to court them, and the ladies forget their sadness.[11]

Each line of the ballad is followed by the exclamation *uvy!* or *prosti!*; this device, particularly the ironic conclusion, is effectively used to parody the chivalric ideal of true love:

Уж три витязя новых в ворота спешат,
увы!
И красотки печали своей говорят:
прости! (3)

Lermontov's ballad 'On byl v krayu svyatom' (1832) is a parody of Zhukovsky's *Staryi rytsar'* (1832), which in turn was a translation of Uhland's *Graf Eberhards Weissdorn*. Zhukovsky's knight, having heroically defended the Faith in Palestine, spends his old age dozing tranquilly under an olive-tree which had grown from a branch he had taken from a tree in the Holy Land and planted. Lermontov's knight returns from Palestine bald and battered, having spent his time there pillaging and raping; he finds his wife pregnant and his children unruly. Each stanza of Lermontov's parody begins in earnest and is followed by an ironic twist which deflates its meaning:

Понес он в край святой
Цветущие ланиты;
Вернулся он домой
Плешивый и избитый.[12] (2)

The final parody, *Yugel'skii baron* (1837), was a joint effort by Lermontov and V. N. Annenkova, a poetess and close friend of Lermontov's grandmother, to caricature Zhukovsky's translation from Scott, *Zamok Smal'gol'm* (1822).[13] Lermontov's baron summons his page to deliver a letter to the baroness; the page refuses, and finally reveals that she has been unfaithful in the

[11] See above, Ch. II, pp. 33–5, on Dmitriev's *Karikatura*.

[12] Cf. Lermontov's *Vetka Palestiny* (1837)—serious lyrical reflections on a similar theme—which also shows Zhukovsky's influence on its vocabulary and syntax.

[13] See above, Ch. III, pp. 69–73.

baron's absence. The baron laughs and explains to the page that 'northern women' are *always* faithful to their husbands:

Там девица верна, постоянна жена;
Север силой ли только велик?
Жизнь там веры полна, счастья там сторона,
И послушен там сердцу язык! (33–6)

The page listens carefully, admits his mistake, and agrees to deliver the baron's message.

Zhukovsky's style is subjected to merciless parody—in Lermontov's excessive use of verbs (*I kusal on, i rval, i pisal, i strochil*),[14] in the interrogative intonation (*Ne devitsa l' ona? . . . i odna li verna?*), and particularly in the choice and use of epithets. On the one hand Lermontov employs precisely those epithets which Zhukovsky used to characterize his heroes: the baron is described as *znamenityi* and *vysokii*, his wife as *odinoka*, *bledna*, *milaya*, *vernaya*; and the page as *molodoi*. On the other hand, Lermontov takes Zhukovsky's unwieldy *topor . . ./Ukreplen dvadtsatifuntovoi*, and replaces it with the splendid *dolgovyazyi lakei/ Tridtsatipyatiletnyi durak*.

In much the same way as Pushkin, Lermontov also proceeded from imitation to parody. From *Nezabudka* (1830) to *Yugel'skii baron* (1837) he attempted to overcome Zhukovsky's influence by parodying the themes and style of ballads he had previously imitated. With his ballad cycle of 1832 Lermontov began to use the form in a creative and individual way.

In 1832 Lermontov composed three literary ballads: *Trostnik*, *Rusalka*, and *Ballada* ('Kuda tak provorno'). Similarities in the treatment of emotional experience in the three works and their pervading lyricism enable the critic to consider them together as a ballad cycle.

The first, *Trostnik*, is a nature-magic ballad which is said to have been influenced by Victor Hugo's poetry.[15] A fisherman plucks a reed and blows through it: the reed relates the sad tale of a young girl who was held prisoner in her stepmother's house. When she spurned the amorous advances of the woman's evil son,

[14] Cf. *Zamok Smal'gol'm*, 25: 2, *I kipel, i gorel, i sverkal*.
[15] B. M. Eikhenbaum, *Stat'i o Lermontove* (M.-L., 1961), 344.

the girl was mercilessly killed. The reeds which grow above her grave contain her sadness.

Sadness (*pechal'*) is the theme of the ballad; Lermontov emphasizes the intimate connection between human suffering and nature, between the girl's soul and the 'animate' reeds (*budto ozhivlennyi*):

И над моей могилой
Взошел тростник большой,
И в нем живут печали
Души моей младой; (6: 1–4)

In contrast to this sadness, the fisherman, whose presence is used to frame the ballad, is described as *veselyi*; he is incapable of helping the girl or even sharing her experience (*A plakat' ne privyk*).

The girl's monologue is related simply and its language is rich in repetitions (*ostav'; rybak*), internal rhymes (*devitsa, krasavitsa, temnitsa*), and folk elements (*slezy goryuchie; na bereg krutoi; na sini volny*), as well as literary elegiac themes (*ya nekogda tsvela; i rannyuyu mogilu*). Lermontov's fisherman, like the *rybak* in Zhukovsky's ballad, is not in spiritual sympathy with nature; but instead of being seduced by the force of nature-magic, in *Trostnik* the fisherman is merely involuntarily employed to express the girl's *pechal'*.

The second work in the cycle, *Rusalka*, is another nature-magic ballad and probably has as one of its sources an early ballad by Heine, *Die Nixen*.[16] It's narrative element is far less important than is that in *Trostnik*. *Rusalka* consists entirely of a mermaid's lament: she begins with a description of her luxurious kingdom beneath the sea and then describes the lifeless corpse of a handsome *vityaz'* who will not respond to her amorous advances. As in *Trostnik*, nature is animate: for example, the waves are described as *revnivy*. Motifs from the earlier ballad (such as *trostniki* and *krutoi bereg*) are repeated in *Rusalka*; however, the theme of *pechal'* has become the vaguer *neponyatnaya toska*, although the word *pechal'* occurs in the original manuscript.[17] The manuscript also contains more

[16] Eikhenbaum, *Lermontov* (L., 1924), 105.
[17] *Sochineniva*, II. 270.

extensive description of the mermaid herself (including *vlazhnaya; khladnaya; belaya grud'; belaya ruka*)[18]—all of which was rejected in the final version.

The subject and characters of *Rusalka* are relatively unimportant compared to the richness of the visual imagery in the description of the mermaid's underwater realm, where a profusion of colours and materials dazzles the senses: *serebristaya pena, zlatye stada (rybok), khrustal'nye goroda, yarkie peski, shelkovye kudri, sinyaya reka,* and so on. Lermontov returned to this underwater motif in a later ballad, *Morskaya tsarevna* (1841), in which the treatment is more narrative than lyrical.

The last work in the 1832 cycle, *Ballada* ('Kuda tak provorno'), is not a nature-magic ballad, although it too is said to have been influenced by Hugo.[19] Here all the emphasis is placed on the action and on the creation of atmosphere. A young Jewess hurries through the streets to warn her Russian lover that their affair has been discovered and that her father has threatened to take revenge on them both. She urges him to flee and swears that she will never reveal his identity. The lover replies by stabbing her and then killing himself. Their corpses are discovered in the morning.

The heroine, an exotic 'alien', is described in the manuscript as having *vlazhnye ochi, volshebnye ochi*[20]—in the final version the only epithet which remains is *bledna* (*Kak mramornyi idol bledna*); the hero, referred to by the Jewess as her *angel prekrasnyi*, remains still and silent in contrast to her movement and agitation: *I mrachen glukhoi byl otvet*. The balladic motifs are numerous: the midnight setting; the father's revenge; the knife (*nozh rokovoi*); and the enigmatic *chto-to*, referring first to the knife (9: 3) and then to the heroine's corpse (10: 1). Whereas in *Trostnik* the theme is *pechal'* and in *Rusalka toska*, in *Ballada* it is the emotion of *strakh* and the heroine's *tainaya nadezhda:*

И страхом и тайной надеждой пылая,
  Еврейка глаза подняла,
Конечно, ужасней минута такая
  Столетий печали была; (4)

The brevity of each of the three ballads in the 1832 cycle, the

[18] Ibid. 269.
[19] Eikhenbaum, *Stat'i*, 344.
[20] *Sochineniya*, II. 270.

lyricism and the imagery of the nature-magic ballads emphasized at the expense of characterization and narrative, and the emotionally charged atmosphere of *Ballada* are an indication of Lermontov's future contributions to the ballad genre.

In 1837–8 Lermontov experimented with certain balladic narrative techniques in his historical poems. The most popular of these, *Borodino* (1837), had been preceded by lyrical work, *Pole Borodina* (1831), in which the account of the battle was presented in fairly conventional language by a participant.[21] In the later, better-known reworking of the theme Lermontov introduced the figure of the young listener, and further characterized the narrator as a simple 'everyman' by means of the alternating *prostorechie* and pathos of his speech and his ironic sense of humour.

Lermontov's next literary ballad, *Tri pal'my* (1839), influenced by Hugo's *Les Orientales*,[22] is a reworking of the theme treated by Pushkin in his *Podrazhanie Koranu IX* (1824). Pushkin's tale, a close rendition of a passage in the Koran,[23] is narrated in the poet's so-called Eastern style, supplemented by humorous details of realistic local colour.[24] In Lermontov's version, three proud palm-trees on a desert oasis complain to God because they seem to serve no useful purpose in the world. Suddenly a caravan appears, and the palm-trees welcome their unexpected guests. That night the travellers chop down the trees and use them for firewood; in the morning the caravan departs, leaving behind only a pile of ashes.

Lermontov preserves Pushkin's Eastern landscape (desert, oasis, and palm-trees), but for Pushkin's one palm, *kladez*, and *putnik* he substitutes three trees, *ruchei*, and *karavan*. He also borrows some of Pushkin's diction with slight modifications; for example, Pushkin rhymes *kholodnyi* with *bezvodnyi* (1: 4), which Lermontov repeats in 9: 4 with an ironic twist: instead of referring to the spring-water, *kholodnyi* modifies the ash left from the charred palms. Pushkin's first line, *I putnik ustalyi na Boga roptal*, supplies Lermontov with two lines: *No strannik ustalyi iz chuzhdoi zemli*

[21] See I. N. Rozanov, *Lermontov—master stikha* (M., 1942), 43–52, for a comparison of *Pole Borodina* with Zhukovsky's *Pevets vo stane russkikh voinov* (1812) and Pushkin's *Poltava*.

[22] Eikhenbaum, *Stat'i*, 344.

[23] See Tomashevsky, *Pushkin*, II. 23.

[24] See Gukovsky, 'Pushkin i poetika russkogo romantizma', *Izvestiya AN SSSR, Otd. literatury i yazyka*, No. 2 (1940), 90–1 for a comparison of Pushkin's *Podrazhanie* with Zhukovsky's *Pesn' araba nad mogiloyu konya* (1810).

(2: 2) and *I stali tri pal'my na Boga roptat'* (3: 1). Pushkin's transition, *I mnogie gody nad nim protekli*, becomes Lermontov's *I mnogie gody neslyshno proshli*.

In spite of the similarities in the Eastern colour and in some of the phraseology, Lermontov significantly altered the meaning of Pushkin's work. Pushkin's subject is the punishment of a tired traveller for his *ropot* against God. When he awakes from his long sleep, the traveller realizes that his youth has vanished; he is restored to his former condition only by means of a miracle, and he continues on his way with true faith in God. Lermontov places the palm-trees in the centre of the ballad: it is their *ropot* against God which results in the arrival of the caravan and in the final destruction of the trees. The palms are punished for their sin of pride (*Tri gordye pal'my*, 1: 2; *I, gordo kivaya makhrovoi glavoyu*, 7: 4) and man is depicted as both the ungrateful despoiler of natural beauty and the involuntary instrument of God's revenge.

Tri pal'my is rich in visual and aural imagery. The oasis setting is described as *zelenyi*, *goluboi*, and *zolotoi*; the caravan as *uzornyi*, *chernyi*, and *belyi*; the ash left behind is *sedoi*. The peaceful silence of the desert, broken only by the *zvuchnyi ruchei*, is shattered with the arrival of the caravan; after its departure, the silence which returns is the silence of death: without the shade of the palm-trees, the stream has dried up. There remains only the *sled pechal'nyi*—a totally subjective expression to convey the poet's own emotional reaction to the events. Having borrowed Pushkin's Eastern landscape and some of his vocabulary, Lermontov, with his reinterpretation of the theme and his introduction of rich imagery, transforms the narrative of *Tri pal'my* into an intensely personal statement about his own favourite themes of pride and inhumanity.

Lermontov's next ballad, *Dary Tereka* (1839), is said to have been influenced both by the spirit of popular Cossack songs and tales[25] and by the style of Hugo's Oriental ballads.[26] The River Terek in the Caucasus flows down to the turbulent Caspian Sea, bearing gifts to placate it. First the river offers the body of a Kabardian warrior, but the sea is not appeased; then the Terek

[25] See N. M. Mendel'son, 'Narodnye motivy v poezii Lermontova', in *Venok M. Yu. Lermontovu* (M.-P., 1914), 193–5.

[26] Eikhenbaum, *Stat'i*, 353–4.

offers the body of a young Cossack woman: the Caspian accepts it greedily, *s ropotom lyubvi.*

The river and the sea are both personified: the Terek is depicted as *lukavyi*, *laskayas'*, and *buinyi*; the Caspian is an indifferent *starik*, until the *kazachka* appears:

И старик во блеске власти
Встал, могучий, как гроза,
И оделись влагой страсти
Темно-синие глаза. (70–4)

The language of *Dary Tereka* combines folk elements—such as the river's ternary address to the sea, various repetitions, and popular expressions—with literary devices, such as the image of the warrior's armour with its inscription from the Koran, and the description of the *kazachka's* corpse:

С темно-бледными плечами,
С светло-русою косой.
Грустен лик ее туманный,
Взор так тихо, сладко спит
А на грудь из малой раны
Струйка алая бежит. (51–6)

The *kazachka*'s wound corresponds to the Cossack's bloodied moustache:

И усов его края
Обагрила знойной крови
Благородная струя. (34–6)

Both wounds are unexplained; the resulting enigma and the poet's non-interference in the ballad are in complete contrast to the more personal themes expressed in *Tri pal'my*.

During the year 1840, while under arrest for his duel with the son of the French ambassador, Lermontov once again experimented with balladic techniques in his narrative verse. *Vozdushnyi korabl'* is a historical poem based on J. C. F. von Zedlitz's ballad *Das Geisterschiff*.[27] In it Lermontov returns to the Napoleonic theme which first attracted him in his lyrics of 1829–30. *Vozdushnyi korabl'* emphasizes the themes of Napoleon's personal loneliness and of his deep love for France. *Sosedka* takes the

[27] In 1836 Zhukovsky translated another of Zedlitz's works on the Napoleonic theme, *Die nächtliche Heerschau*, as *Nochnoi smotr*.

form of an extended lyrical reflection by a prisoner who would waste away were it not for the fact that his *sosedka*, the gaoler's daughter, suffers the same spiritual confinement as he does.[28] In *Plennyi rytsar'* a knight compares his own glorious past with the squalor of his present imprisonment. The lyric *Lyubov' mertvetsa* (1841) is based on motifs borrowed from Bürger's *Lenore*.[29] It was not until 1841 that Lermontov returned to the literary ballad to make what was to be his most original contribution to the genre.

The first of these ballads, *Spor*, is in the form of a debate between two mountains in the Caucasus: the wise Shat and the impetuous Kazbek. Shat warns Kazbek that he too, like his predecessors, will be conquered and exploited by the peoples of the East. Kazbek replies that he does not fear the *dryakhlyi Vostok*. Suddenly the two mountains notice the advance of Russian regiments towards the East; Kazbek tries to count them, but fails and sinks into silence.

This ballad has been interpreted as an expression of Lermontov's sympathy for the Caucasian peoples and of his recognition that Russian annexation of the Caucasus would lead to economic and cultural betterment of the area.[30] In fact this ideological theme is as unimportant as the narrative element. *Spor* consists of three distinct groups of visual and aural images. The first, presented by Shat, describes man's destructive power and its effect on the Caucasus (*dymnye kelii, zheleznaya lopata, strashnyi put'*). The second, presented by Kazbek, is a colourful characterization of the slumbering peoples of the East (*pena sladkikh vin; uzornye shal'vary, tsvetnoi divan, zadumchivyi fontan, raskalennye stupeni*). The third group of images, provided by the narrator, describes the colours and sounds of the advancing army (*strannoe dvizhen'e*), followed by the emotional reaction of Kazbek (*tomim zloveshchei dumoi; polnyi chernykh snov; grustnyi vzor*).[31] As in *Tri pal'my*, Lermontov's theme in *Spor* is man's destruction of natural beauty; the poet's method is the creation of vivid imagery.

Lermontov's most original literary ballad, *Tamara* (1841), is

[28] Cf. Zhukovsky's *Uznik* (1819).

[29] This work was called *Novyi mertvets, Zhivoi mertvets*, and *Vlyublennyi mertvets* in manuscript versions; see *Sochineniya*, II. 294–5.

[30] See *Sochineniya*, II. 359–60.

[31] The manuscript version contains the following variants for the epithets in the description of Kazbek: *tomim tyazheloi/nadmennoi dumoi; polnyi gordykh snov;* and *mrachnyi vzor;* see *Sochineniya*, II. 298–300.

probably based on an old Georgian legend, although no immediate source has been identified.[32] It tells the story of the beautiful princess Tamara whose seductive voice attracts travellers to her castle; there they are treated to a night of amorous delights while strange sounds echo through the forest. In the morning the only sounds are those of the roaring Terek carrying away the bodies of the hopeless victims and the sweet farewells of Tamara.

The tale is related in pure romantic Russian, with few folkloric expressions. The manuscript version in particular shows Lermontov's attempts to overcome the continuing influence of Zhukovsky's style. The setting of *Tamara* is mysterious and foreboding; the tower is described as *starinnaya*, *vysokaya*, and *tesnaya* (in the manuscript, as *ugryumaya* and *zubchataya*);[33] it stands on a black cliff (*cherneya na chernoi skale*) overlooking a deep ravine. The visual details and the language of the landscape description closely resemble the settings in Zhukovsky's ballads.

The heroine of Lermontov's ballad, however, is unlike Zhukovsky's idealized Svetlanas and Minvanas (*Eolova arfa*). Tamara combines the principles of both good and evil:

Прекрасна, как ангел небесный,
Как демон, коварна и зла. (2: 3–4)

Her supernatural charms are described as *vsesil'nye* (in the manuscript as *moguchie* and *volshebnye*);[34] her power is *neponyatnaya*.[35] The nights of passionate love are accompanied by *strannye*, *dikie zvuki*, the explanation for which again emphasizes the heroine's dual nature:

Как будто в ту башню пустую
Сто юношей пылких и жен
Сошлися на свадьбу ночную
На тризну больших похорон. (8)

The *mrak i molchanie* of the morning after replaced the original *glukhoe smerti molchan'e*,[36] which is typical of Zhukovsky's style

[32] Eikhenbaum, *Stat'i*, 356. Eikenbaum refers to A. Veselovsky's articles in *Kavkaz*, No. 6–7, No. 66 (1898), in which he cites two French books about the Caucasus containing mention of a similar legend.

[33] *Sochineniya*, II. 303.

[34] Ibid.

[35] Cf. Lermontov's *Rusalka*, 7: 2, *neponyatnaya toska*.

[36] *Sochineniya*, II. 304.

in its explicitness and in its choice of epithet. Similarly the *bezglasnoe telo* was originally described as *ch'e-to bezglasnoe telo*,[37] the vague *ch'e-to* being another favourite Zhukovsky device. Lermontov eliminated the most imitative Zhukovsky-like elements from his final text, and the result is an original literary ballad, haunting and enigmatic. *Tamara* is, in a sense, Lermontov's own interpretation of the nature-magic theme treated by Zhukovsky in *Rybak* and by Pushkin in *Rusalka*: the attraction of the supernatural and the subordination of human will to higher powers.[38] But in Lermontov's version the implicit ambiguity is made explicit in the nature of the heroine (good and evil) and in the consequences for the victims (love and death).

Lermontov's last literary ballad, *Morskaya tsarevna* (1841), treats the same nature-magic theme as *Tamara*, and is, in fact, a reworking of his own *Rusalka* (1832). Whereas in the earlier ballad both the narrative element and the theme are relatively unimportant when compared with the imagery, *Morskaya tsarevna* has both an engaging narrative and a meaningful theme. A young tsarevich, while bathing his horse in the sea, is invited by a mermaid to spend one night with her. The impetuous youth seizes the poor mermaid and pulls her ashore despite her angry protests. When his comrades rally to inspect his catch, instead of a beautiful creature, they discover only a scaly sea-monster muttering incomprehensible reproaches.

Once again Lermontov's theme is the mysterious attraction of supernatural beauty; however, instead of submitting to its power, man attempts to capture that beauty and to bring it back into his own world in order to exert his will over it and to preserve it. This attempt to master the supernatural is doomed to failure; the tsarevich remains *zadumchivyi*, and is left with only an image of the beautiful mermaid in his memory.

The language of the ballad is simple and dynamic; verbs tend to replace epithets as the principal means of description:

Фыркает конь и ушами прядет,
Брызжет и плещет и дале плывет. (2)

Держит, рука боевая сильна:
Плачет и молит и бьется она. (8)

[37] Ibid.
[38] See above, Ch. III, pp. 47–9 and Ch. VII, pp. 148–51.

Tamara and *Morskaya tsarevna*, both written between May and July 1841, demonstrate Lermontov's success in overcoming what he perceived as the limitations of Zhukovsky's style.[39]

While Lermontov's most original ballads are similar to Pushkin's inasmuch as they avoid the tendency to 'show off' their 'ancient lore', to 'put wild . . . sentiments in stilted eighteenth-century dialogue', and to 'revel in the . . . pathetic',[40] they are not 'models' in the sense that Pushkin's ballads are, nor do they share the characteristics of the traditional folk genre. For Lermontov, the literary ballad was merely one available lyrical form, not *the* most fashionable genre in Russian poetry.[41] When Belinsky wrote in 1843 that 'the reading of marvellous ballads no longer provides any pleasure, but produces apathy and boredom',[42] his description of the demise of the genre was all too accurate.

[39] The results of a survey of 208 epithets from eighteen of Lermontov's ballads (940 lines) are as follows: of the total number, 140 epithets are used only once each; 40 are used twice each; 9 are used 3 times each; and 19 are used 4 or more times each: *belyi, blednyi, boevoi, bol'shoi, vysokii, dikii, zolotoi, krovavyi, milyi, mladoi, moguchii, mrachnyi, nochnoi, pechal'nyi, prekrasnyi, rodnoi, sinii, kholodnyi, chernyi*. Lermontov's epithets are closer in frequency, range, and meaning to Zhukovsky's epithets than to Pushkin's. Repetition of a limited number of epithets and formations with the prefixes *bez-* and *ne-* are characteristic of Lermontov's style.

[40] Bayley, *Pushkin*, 57.

[41] See also J. L. Wilkinson, 'The Literary Ballads in Russia from 1789–1841: Tradition and the Poetry of M. Ju. Lermontov', Ph.D. thesis in progress (University of Kansas).

[42] See above, Ch. V, p. 120.

CONCLUSION

Ideas can be, and are, cosmopolitan, but not style, which has a soil, a sky, and sun all its own.

—Chateaubriand[1]

WIDESPREAD enthusiasm for the ballad in late eighteenth-century European literature inspired Russian poets to experiment with the new genre during the 1790s. After the publication of *Lyudmila* in 1808 the literary ballad became the most influential and controversial genre in Russian literature for almost two decades, and Zhukovsky was considered its most talented practitioner. While the ideas in his forty literary ballads are 'cosmopolitan' in that they were frequently borrowed from English and German sources, the style of his ballads, particularly the frequency, range, and meaning of his epithets, is original. These epithets created the foundation for the vocabulary of Russian romantic poetry. The polemics in Russian criticism from 1815 to 1825 help to clarify the nature of Zhukovsky's stylistic innovations, while the ballads of his imitators provide valuable material for comparison. Pushkin and Lermontov also began their literary careers by writing imitations of Zhukovsky's ballads; both progressed through parody to original use of the genre.

By the beginning of the 1840s the literary ballad had lost its magic. The particular characteristics of the genre, its narrative unit, method, and attitude, and its intangible 'world', had disappeared. The ballad was relegated to a position of equality with other lyrical genres; the term became a synonym for a 'lyrical story in verse'.

In the late thirties and early forties Nekrasov made use of the genre in some of his early works (*Voron*, *Rytsar'*, *Vodyanoi*). During the 1850s the ballad once again became the object of parody, particularly in the comic verse of 'Koz'ma Prutkov'[2]

[1] Schenk, *The Mind of the European Romantics*, xxiii.

[2] A pseudonym for a 'collective' consisting of A. K. Tolstoy, Vladimir and Aleksandr Zhemchuzhnikov, and the Alekseev brothers. See B. H. Monter, *Koz'ma Prutkov* (The Hague, 1972).

(*Nemetskaya ballada*, *Putnik*) and I. P. Myatlev (*Artamonych*). In the sixties A. K. Tolstoy revived the genre in his stylized historical and folkloric narrative poems. Later, during the symbolist period, Vladimir Solov'ev parodied the form in *Osennyaya progulka rytsarya Ral'fa* (1886), while Valerii Bryusov chose the ballad to express his most personal lyrical themes (*Putnik; U morya; Ballada o lyubvi i smerti; Ballada vospominanii*).[3] Among Soviet poets, the genre has been successfully used by Nikolai Tikhonov, Sergei Esenin, and Aleksandr Tvardovsky, among others.[4]

A comprehensive account of the ballad revival in nineteenth-century European literature still remains to be written. In addition to English, German, French, and Russian ballads, this future literary history must consider related developments in other Slavonic literatures, including Polish,[5] Ukrainian,[6] and Czech.[7]

The Russian literary ballad is only one manifestation of that enthusiasm for the genre, which is 'one of the universal characteristics of the Romantic temperament, whatever its incarnation'.[8]

[3] See D. L. Burgin, 'The Literary Ballad in the Symbolist Period', unpublished Ph.D. thesis (Harvard University, 1973).

[4] See V. Lartsev, 'Ballada v sovremennoi poezii', *Zvezda vostoka* (Tashkent), 9 Sept. 1963, 123–33.

[5] For example, Mickiewicz's *Ballady i romanse* (1822); see W. Weintraub, *The Poetry of Adam Mickiewicz* (The Hague, 1954,) 31–45.

[6] For example, Shevchenko's literary ballads (1840s); see W. Smyrniw, 'The Treatment of the Ballad by Shevchenko and his Contemporaries in Relation to Western Balladry', *Canadian Slavonic Papers*, XII, No. 2 (1970), 142–74.

[7] For example, Erben's *Kytice* (1853); see M. Součková, *The Czech Romantics* (The Hague, 1958), 87–127.

[8] K. H. and W. U. Ober, 'Žhukovskij's Early Translations', 182.

APPENDIX A THE EPITHET IN FOLK AND LITERARY BALLADS

THE EPITHET IN RUSSIAN FOLK BALLADS[1]

	epithet	substantives
(1a)	белый	руки, груди, тело, снег
	зеленый	сад, луга, вино
	родной	матушка, сестрица
	сладкий	меды, водочки
	черный	кудри, брови, вороны
(1b)	высокий	терем
	грозный	тучи, сон
	добрый	конь, молодец
	злой	жена, мачеха, змея
	красный	девица, золото, солнце
	любимый	дочь, зять
	лютый	зелье, змея
	милый	друг
	младой/ молодой	княгиня, сестрица
	новый	горница, гробница
	острый	сабля
	темный	лес, ночь
	чистый	поле, серебро
	широкий	двор, ворота, улица
	ясный	очи, сокол
(2)	божий	церковь, масло, звон
	булатный	нож, меч
	дубовый	столы, гроб
	золотой	перстень, казна, цепочка, венец
	шелковый	пояс, платок, платье

1. Texts selected from *Narodnye ballady*, 45–174; see above, Ch. IV, p. 81.

THE EPITHET IN ENGLISH LITERARY BALLADS[1]

	epithet	uses	substantives
(1a)	black	5	horse, eyes, arms
	red	5	light, brow
	white	8	face, countenance, cheeks, waves
(1b)	bright	8	eyes, lady
	cold	9	hands, corpse, dew
	dark	9	night, water, eyes, brow
	deep	6	sounds, water, river
	fair	18	strand, stream, chamber, lady, sky
	gay	4	heart, lady
	holy	10	water, hymns, eve, sacrament
	little	10	boat, foot-page
	pale	10	face, cheek, brow, light, hue
	wild	4	alarm, winds, water
	young	7	Edmund, Eberhard
(2)	silver	3	chain, pound

English folk ballads: used 10 × or more per 1,000 lines[2]	English literary ballads: uses in sample of 1,000 lines
bonny	—
dear	—
fair	18
golden	—
good	—
green	—
handsome	—
old	1
red	5
silver	3
young	7

1. Sample of 1,000 lines from English literary ballads by Scott and Southey; see above, Ch. IV, p. 83.
2. Miles, *A Tabular View*, see chart 'Major Adjectives'.

THE EPITHET IN GERMAN LITERARY BALLADS[1]

	epithet	uses	substantives
(1a)	schwarz	3	Tat, Mantel, Mund
	tot	3	Kind, Fräulein
(1b)	alt	6	Sitte, Zeit, Held
	dunkel	3	Gefühle, Hain
	fromm	3	Schauder, Dichter
	furchtbar	4	Stimme, Macht
	gross	3	Leid, Trauer, Tat
	hoh	4	Balkon, Schloss
	kühn	5	Auge, Held
	schwer	3	Traum, Tat
	schön	3	Spiele, Gestalt
	still	6	Weiner, Hoffnung, Antlitz
	süss	4	Mund, Lieder, Freundin
	teuer	5	Lohn, Bild
	tief	6	Gruft, Traum, Himmel
	wild	4	Wald, Gewalt
(2)	golden	3	Stern, Becher
	irdisch	3	Leid, Gut

German folk ballads: used 4 × or more in 350-line sample[2]	German literary ballads: uses in sample of 1,000 lines
breit	1
edel	2
gross	3
grün	2
hoh	4
rot	–
schön	3
weiss	1
zart	2

1. Sample of 1,000 lines from German literary ballads by Bürger, Goethe, Schiller, and Uhland; see above, Ch. IV, p. 83.
2. Texts selected from *The Penguin Book of German Verse*, ed. L. Forster (Harmondsworth, 1959), 44–64.

APPENDIX B. THE EPITHET IN ZHUKOVSKY'S LITERARY BALLADS

KEY TO CHARTS[1]

(1b)

Definition: *Slovar' Akademii Rossiskoi* (SPb., 1789–94). Asterisks denote figurative meanings as indicated in the dictionary. Parentheses contain examples cited in the definition.

I, II, III: Examples are selected from the Academy of Sciences' Dictionary of Eighteenth-Century Russian (in preparation), supplemented with examples from an original survey. Examples are arranged by thirds of the eighteenth century (I, II, III). The following is a list of abbreviations used to designate the source of each example:[2]

I.	Гист.	*Гистория о российском матросе Василии Кориотском*
	Кант.	Кантемир
	Тред.	Тредиаковский
II.	Елаг.	Елагин
	Княж.	Княжнин
	Лом.	Ломоносов
	Лук.	Лукин
	Май.	Майков
	Пет.	Петров
	Поп.	Попов
	Сум.	Сумароков
	Тред.	Тредиаковский
	Фон.	Фонвизин
	Чулк.	Чулков
III.	Бог.	Богданович
	Дер.	Державин
	Дмит.	Дмитриев
	Кап.	Капнист
	Кар.	Карамзин
	Кост.	Костров
	МЖ.	*Московский журнал*
	ММерк.	*Московский Меркурий*
	Мур.	Муравьев
	Нел.	Нелединский-Мелецкий
	Пант.	*Пантеон иностранной словесности*
	Рад.	Радищев
	СПбМерк.	*Санкт-Петербургский Меркурий*
	Хем.	Хемницер

1. See above, Ch. IV, p. 93, for a discussion of Zhukovsky's epithets; and see below, p. 220, for Charts (1a) and (2).
2. Examples listed without any specific source were in general usage in eighteenth-century Russian.

Folk — Examples are selected from *Narodnye ballady*, 45–174.

W. Eur. — Examples are selected from English literary ballads by Scott and Southey, and from German literary ballads by Bürger, Goethe, Schiller, and Uhland—all of which were 'translated' by Zhukovsky.

Lit. — Examples are selected from Russian literary ballads of the 1790s and early 1800s. Each substantive is followed by a 'code' which identifies ballad/stanza (if in verse)/line. The following is a list of abbreviations used to designate ballad titles:

ЭМ	*Эдвин и Малли*
АР	*Алвин и Рена*
ЛБ	*Леонард и Блондина*
ВМ	*Вилльям и Маргарита*
М	*Милон*
ЛС	*Лаура и Сельмар*
Б	*Быль*
К	*Карикатура*
СЛ	*Старинная любовь*
ГГ	*Граф Гваринос*
Р	*Раиса*
А	*Алина*[1]

Zhukovsky: Full examples from the forty literary ballads are recorded and are arranged chronologically within each subdivision of the definition. Literal meanings are listed first; figurative meanings follow. Numbers (1), (2), (3), etc., refer to more or less distinct meanings; letters (a), (b), (c), etc., refer to groups of substantives to which each given meaning is applied. There is no correspondence intended between the subdivisions of one chart and those of another. Each substantive is followed by a 'code' which identifies ballad/stanza/line. If an epithet has been translated from, or has any equivalent in, the foreign source, then the original word is included in parentheses after the 'code'. An oblique stroke indicates that, although the ballad itself has a specific source, the given epithet was supplied by Zhukovsky where none was present in the original. No mark indicates that the ballad has no specific source. The following is a list of abbreviations used to designate ballad titles:

Л	*Людмила*
Ка	*Кассандра*
Св	*Светлана*
П	*Пустынник*
Ад	*Адельстан*
ИЖ	*Ивиковы журавли*
Ва	*Варвик*
АА	*Алина и Альсим*
ЭЭ	*Эльвина и Эдвин*
Ах	*Ахилл*
Э	*Эолова арфа*
М	*Мщение*

1. The code for *Alina* consists of the page number (84–9) in N. M. Karamzin, *Polnoe sobranie stikhotvorenii* (M.-L., 1966) and the line.

Га	*Гаральд*
ТП	*Три песни*
Г	*Громобой*
В	*Вадим*
Ры	*Рыбак*
РТ	*Рыцарь Тогенбург*
ЛЦ	*Лесной царь*
ГГ	*Граф гапсбургский*
У	*Узник*
З	*Замок Смальгольм*
Т	*Торжество победителей*
К	*Кубок*
ПП	*Поликратов перстень*
ЖЦ	*Жалоба Цереры*
Д	*Доника*
С	*Суд божий над эпископем*
А	*Алонзо*
L	*Ленора*
По	*Покаяние*
КУ	*Королева Урака и пять мучеников*
РО	*Роланд оруженосец*
ПКВ	*Плавание Карла великого*
РР	*Рыцарь Роллон*
СР	*Старый рыцарь*
Бр	*Братоубийца*
Ул	*Уллин и его дочь*
ЭП	*Элевзинский праздник*
НС	*Ночной смотр*[1]

Comments. The examples from Zhukovsky's ballads are followed by brief comments concerning: *Frequency*—the total number of times each epithet is used, and the number of ballads in which it occurs; *Source*—the number of times an epithet was translated from a foreign source and what English, German, or French epithets the Russian replaced; and *Usage*—comments on Zhukovsky's individual use of each epithet, including comparison with eighteenth-century Russian usage if relevant.

1. Although not strictly a literary ballad, *Nochnoi smotr* has been included in the survey because its epithets provide examples similar to those in the literary ballads.

БЛЕДНЫЙ

Definition

(1) Относительно к лицу, значит что цвет оного без всякой румяности, живости;
(2) Когда речь о цветах, значит блеклый, поблеклый, белесоватый;
(3) Говорится также бледное солнце, бледная луна: в сем смысле значит тусклый, слабое сияние производящий, неиздающий полного света.

I	II	III
он (Кант.)	луна (Пет.)	смерть (Дер.)
она (Тред.)	свет (Лом.)	вид (Бог.)
	лицо (Тред.)	тени (Кар.)
	труп (Лом.)	молнии (Кар.)
	цвет (Елаг.)	ужас (Кар.)
	зависть (Тред.)	осень (Кар.)

Folk	W. Eur.	Lit.
/	pale: face, cheek, hue, splendour bleich: Fenster	Рена АР 19:2 щеки ЭМ:20 привидения ЭМ:176 тень ЛБ 3:3 Лаура ЛС 1:3 она Р 4:1

Zhukovsky

(1) Of persons, their complexion etc., pale, pallid, wan; in context reflects:

(a) emaciation

гости	С 6:2 /
пост	Бр 5:3 /

(b) death

толпа	Ка 14:1 (bleich)
он	Св 8:14
друг	Св 9:14
лик	ЭЭ 19:4 /
она	ЭЭ 25:2 /
лик	Ах 21:7
некто	В 56:7
он	РТ 10:7 (bleich)
труп	Д 27:2 (livid)
он	Бр 11:4 (bleich)

(c) fear

он	ИЖ 23:1 (schreckenbleich)
лик	Б 22:1 /
Громобой	Г 43:2
жена	З 33:1 /
убийца	По 15:3 /
посланный	РР 5:1 (bleich)

(d) general emotional distress

лик	Ва 10:4 /
лик	Ва 19:3 (pale)
лик	Ва 35:4 (pale)
он	АА 14:3 /
барон	З 4:2 (sad and sour)
он	По 10:4; 13:4 /
Тюрпин	РО 23:2 /

(2) Dim, reflecting, or producing weak light;

свет	Св 8:14
месяц	Ад 28:3 /
цвет	АА 14:7 (pâleur)
пламень	Г 71:4
день	Г 72:7
луч	В 6:8
пламень	В 55:4
дым	В 57:6

Compound:
бледноликая Изолина А 9:1 /

Comments

Frequency: Used 34 times; occurs in 20 ballads.
Source: Translated from foreign source 9 times; once replaces *sad and sour*.
Usage: Zhukovsky develops late 18th-c. usage of the epithet and expands its applicability. Depending on its context, *blednyi* can reflect emaciation (including the transferred usage *blednyi post*), death, fear, or general emotional distress.

ВЕРНЫЙ

Definition

(1) Надежный, неложный, истинный;
(2) Относительно к вере: исповедующий Християнскую веру.

I	II	III
слуга (Кант.) друг (Гист.)	сердце (Лом.) жена (Фон.) друг (Сум.) раб слуга служба человек	дружба (Кар.) чувство (МЖ.) знак признак источник

Folk	W. Eur.	Lit.
нянька слуга	faithful: Eberhard treu: Schwesterliebe	сын Б 8: 1 кров Р 2: 2 Раиса Р 16: 2 он А 89: 4

Zhukovsky

(1) faithful, loyal, true, reliable; referring to:
- (a) friends

друг	Ах 8: 1
друг	Э 21: 4
товарищ	РР 13: 3

- (b) spouse

жена	АА 26: 3

- (c) servants, companions, etc.

провожатый	ИЖ 3: 2 (befreundet)
пес	В 1: 10
слуга	РР 11: 3 (treuest)

- (d) abstractions

обеты	Св 18: 11
струны	Э 20: 3
сон	В 64: 3
обет	Д 24: 2 (sacred)

Comment

Frequency: Used 11 times; occurs in 8 ballads.

Source: Translated from foreign source once; also replaces *befreundet* and *sacred*. The folk epithet *vernyi sluga* is common in 18th-c. poetry.

Usage: *Vernyi* is related to the poet's theme of ideal friendship; it is also one of a series of equivalent epithets applied to *struny* as a metaphor for poetry (cf. *milyi*, *sladkii*).

ВЕСЕЛЫЙ

Definition

(1) Радостный, у кого сердце приятными чувствованиями наполнено;
(2) Вливающий приятные чувствования в других, забавный чувствам.

I	II	III
лицо (Кант.) нрав (Кант.) дух (Тред.) место (Тред.)	природа (Елаг.) жизнь (Лук.) глас (Лом.) вид (Чулк.) нрав пир	взоры (Рад.) улыбка (Кар.) дни (СПб Мерк.) мечты (Дер.) песни (Кар.)

Folk	W. Eur.	Lit.
пир	gay: heart froh: Braut Ziel	вид АР 6:2 девица ЭМ:67 гости ЭМ:177 пир ЭМ:196

Zhukovsky

(1) experiencing joy, joyous; referring to:
- (a) people or mythological figures
  - Людмила — Л 10:3 /
  - девы — Ка 2:4 /
  - посетитель — Ва 12:3 /
  - пахарь — Г 15:7
  - Вадим — В 46:2
  - толпа — Ку 16:4
  - Ком — ЭП 16:2 /
  - Камены — ЭП 22:5 /
- (b) places
  - вместе — Э 15:2
  - ад — Г 7:7
- (c) events
  - пир — ИЖ 1:1 (froh)
  - пир — Г 28:4

(2) expressing joy:
- очи — ЭЭ 5:3 (mild)
- песня — ТП 1:1 (schönste)
- взор — Т 7:1 /
- разговор — РО 1:6 /

(3) evoking joy:
- блеск — Б 25:1 /
- утро — Э 16:2
- природа — Э 16:2
- луч — В 4:4
- бег — В 69:8

Comments

Frequency: Used 21 times; occurs in 13 ballads.

Source: Translated from foreign source once; also replaces *mild*, *schönste*. The folk epithet *veselyi pir* occurs in 18th-c. poetry and in pre-Zhukovsky literary ballads.

Usage: Zhukovsky expands the applicability of the epithet particularly in descriptions of locations such as *vmeste* (*minutnaya sladost' / Veselovogo vmeste*) and *ad*; he also uses *veselyi* to express his own subjective reaction to phenomena (*blesk*, *beg*, *priroda*). The epithet implies the poet's emotional sympathy.

ВЫСОКИЙ

Definition

(1) Возвышенный, в верх поднявшийся, или поднятый, внесенный;
(2) Выспренный, далеко в верх отстоящий;
(6) В смысле* и нравственном означает: важный, превосходный, могущественный, крепкий, гордый, величавый. . . .

I	II	III
/	дух (Лом.) мысли (Лом. Трут.) чело (Лом.) гора (Лом.)	таинства (МЖ.) добродетель (МЖ.) творец (Кар.) песнь (Дер.) ум (Дер.)

Folk	W. Eur.	Lit.
терем крылец	high: walls tower Mass hoh: Schloss Bergesrücken Luft	теремы СЛ 1:2 цель ГГ 17:2 холм Р 19:1

Zhukovsky

(1) high; of considerable upward extent or magnitude:

стан	В 4:5	
брег	В 25:8	
окно	У 2:1	
скала	К 2:1	(von der Höh)
замок	Д 1:3	(high)
окно	А 4:1	/

(2) elevated, lofty:

душа	П 29:3	/
венец	Э 14:2	
даль	Д 14:3	/

Comments

Frequency: Used 9 times; occurs in 7 ballads.
Source: Translated from foreign source twice.
Usage: Zhukovsky develops the figurative meanings which the epithet acquired in the 18 c. and expands its applicability to include other abstract concepts; thus *vysokaya dusha* replaces the classical *dukh* and *mysli*; *vysokaya dal'* indicates an indefinite, spiritual location.

ГЛУБОКИЙ

Definition

(1) Имеющий дно далеко в низ от поверхности лежащее;
(2) *Трудный к познанию, к постижению умом;
(3) *Чрезмерный, великий, крайный (молчанье, печаль, знание);
(4) Проницательный, остроумный (мысль).
—ночь—поздные часы ночи
—сон—крепкий сон

I	II	III
мысли (Тред.) труд (Кант.) темнота (Кант.)	вечность (Лом.) мрак (Лом.) молчание (Елаг.) тоска (Елаг.) задумчивость (Лук.) тишина (Лом.)	чувствительность (Кар.) меланхолия (МЖ.) размышление (МЖ.) уныние (М. Мерк.)

Folk	W. Eur.	Lit.
погреб ямы снежочки	deep: water sounds tief: Gruft Himmel Traum	вздох АР 7:3 сон ВМ:3

Zhukovsky

(1) deep; having great extension downward; extending far inward:

снег	Св 9:2
река	М:4 (tief)
пучина	К 11:5 /
свод	По 32:3 /
голос	Д 14:1 /
рев	ЭП 18:6 /

(2) intense, profound:

(a) referring to sleep etc.

сон	Св 13:5
сон	Г 17:11
сон	З 38:3 (heavy)
сон	РО 6:8 /
сон	РО 17:2 /
тишина	ИЖ 12:7 /
ночь	Г 28:10

(b) concerning the emotions:

нежность	Д 22:2 (deep)
размышление	По 40:2 /
унижение	ЭП 4:7 /

Comments

Frequency: Used 16 times; occurs in 10 ballads.
Source: Translated from foreign source 3 times.
Usage: Zhukovsky develops the figurative meaning of the epithet which originated in the 18th c., and extends its applicability to include emotional substantives, following late 18th-c. developments.

ГРОЗНЫЙ

Definition

(1) Строгий, свирепый, суровый;
(2) Наполненый угроз;
(3) Иногда значит: страшный, ужасный, наводящий страх (туча, буря).

I	II	III
голос (Кант.)	взор (Лом.) звук (Лом.) судьбина (Лом.) слова (Елаг.) тучи облака	голос (Кар.) ночь (МЖ.)

Folk	W. Eur.	Lit.
сон тучи король	/	волны ЛС 4:3 голос ГГ 10:2 луч Р 1:2

Zhukovsky

(1) dreadful, awful; inspiring fear, horror; referring to:

(a) sight

очи	Св 15:8	
сон	Св 16:9	
когти	Ад 45:2	/
призрак	Ва 17:1	/
луч	Ах 21:4	
лица	ТП 4:2	/
сонм	Г 25:1	
тучи	Г 29:6	

(b) sound

глас	Ах 7:6	
вой	Г 28:9	
речь	В 23:1	

(c) people

рать	Л 1:12	/
старец	Г 59:7	
Зверолов	ЭП 2:6	/

(d) time

времена	ГГ 2:6 (schrecklich)

(e) place

море	К 3:3 (wild)

(2) stern, cruel, severe:

закон	Г 33:11
сын (небес)	Г 55:1

Comments

Frequency: Used 18 times; occurs in 10 ballads.

Source: Translated from foreign source twice: *schrecklich, wild* (Ger.) > *groznyi*.

Usage: Zhukovsky expands the applicability of the epithet, applying it to a wide range of phenomena. *Groznyi* is used as a synonym for the more frequent epithets *strashnyi*, *uzhasnyi* (e.g. 'Akh! uzhasnyi, groznyi son!' CB 16:9).

ГУСТОЙ

<table>
<tr><td colspan="3">

Definition

(1) Говоря о прозябаемых: частый, непроходимый, изобильный (лес, роща);
(2) Говоря о деревах: ветвистый, многолиственный;
(3) В отношении к волосам: волосистый, много волосов имеющий;
(6) В отношении к воздуху и к облакам: мрачный, непроницаемый, от скопившихся паров.

</td><td rowspan="2">

Zhukovsky

(1) thick, dense; filled with objects or individuals:
лес Га 1:4 (wild)
лес Га 8:4 (weit)
лес Га 12:2 /
лес В 25:7
лес РО 18:1 /
толпа Т 2:1 /

(2) thick, bushy (of hair):
борода АА 14:3 (longue)
борода ЛЦ 2:3 /
кудри Э 5:5
кудри В 36:5

(3) dense, impenetrable:
тьма П 2:1 /
мгла ИЖ 19:4 /
дым Б 34:2 /
пыль В 43:6

</td></tr>
<tr><td>

I

мгла (Тред.)
воздух (Тред.)

</td><td>

II

тень (Лом.)
мрак (Тред.)
лес (Тред. Сум.)
ночь (Сум.)

</td><td>

III

печаль (Рад.)
туман (Рад.)
власы (Рад.)

</td></tr>
<tr><td>

Folk
/

</td><td>

W. Eur.
/

</td><td>

Lit.
/

</td><td>

Comments

Frequency: Used 14 times; occurs in 10 ballads.
Source: Never translated from foreign source; replaces *wild* (Ger.), *weit*, *longue*.
Usage: Zhukovsky uses *gustoi* as a synonym for *mrachnyi* in the description of ballad settings; however, the epithet did not acquire the emotional overtones which were characteristic of *mrachnyi*.

</td></tr>
</table>

ДИКИЙ

Definition

(1) Тоже что дивий;
(2) Иногда значит: неручный, не привыкший к человеческому общежитию;
(3) Необходительныий, грубый, не знающий обращения;
(4) Говоря о месте: ненаселенный, необитаемый, пустый;
(5) Странный, чудный, необычайный (голос).

I	II	III
мысли (Тред.)	печаль (Тред.) голос (Чулк.) нрав (Тред.) места камень звери народ	природа (МЖ.) взор (МЖ.) радость (МЖ.) уныние (Дер.) берега (Кар.)

Folk	W. Eur.	Lit.
степь	wild (Eng.): look Margaret waters wild (Ger.): Meer Wald Gewalt	брег ЛБ 17:4

Zhukovsky

(1) wild, in a state of nature:
- бор — В 51:7
- поляна — По 24:3 /
- вепрь — КУ 25:1 (wild)
- берег — Бр 1:2 /

(2) unusual, abnormal, terrible; referring to:
- (a) sight
  - взор — Г 43:6
  - свет — ЭП 3:4 /
- (b) sound
  - рев — ИЖ 8:5 /
  - хор — ИЖ 15:2 /
  - глас — В 21:5
  - песня — Т 2:5 /
- (c) people or mythological figures
  - сторож — Г 79:1
  - Троглодит — ЭП 2:1 /
- (d) emotions
  - исступление — С 19:2 /

(3) strange, uncivilized, savage:
- он — Г 26:11
- он — По 34:1 /

Comments

Frequency: Used 15 times; occurs in 9 ballads.
Source: Translated from foreign source once.
Usage: Zhukovsky expands the figurative meaning acquired during the 18th c.; he applies the epithet to a wide range of natural and supernatural phenomena. *Dikii* also acquires overtones of mystery and uncanniness.

ЗАДУМЧИВЫЙ

<table>
<tr><td colspan="3">Definition
(1) Тот, который задумывается; подверженный задумчивости;
(2) Печальный, в печали находящийся.</td><td rowspan="2">Zhukovsky
(1) pensive; plunged in meditation or reflection:
он — ЭЭ 14: 1 /
она — Г 75: 10
рыбак — Ры 1: 2 (ruhevoll)
он — У 20: 3 /
он — По 23: 3 /
Оливер — РО 25: 2 /

(2) expressing pensiveness:
пламень (во взорах) — Э 6: 2
очи — Э 23: 2

(3) evoking pensiveness:
звон — Э 29: 2
лира — Г: Введ. 3: 8</td></tr>
<tr><td>I

он
(Кант.)</td><td>II

щеголь
(Чулк.)
упражнение
(Елаг.)
тиран
(Сум.)
я
вы
он</td><td>III

супруг
(Бог.)
девы
(Дер.)
луна
(Дмит.)
краса
(Дер.)</td></tr>
<tr><td>Folk

/</td><td>W. Eur.

pensive:
guest</td><td>Lit.

Милон
А 85: 7</td><td>Comments
Frequency: Used 10 times; occurs in 6 ballads.
Source: Translated from foreign source once: *ruhevoll* > *zadumchivyi*.
Usage: Zhukovsky develops late 18th-c. usage in which *zadumchivyi* is used not only to describe the emotional state of objective characters but also to express the poet's subjective reaction to phenomena (*zvon*, *lira*).</td></tr>
</table>

ЛЕГКИЙ

Definition

(1) Собственно: нетяжелый, невеский;
(2) *Удобоисполяемый, или удобосносимый;
(3) *Поворотливый, расторопный;
(4) *Малый, маловажный (ссора); . . .
(7) Небольшой, слабый, неопасный (ветер);
—сон—некрепкий
—голос—ясный
—слог—плавный

I	II	III
работа (Кант.)	ветер (Сум.) прах (Лом. Пет.) крилы (Лом.) зефир (Тред.)	полет (МЖ.) крыло (МЖ.) облака (Дер.) мгла (Рад.) сон (Мур.)

Folk	W. Eur.	Lit.
/	leicht: Stab Schar luftig: Gesindel	/

Zhukovsky

(1) light, of little weight:

рука	Св 4: 11
цепь	Ад 29: 4 (silver)
цепь	Ад 31: 2 (silver)
клюка	ИЖ 1: 7 (leicht)
челн	В 47: 11
лодка	С 15: 1 /

(2) airy, ethereal:

хоровод	Л 16: 6 (luftig)
крилы	Св 15: 2
тень	Ах 18: 7
тень	Э 21: 3
хоровод	Га 5: 1 (leicht)
дыханье	Д 17: 3 /
рой	L 26: 1 /
тень	По 39: 4 /
Оры	ЭП 20: 6 /

(3) swift:

конь	В 23: 6
скок	L 13: 1 /
кони	НС 2: 11 (luftig)

(4) insignificant, small, weak:

ветерок	Л 16: 11 /
шепот	Св 6: 11
журчанье	Св 13: 8
плесканье	Э 11: 8
ветерок	Г 41: 9
сон	В 3: 3
шорох	В 53: 7
пламень	В 55: 4
пламень	ЖЦ 4: 3 /

Compound:
легкокрылый ветерок Ад 5: 2 (gentle)

Comments

Frequency: Used 27 times; occurs in 16 ballads.
Source: Translated from foreign source 4 times; twice replaces *silver*.
Usage: Zhukovsky, strongly influenced by German sources, develops the meaning *legkii* = airy, ethereal; the epithet acquires overtones of mystery and uncanniness, and is usually applied to supernatural phenomena.

МИЛЫЙ

Definition

(1) Приятный, любезный, пленительный, привлекательный; (взор, дитя).

I	II	III
дружки (Тред.)	зрак (Сум.)	улыбка (Нел., Кар.)
	вид (Пет.)	друг (Мур.)
	невинность (Княж.)	мечта (Нел.)
	утехи (Май.)	тайна (МЖ.)
	она	душа (Кар.)
	он	тени (Кар.)
	я	скорбь (Кар.)
	вы	
	ты	

Folk	W. Eur.	Lit.
сестрица	dear: children	тень ЛБ 17:3
чадо	kind: he, she	супруг M 23:4
	lieb: Sonne, Kind	Кронид Р 9:1
	traut: Reiter, Kind	чувствительность A 84:4
		подруга A 85:8
		тень A 86:30
		слезы A 87:17

Zhukovsky

(1) kind, sympathetic, pleasant, attractive:

вид	Л 20:4	/
взор	Ка 13:3 (schön)	
разговоры	Св 18:8	
живость	АА 14:5	/
взгляд	Г 30:3	
встреча	Г 33:2	
смятенье	В 36:10	
мечта	В 39:1	

(2) dear, favourite, close to the heart:

друг	Л 4:4	/
Светлана	Св 2:4	
друг	Св 3:2	
друг	Св 15:13	
тень	П 35:3	/
жизнь	П 39:3	/
струны	Э 32:1	
цветок	Э 32:7	
творенья	Г 31:6	
рыцарь	РТ 1:2	/
край	РТ 4:7 (teuer)	
родина	Т 4:12	/

Comments

Frequency: Used 20 times; occurs in 10 ballads.

Source: Translated from foreign models once; also replaces *schön*.

Usage: Zhukovsky develops late 18th-c. usage of the epithet, especially that of Karamzin. As *kind*, *milyi* is applied to abstract substantives (*zhivost'*, *smyaten'e*); as *dear* it is used to describe persons (even *ten'*), natural phenomena, homeland, etc. *Milyi* conveys the poet's warmest emotional approval; it comes to replace its 18th-c. synonyms *prekrasnyi* and *priyatnyi*.

МРАЧНЫЙ

Definition

(1) Темный, лишенный света (солнце, день, места);
(2) *Невеселый, печальный, угрюмый (взор, лица).

I	II	III
печаль (Кант.)	мысли (Сум.) глаза (Елаг.) глубина (Лом.) древность (Лом.)	осень (Кар.) тишина (Дер.) тень (Кар., Рад.) природа (Мур.) ад (Княж.) задумчивость (МЖ.) уединение (МЖ.)

Folk	W. Eur.	Lit.
/	dreary: place days and nights	час ВМ: 29 грот М 8: 4 лес А 86: 29

Zhukovsky

(1) dark, poorly illuminated:

дол и лес	Л 7: 12	/
Эльдон	З 30: 2	/
пустыня	По 26: 4	

(2) gloomy, sombre:

конь	Ах 16: 6	
пришлец	З 27: 2	/
монах	З 48: 3	/
монах	З 49: 1	/
лица	Бр 5: 3	/
лоб	Бр 6: 4	/

(3) evil, mysterious:

ад	Ка 14: 3	/
Он	Б 41: 2	/
бес	Д 27: 3	/

Comments

Frequency: Used 12 times; occurs in 8 ballads.

Source: Never translated from foreign source.

Usage: Zhukovsky follows the figurative usage of the epithet which developed in the 18th c. Even as *dark*, *mrachnyi* implies *gloomy*. The figurative meaning is expanded to include *kon'*, and it acquires overtones of mystery when referring to the devil (cf. *chernyi*).

НЕЖНЫЙ

Definition

(1) Мягкий, не имеющий грубости;
(2) Слабый (дитя);
(3) Разборчивый, отменно чувствительный;
(5) *Чувствительный к дружбе, к состраданию, к любви, и проч. (друг, сердце); . . .
(6) *Трогательный, привлекательный (голос, взгляд).

I	II	III
постель (Кант.)	взгляд (Сум.) любовь (Сум., Лом., Елаг.) весна (Лом.) душа (Сум.) взоры (Трут.)	чувства (Кар.) томность (Кар.) горесть (МЖ.) дух (Нел.) мечты (Мур.)

Folk	W. Eur.	Lit.
руки тело	zart: Saite Erbarmer	сердце АР 11:1 девица ЭМ: 118 красы ЛБ 11:1 желанье ЛС 2:1 вздох Р 12:2 пламень А 85:24

Zhukovsky

(1) tender, loving, affectionate:

Лора	Ад 15:1	/
матери	Г 14:1	
любовь	Д 22:1	/
друг	L 3:5	/

(2) pleasant, delightful:

взор	Ах 19:5	
звуки	Г 30:6	
глас	В 21:3	
клик	ЖЦ 7:10	/

(3) gentle, soft:

рука	Л 14:3 (Lilienhände)	
рука	Га 4:2	/

(4) weak, delicate:

чада	ЖЦ 8:2 (Frühlings Kinder)	
пол	П 21:2	/

Comments

Frequency: Used 12 times; occurs in 10 ballads.

Source: Never translated from foreign source; twice the epithet replaces substantives of related meaning.

Usage: Zhukovsky follows the usage which developed in early literary ballads, especially those by Karamzin. He uses *nezhnyi* to describe persons, countenance, and sounds, and, less frequently, abstract substantives (*lyubov'*).

ОДИНОКИЙ

Definition

(1) Таковый же, схожий, похожий;
(2) Холостый или безсемейный.

I	II	III
/	/	/
Folk	W. Eur.	Lit.
дочь	lone: hour lonely: night lonesome: hill solitary: way	/

Zhukovsky

(1) solitary, lonely, alone; referring to:
  (a) persons
    девица Св 11: 5
    рыцарь Ад 14: 4 /
    Вадим В 46: 4

  (b) places, things, etc.
    грусть Св 3: 4
    храм Св 9: 4
    путь В 60: 9
    огонь З 13: 3 (lonely)
    путь З 18: 3 (alone)
    путь РР 4: 2 /

Compound:
    одиноко-уньылая жена З 32: 4 (fair)

Comments

Frequency: Used 10 times; occurs in 6 ballads.
Source: Translated from foreign source twice; also replaces *fair*.
Usage: Since there are no examples recorded in Dictionary of 18th-Century Russian or in pre-Zhukovsky ballads, the use of *odinokii* as a descriptive epithet seems to have originated with Zhukovsky.

ПЕЧАЛЬНЫЙ

Definition

(1) В печали находящийся;
(2) Причиняющий печаль.

I	II	III
песни (Тред.) жизнь (Тред.) сердце (Тред.) лицо (Кант.) разговор (Кант.)	слова (Скм.) уста (Елаг.) вопль (Елаг.) мысль (Сум.)	уединение (МЖ.) уныние (МЖ.) душа (МЖ.) луна (Кап.) лира (Дер.)

Folk	W. Eur.	Lit.
речь	sad: looks traurig: Öde	луч АР 12:3 Блондина ЛБ 10:1

Zhukovsky

(1) sad, experiencing sorrow:

она	ЭЭ 12:4 /
матерь	В 10:5
я	ЖЦ 4:1 /
Милон	РО 27:2 (traurig)

(2) expressing sorrow:

глас	Ах 4:2
лицо	А 5:2 /
вой	L 21:8 /
око	ЭП 4:5 /

(3) evoking sorrow:

денница	Ах 5:1
сумрак	Б 22:2 /
жребий	Г 2:3
вестия	КУ 41:2 /

Compound:
торжественно-печальный гимн КУ 37:2

Comments

Frequency: Used 12 times; occurs in 11 ballads.
Source: Translated from foreign source once.
Usage: Zhukovsky expands the meaning of *pechal'nyi* to include not only the emotional state of objective characters as experienced by them or as expressed in their countenance, but also to express the poet's own subjective reaction to phenomena (*dennitsa, sumrak*).

СВЕТЛЫЙ

Definition

(1) Сияющий, блистающий, изпускающий свет;
(2) Чистый, ясный;
(3) *Говоря о цвете: походящий к яркому, белому;
—голос—яркий, звонкий, приятный.

I	II	III
день (Кант.)	взор (Лом.)	воздух (Кар.)
вода (Кант.)	дом (Лом.)	блеск (Дер.)
ум (Кант.)	месяц (Княж.)	вечер (Дер.)
	ночь (Чулк.)	голос (Дер.)
		спокойствие (Пант.)
		лицо (Нел.)

Folk	W. Eur.	Lit.
светлица	bright: bloom, eyes, silver	воды A 84:8
	bunt: Blume	

Zhukovsky

(1) bright, shining; emitting, reflecting, or pervaded by, much light:

взор	Л 1:6
сумрак	Л 8:9
хоровод	Л 16:6 (halb sichtbarlich)
глаза	Св 13:11
огонек	П 12:3 (little)
рог	Ах 2:2
краса	Г 16:7
дом	Г 28:1
день	Г 48:1; 65:4
юг	В 7:1
венец	В 44:11
крест	В 68:11
день	ЖЦ 7:8

(2) pure, clear:

воды	Ах 14:1
бездна	Бр 3:6

(3) happy, joyful, glad:

жизнь	Св 20:12
сонм	ЭП 15:2

(4) holy, sacred:

рай	Г 36:2
час	В 72:1
Иванов день	З 16:2 (holy)
праздник	Бр 3:2

Compound:
светлоглавый Аполлон ЭП 15:2

Comments

Frequency: Used 22 times; occurs in 10 ballads.
Source: Never translated from foreign sources; replaces *little*, *holy*, *halb sichtbarlich.*
Usage: The literal meaning of *svetlyi* = bright, shining acquires overtones of mystery (*sumrak*, *khorovod*). Zhukovsky also develops the figurative meanings of the epithet (*zhizn'*, *rai*, *chas*, etc.).

СВЯТОЙ

Definition

(1) Всесовершенно чистый, праведный;
(2) Живущий по правилам верою предписанным;
(3) Богу посвященный.

I	II	III
муж (Кант.)	правда (Лом.) добродетель (Сум.) слово (Сум.) страх (Тред.)	язык (Кар.) поэзия (Кар.) восторг (Кар.) чувство (Пант.)

Folk	W. Eur.	Lit.
тела монах мощи	holy: water hymns men heilig: Macht Pflicht	Мать ГТ 19:3

Zhukovsky

(1) holy; belonging to, dedicated to, devoted to God; referring to:

(a) religious concepts, events, etc.

провиденье Л 4:10 /
союз ЭЭ 6:1 /
милость Г 44:7
любовь В 12:4
награда В 64:4
жизнь В 71:10
обычай ГТ 3:9 /
благодать ГТ 8:8; 11:2 /
треба ГТ 9:7 /
союз Д 9:4 /
слово L 8:2 /
усыпленье По 35:3 /
воля КУ 5:2 (divine)
процессия КУ 20:2 /
власть ПКВ 13:4 /

(b) religious objects

икона Л 5:8 (hochgelobt)
налой Св 2:14
дары Б 10:4; 12:1; 18:4; 20:1 (holy)
риза Г 57:10
рука В 11:4
налой В 67:3
облачение По 1:2 /
фимиам По 3:2 /
кости КУ 15:3 /
раки КУ 27:2 /
мощи КУ 32:3 /
глава КУ 36:4 /
олива СР 2:1 /

(c) people

анахорет П 1:2 (gentle)
чернец Б 3:1 /
угодник Г 37:4
боги ЖЦ 7:11 (ewig Hohen)
чудотворцы По 43:1 /
угодники КУ 22:4; 29:1; 39:1 (holy)
пришельцы КУ 38:2 (blessed)

(d) places

стены Г 12:5
обитель Г 36:4; 36:5
приют В 16:11
монастырь РТ 7:4 /
Илион Т 2:8 /
храм По 5:1 /
монастырь По 17:1; 21:1 /
земля ПКВ 1:3; 14:3 (heil'gen)
места ПКВ 6:1 (Heiland)
скала Бр 4:8 (schroff)
храм Бр 5:7 /

(e) time

час По 10:1 /

Comments

Frequency: Used 61 times; occurs in 18 ballads.
Source: Translated from foreign sources 8 times; also replaces *gentle*, *ewig*, *schroff*.
Usage: The epithet *svyatoi* occurs in almost exclusively religious contexts, and is not used to sanctify or elevate secular themes as in Karamzin's lyrics.

СВЯЩЕННЫЙ

Definition

(1) Церковный, до веры касающийся;
(2) Заслуживающий особенное почтение, благоговение наше.

I	II	III
/	огнь (Тред.) места (Пет.) ужас (Лом.)	красота (МЖ.) песнь (МЖ.) холм (Мур.) лес (Мур.)

Folk	W. Eur.	Lit.
/	sacred: rite day hochgelobt: Sakrament	трепет М 8: 1 радость М 23: 1 остаток (древности) А 86: 32

Zhukovsky

(1) revered, honoured, mysterious; referring to:

(a) religious concepts

страх	ИЖ 13: 3	/
узы	Г 11: 12	
прах	В 69: 3	
ноша	ГГ 7: 10	/

(b) people

провозвестница	Ка 3: 7	/
Гелиос	ИЖ 9: 7	/
пришлец	В 8: 6	

(c) places

лес	Ка 16: 2	/
брег	Ах 23: 1	
вид	В 68: 5	
град	Т 1: 1	/

(d) time

час	Г 13: 9

Comments

Frequency: Used 12 times; occurs in 7 ballads.
Source: Never translated from foreign source.
Usage: Unlike *svyatoi*, Zhukovsky applies *svyashchennyi*, an 18th-c. elevated equivalent for *svyatoi*, to secular words (*les*, *vid*).

СМУТНЫЙ

Definition

(1) Тоже что смущенный (взор);
(2) *Мятежный, неспокойный (время).

I	II	III
дружок (Кант.) лицо	взоры (Княж.) глаза (Елаг.)	дни (Рад.) надежда (Нел.) души (Мур.) эфир (Дер.)
Folk	**W. Eur.**	**Lit.**
	restless: conscience sullen: thought	

Zhukovsky

(1) agitated, restless; indicative of emotional disturbance:

дух	Св 16: 8
думы	Ад 34: 4 (sullen)
океан	ИЖ 11: 4 /
он	В 47: 3
день	Бр 8: 5 /

(2) indistinct, indefinite:

крик	Ва 32: 2 /
желанье	У 11: 5
огонь	У 21: 5
все	К 19: 1 /

Comments

Frequency: Used 9 times; occurs in 8 ballads.
Source: Translated from foreign source once.
Usage: The epithet acquires overtones of mystery, particularly in combinations such as *smutnyi* + *zhelan'e, vse.*

СТРАШНЫЙ

Definition

(1) В ужас, в страх приводящий; ужасный; (вид, буря).

I	II	III
стремнины (Кант.)	сон (Сум.) час (Лом.) вид (Елаг., Лом.) рок (Елаг.) гром (Лом., Сум.)	тишина (Дер.) лицо (Кар.) веселие (МЖ.) минута (Пант.) гром (Кар.) филины (Мур.)

Folk	W. Eur.	Lit.
сон	awful: sign distressful: cry, voice fearful: day ghastly: eyes hideous: roar furchtbar: Stimmen grasslich: Wunder schrecklich: Zeit	громада AP 18:3 могилы BM:31 судьбина M 18:3 волны ЛС 11:1 Марлотес ГГ 12:4 вой P 3:3

Zhukovsky

(1) terrible, frightful; exciting terror; referring to:

(a) sight

вид	Л 10:4 /
сны	Св 20:1
мрак	Ад 40:4 /
ряд (зубов)	ИЖ 14:8 /
лик	Ва 10:4 /
сумрак	Б 22:2 /
след	Б 47:2 /
молния	Г 58:8
вид	ЖЦ 2:9 /
сон	L 1:1 /

(b) sound

хор	Л 21:8 /
молчанье	Св 13:6
хор	ИЖ 15:6 /
крик	Ва 38:4 /
колыханье	Б 5:4 /
голос	Г 29:12
речи	Г 47:9
гром	В 31:2

(c) emotions

ревность	По 29:1 /
мщенье	По 30:4 /

(d) people

житель	Св 12:7
она	ЭЭ 4:2 /
враг	Г 25:7
пришлец	Г 55:3
мертвый	Г 65:8
жильцы	К 21:6 /
гости	КУ 15:2 /
гость	РР 7:1 /
грешник	РР 14:2 /

(e) time

миг	Л 12:10 /
час	Г 20:10
день и ночь	Г 28:7
час	Г 50:11

(f) place

места	Св 11:7
берег	Ад 39:1 (desolate)
стремнина	Г 1:2
одр	Г 43:1
утес	В 57:10

(g) event and misc.

путь	Ка 15:6 /
призванье	Б 44:2 /
бой	Г 19:9
отрада	Г 26:4
мир	Т 5:12 /
что-то	Д 20:4 (strange)
дело	С 4:2 /
жизнь	Бр 8:8 /
пир	ЭП 8:8 /

Comments

Frequency: Used 47 times; occurs in 21 ballads.

Source: Never translated from foreign source; replaces *desolate*, *strange*.

Usage: *Strashnyi*, Zhukovsky's second most frequent epithet, is applied to a wide range of phenomena in order to explain, rather than to demonstrate, how 'terrible' something is. (Cf. *uzhasnyi*.)

Definition

(1) Сокровенный, никому неизвестный, кроме одного или весьма немногих; (намерение, разговоры).

I	II	III
разговоры (Тред.) злоба (Тред.)	устав (Сум.) радость (Сум.) место (Елаг.) глас (Елаг.) печаль (Елаг.) мучение (Елаг.)	беспокойство (МЖ.) удовольствие (МЖ.) грусть (Дмит.) сила (Пант.) стезя (Мур.)

Folk	W. Eur.	Lit.
/	secret: pair foe verborgner: Fiend	/

Zhukovsky

(1) secret:

(a) known by few

враг ИЖ 9: 6 (verborgner)
часы Э 10: 4
рука В 26: 10
сила В 52: 2
звезда У 23: 3
логибель ПП 7: 4 /
узы ЖЦ 7: 5 /
дар ЖЦ 8: 10 /
свидетель По 49: 1 /

(b) concealed, not openly avowed

робость Св 5: 3
чувство В 2: 3
страх В 56: 1
скорбь Д 22: 3 /
дума По 37: 4 /
грех По 45: 3 /

(2) unknown to anyone; mysterious:

мрак Св 16: 12
рок Ах 16: 2
дары Б 3: 3 /
чудеса В 73: 1

Compound:

небесно-тайный удел У 14: 6

Comments

Frequency: Used 19 times; occurs in 12 ballads.
Source: Translated from foreign source once.
Usage: Zhukovsky develops late 18th-c. usage of the epithet, expanding its applicability (*chuvstvo*, *strakh*, etc.). *Tainyi* also acquires overtones of mystery and uncanniness (*mrak*, *rok*, etc.).

ТЕМНЫЙ

Definition

(1) Мрачный, чуждый света (место, ночь);
(2) В цветах называется цвет противоположный светлому;
(3) *Неудобопонятный, невразумительный, (выражение).

I	II	III
лес (Гист.)	зависть (Лом.)	аллея (МЖ.)
ночь (Тред.)	печаль (Тред.)	чувства (МЖ.)
язык (Тред.)	век (Княж.)	прохлада (Мур.)
	гроб (Княж.)	могила (Кар.)
	ночь	бездна (Дер.)
	лес	небеса (Дер.)
	мысль	
	понятие	

Folk	W. Eur.	Lit.
лес	dark:	/
ночь	night	
темница	water	
	eyes	
	dim:	
	eyes	
	light	
	dunkel:	
	Knäuel	
	Gefühle	
	düster	
	Ort	
	Linden	

Zhukovsky

(1) dark; devoid of or deficient in light; referring to:

(a) place or object

кельи	Л 11:6 /
даль	Св 10:7
луч	Ад 32:4 (dim)
свет	ИЖ 14:3 (düsterrot)
своды	Э 9:1
лес	Г 1:11
глубина	Г 3:3
вершины	Г 27:4
сень	Г 41:3
ночь	В 16:11
лес	В 19:9; 28:7
бор	В 53:10; 63:1
липы	РТ 7:3 (düster)
ветви	ЛЦ 6:2 (düster)
небо	У 22:3
ночь	З 19:3 /
громада	Д 1:3 /
дорога	С 13:2 /
свод	L 12:7 /
приют	L 18:4 /
ограда	По 21:2 /
свод	По 32:3 /
лес	РО 2:7 /

(b) death

могила	Л 20:10 /
гроб	К 14:5 /
гробы	НС 1:5 /
могилы	НС 2:5 /

(2) of dark colour:

ресницы	Э 6:3
корона	ЛЦ 2:3 /
очи	Д 12:2 (dark)

(3) vague, indefinite:

чувство	ГГ 5:9 (dunkel)

Comments

Frequency: Used 33 times; occurs in 19 ballads.

Source: Translated from foreign source 5 times; also replaces *düsterrot*.

Usage: Zhukovsky develops late 18th-c. usage of the epithet. *Temnyi* acquires overtones of mystery and vagueness, particularly when applied to abstract locations (*dal'*, *glubina*, *vershiny*) and to emotions (*chuvstva*).

ТИХИЙ

Definition

(1) Смирный, кроткий (человек, нрав);
(2) *Медленный, небыстрый (походка);
(3) *Противополагается слову громкий (голос);
(4) *Относительно к ветру: слабый;
(5) *Спокойный, благонадежный.

I	II	III
муж (Кант.)	реки (Лом.)	месяц (МЖ.)
нрав (Кант.)	зефиры (Лом., Сум.)	чувство (Кар.)
голос (Тред.)	роща (Сум.)	долина (Кар.)
сердце (Кант.)	воды (Лом.)	душа (Рад.)
дети (Кант.)	слова (Елаг.)	трепет (Мур.)
		светлость (Мур.)
		шепот (Мур.)

Folk	W. Eur.	Lit.
Дон	calm: lake silent: hour thought ruhig: Kind still (Ger.): Weiner Hoffnung Wasserschlund Hochzeitbettchen	покров (ночи) ЭМ: 163 век М 1:2

Zhukovsky

(1) quiet, barely audible, making little noise:

шепот	Л 9:9 (vernehmlich)
шорох	Л 16:1 /
глас	Л 18:11 /
хор	Л 21:8 /
шепот	Св 6:11
глас	Ах 4:2
пенье	Г 21:6
хор	Г 34:11
глас	Г 44:11
глас	В 36:9
шаги	В 47:2
шум	В 57:2
говор	В 70:11
стон	Т 2:6 /
голос	Д 14:2 /
пенье	КУ 33:3 /

(2) peaceful, secluded, still, calm; referring to:

(a) place

дубрава	Л 8:2 /
дом	Л 13:9 (still)
могила	П 35:1 /
склон (брегов)	Ва 5:1 /
гроб	Б 22:3 /
лес	В 49:9
сень	В 50:6
замок	В 58:5
дол	РТ 8:7; 10:3 (ruhig)
равнина	Д 13:4 /
приют	L 18:4 (still)
земля	По 35:3 /

(b) time

утро	П 22:3 /
сон	Г 54:7
ночь	З 19:3 (sweet)
вечер	По 32:1 /

(c) people

ангел	Г 66:3
дитя	В 35:3
он	У 20:6
жена	З 33:1 /

(d) landscape, weather, etc.

Ксант и Симоис	Ах 23:6
ветерок	Э 17:8
сиянье	Г 38:8
трепетанье	В 34:8
ветер	Д 10:1 /

(e) emotions

радость	Э 11:4
желанье	Г 32:6

(3) slow, measured:

стопа	ИЖ 18:5 (langsam)
стопа	Э 23:7

Compound:

тихоструйный:	волны Ал 22:3 /
сумрачно-тихий:	Доника Д 15:2 /

Comments

Frequency: Used 46 times; occurs in 18 ballads.

Source: Translated from foreign source 5 times; also replaces *sweet*.

Usage: Zhukovsky expands the applicability of the epithet, applying it to a wide range of sounds, and to both locations and persons to indicate physical and/or spiritual tranquillity.

ТЯЖЕЛЫЙ

Definition

(see *tyazhkii*)

I	II	III
/	работа (Сум.) оковы (Елаг.) урон (Елаг.) рука (Трут.)	вздох (СПб Мерк.) власть (Рад.) язык (Мур.)

Folk	W. Eur.	Lit.
/	heavy: weight schwer: Traum Tat Panzer	разлука AP 3:4 вздох AP 7:3 палаш К 4:3

Zhukovsky

(1) heavy, ponderous, of great weight:

труп	Ва 37:4 (heavier)
панцырь	М: 12 (schwer)
винты	В 54:4
седок	З 4:4 /
шуйца	З 46:1 /
мечи	РО 3:6; 9:2 /
щит	РО 11:3 /
плот	ЭП 20:4 (schwer)

(2) oppressive, grievous, hard to bear:

крест	Г 2:5

(3) massive, dark:

облака	В 30:7

Comments

Frequency: Used 11 times; occurs in 7 ballads.

Source: Translated from foreign source 3 times.

Usage: Zhukovsky employs the epithet in the literal sense, except when combined with *krest* to indicate a spiritual burden. (Cf. *tyazhkii*.)

ТЯЖКИЙ

Definition

(1) Имеющий тяжесть, силу стремящую тело к падению;
(2) Имеющий великую, нарочитую пред другими тяжесть (бремя, ноша);
(3) *Весьма трудный, неудобосносимый (работа).

I	II	III
мысли (Кант.)	узы (Лом.)	скорбь (Кап.)
несчастие (Кант.)	стон (Сум.)	милость (Хем.)
раны	оковы (Сум.)	слеза (Рад.)
болезнь	горесть (Сум.)	тьма (Дер.)
работа	размышление (Елаг.)	

Folk	W. Eur.	Lit.
грехи	(see *tyazhelyi*)	цепи ГГ 12:1

Zhukovsky

(1) heavy, ponderous, of great weight:

винты	Б 19:2 (strong)	
врат	Б 24:3	/
цепь	Г 59:5	
гроб	L 21:6	/
дротик	ЭП 10:2	/

(2) oppressive, grievous, hard to bear:

долг	АА 26:5	/
мýка	Э 30:1	
мýка	Г 73:10	
слезы	Бр 5:2	/

(3) loud, deep:

стон	Ва 27:4; 29:4	/
стон	Б 44:1; 47:3	/
звон	ЭЭ 24:2	/
топот	В 53:8	
храп	Ул 5:3 (hard)	

(4) serious:

болезнь	КУ 18:4	/

Comments

Frequency: Used 17 times; occurs in 12 ballads.

Source: Never translated from foreign source; replaces *strong*, *hard*.

Usage: Zhukovsky employs the epithet *tyazhkii* as an elevated variant of *tyazhelyi*: *tyazhkii* + *vrat*, *tsep'*; in the figurative sense the epithet is applied to psychological substantives (*múka*).

УЖАСНЫЙ

Definition

(a) [illegible] (взор, шум, буря).

I	II	III
стремнины (Кант.)	сила (Лом.)	величина (МЖ.)
час (Кант.)	звуки (Лом.)	ад (Рад.)
грозы (Тред.)	сон (Сум.)	муки (Нел.)
	слово (Сум.)	
	страх (Чулк.)	

Folk	W. Eur.	Lit.
/	(see *strashnyi*)	явленье ЭМ: 215
		час ВМ: 29
		ветр М 11: 2
		день и ночь Б 15: 3
		тьма Р 9: 4
		минуты Р 20: 1

Zhukovsky

(1) horrible, dreadful, exciting horror; referring to:

(a) sight

сон	Св 16: 9
созданья	ИЖ 16: 8 (furchtbar)
вид	Б 24: 1 /
мрак	Г 42: 9
млат	Г 67: 9
сон	З 42: 2 /
вихорь	К 17: 4 /

(b) sound

песни	ИЖ 18: 1 /
вой	Б 25: 3 /
шум	Б 25: 3 /
песня	ТП 3: 1 /
тишина	Г 19: 1
шепот	Д 4: 4 /
слово	По 11: 2 /

(c) people

он	Ах 21: 1
он	Г 7: 8
он	В 1: 7
он	З 23: 2 /
ездок	РР 18: 3 (schwarz)

(d) place

лес	ИЖ 5: 3 /
ад	Г 20: 6
гроб	Г 33: 7

(e) time

день	Ва 15: 1 /

(f) event, misc.

истина	Ка 8: 7 (schrecklich)
жизнь	Ка 11: 7 /
цена	Ад 36: 3 /
суд	ИЖ 22: 4 /
страшилище	Ва 11: 3 /
молва	РТ 5: 3 /
казнь	Т 12: 3 (schwer)
дело	По 27: 1; 47: 4 /
что	По 38: 2 /

Comments

Frequency: Used 33 times; occurs in 17 ballads.

Source: Translated from foreign source twice; also replaces *schwarz*, *schwer*.

Usage: Zhukovsky applies the epithet to a wide range of phenomena in order to explain, rather than demonstrate, how 'horrible' something is. (Cf. *strashnyi*.)

УНЫЛЫЙ

Definition

(1) Лишившийся бодрости духа, предавшийся печальному возчувствованию (вид).

I	II	III
голос (Кант.)	лицо (Тред.) взор (Елаг.) дух (Елаг.) сердце (Пет.)	душа (Нел.) вопль (Кап.) песни (Кар.) поэт (Кар.) леса (Кар.) мысли (Дмит.)

Folk	W. Eur.	Lit.
/	distressful: cry, voice mournful: mood düster: Ort, Linden traurig: Öde	луна ЛС 3:1 вопль СЛ 6:6 вид А 85:9 томность А 85:22

Zhukovsky

(1) experiencing despondency, dejection:

он	Св 8:14; 9:14
гость	П 12:2 (pensive)
он	АА 15:5 (Tant de chagrins)
душа	Э 12:2
сердце	Э 13:1
певец	Э 19:1
странник	Э 32:5
призрак	Г 40:8
душа	РТ 8:1
он	По 39:1 /

(2) expressing despondency:

взор	Ва 19:3 /
очи	В 55:8
гармония	Д 6:3 (strange)
голос	Л 14:1 /
лицо	По 13:3 /

(3) evoking despondency:

земля	Ах 8:3
дни	Г 26:5
лес	Г 73:4

Compound:

сумрачно-унылый Гаральд **Га 8:1** /

Comments

Frequency: Used 19 times; occurs in 11 ballads.

Source: Translated from foreign source twice; also replaces *strange*.

Usage: Zhukovsky develops late 18th-c. usage, especially that of Karamzin, and applies the epithet *unylyi* not only to describe the emotional state of objective characters, but also to express the poet's own subjective reactions to phenomena (*zemlya*, *dni*, *les*).

ЧИСТЫЙ

Definition

(1) Незамаранный, незагаженный;
(2) Не имеющий в себе никакой примеси;
(3) *Относительно к голосу: светлый, ясный; . . .
(6) *В нравственном смысле: непорочный, нелицемерный, непритворный (вера, сердце, совесть, любовь, душа).

I	II	III
совесть (Кант.)	голос (Лом.)	душа (МЖ., Дер.)
девицы (Кант.)	сердце (Сум.)	чувства (МЖ.)
воздух (Тред.)	луга (Сум.)	роса (Мур.)
	день (Княж.)	стихи (Кар.)

Folk	W. Eur.	Lit.
поле	rein: Seele	души М 5:3
серебро		поле К 2:1
		дева ГГ 19:4

Zhukovsky

(1) clean, pure, spotless:

вода	Св 1:9
стекло	Св 4:7
поток	Э 10:1
свод	По 32:3 /

(2) pure, unspoiled, free from corruption:

кто	ИЖ 16:2 (rein)
все	В 7:2
перси	В 36:3
жертва	ЭП 13:1 /
душа	П 30:3 /
душа	ЭЭ 3:1 /
душа	Г 45:1; 63:6; 76:6

(3) open, spacious:

поле	В 17:2

Comments

Frequency: Used 14 times; occurs in 8 ballads.
Source: Translated from foreign source once.
Usage: Zhukovsky develops late 18th-c. usage. The epithet acquires overtones of mystery and vagueness when applied to substantivized pronouns (*kto*, *vse*) and is almost synonymous with *svyatoi* when used to modify *dusha*.

APPENDIX B

KEY TO CHARTS

(1a) and (2)

Folk as for (1b).
W. Eur. as for (1b).
Lit. as for (1b).

Zhukovsky. Examples are selected from Zhukovsky's ballads and are arranged within each subdivision chronologically. Each of these epithets crosses the boundary from (1a) qualitative absolute or (2) relative epithets to the (1b) qualitative relative epithets. The (1a) or (2) meaning of each epithet is listed first with examples; then the (1b) meaning follows, also with examples. The 'code' which identifies ballad/stanza/line, and the abbreviations of ballad titles are the same as for (1b). If an epithet has been translated from, or has any equivalent in, the foreign source, then the original word is included in parentheses after the 'code'. An oblique stroke indicates that although the ballad itself has a specific source, the given epithet was supplied by Zhukovsky where none was present in the original. No mark indicates that the ballad has no specific source. The examples are followed by brief comments on Zhukovsky's usage, including comparison to eighteenth-century Russian usage if relevant.

БЕЛЫЙ

Folk	W. Eur.	Lit.	Zhukovsky	
			(1 a) white	
ручки	white:	одежда	плат	Св 1: 12
тело	countenance	ЭМ 2: 11	полотно	Св 14: 3
груди	cheek	саван	голубочек	Св 14: 14
снег	billows	БЛ 2: 2	лебедь	Ад 4: 2; 6: 1
платье	robes	грудь		
голубушка		Р 5: 1	(1b) holy, pure:	
лебедушка			одежда	В 6: 8
	weiss:		одежда	КУ 10: 4 (white)
	Schaum			

Comments

(1a) B*elyi* is used in a conscious attempt to imitate the language of folklore. Its use is restricted to primarily *narodnyi* contexts.

(1b) The epithet also acquires overtones of sanctity and mystery, and occurs in religious contexts.

ЖИВОЙ

Folk	W. Eur.	Lit.	Zhukovsky
вода	lively: hue lebende: Seele	жена К 19:4; 20:3 он А 89:3	(1a) alive: спутник В 11:11 душа К 10:6 (lebende) он L 1:3 / (1b) vivid, bright: цветы У 12:5 белизна К 13:2 (schwanenweiss) звук К 21:5 /
			Comments (1a) *Zhivoi* is used in the conventional sense. (1b) The epithet is used as a synonym for *svetlyi*, parallel to the English *lively* (although not directly translated from it), and to the French *vif*.

НЕМОЙ

Folk	W. Eur.	Lit.	Zhukovsky
/	mute: he she stumm: Harm	отчаяние ЭМ: 165	(1a) mute: голова PO 22: 2 / бездна K 10: 5 (heulende) (1b) deep; inexpressible: печаль PT 2: 1 (stumm) грусть У 20: 3
			Comments (1a) *Nemoi* is used figuratively (+ *bezdna*) to replace *heulende Tiefe* (cf. *glukhaya bezdna*, K 19: 3). (1b) The epithet is used to imply profound spiritual condition.

РОДНОЙ

Folk	W. Eur.	Lit.	Zhukovsky
матушка сестрица бабушка	dear: children native: field land lieblich: Tochter teuer: Land	/	(1a) blood-related: отец Г 14:9 семья У 20:1 (1b) spiritually related: душа ЭЭ 6:2 / душа Ах 19:4 (1b) dear, beloved: страна Л 10:12 / страна ИЖ 3:4 / страна Ка 15:7 / брега Ва 11:1 / дно Ры 2:3 / холмы Т 2:9 (geliebt) глас ЖЦ 10:8 /
			Comments (1a) *Rodnoi* is used in the conventional sense and does not occur in folkloric contexts. (1b) The meaning of the epithet is extended from blood-relatedness to spiritual similarity (*rodnaya dusha*); it is also used to express the poet's warm emotional relationship with his homeland and with specific features in its landscape.

СЕДОЙ

Folk	W. Eur.	Lit.	Zhukovsky
/	white: foam billows weiss: Schaum grau: Weiden Bart	старина К 1:2	(1a) grey-white: пена К 7:2 (weiss) глубина К 13:1 / брега Г 69:9 мох В 52:7 призраки В 58:10 ветлы ЛЦ 6:4 (grau) бездна Ул 6:4 (white) (1b) possessing grey-white hair; therefore, old, brave, strong, etc.: боец Га 1:2 (kühn) боец Га 8:2 (stolz) боец Га 12:4 (alt) Риоль ПКВ 9:1 (grau) старик СР 5:1 (getreu) гусары НС 2:7 (weiss) **Comments** (1a) *Sedoi* is used in descriptions of the sea (cf. Lomonosov—*sedaya pena*). (1b) The epithet replaces a variety of German epithets, which indicates that it has acquired overtones of strength, maturity, courage, etc.

СЛАДКИЙ

Folk	W. Eur.	Lit.	Zhukovsky
меды водочки	sweet: eve stream paths süss: Mund Lieder Freundin	разговоры ЭМ: 153	(1a) sweet (to the taste): вино ПКВ 11: 3 (rot) грозды ЭП 4: 1 (süss) (1b) pleasant, delightful: час Л 3: 1 / покой П 5: 4 / глас Ах 19: 4 смятенье Э 6: 4 воспоминанье Г 1: 8 песни А 4: 3 / лира ЭП 25: 2

Comments

(1a) *Sladkii* is used in the conventional sense.

(1b) Zhukovsky develops late 18th-c. usage of the epithet (cf. *sladkii* + *vostorg*, *volnen'e*, *zadumchivost'*), by applying *sladkii* to abstract psychological substantives, such as *smyaten'e* and *vospominan'e*. The epithet is used to express the poet's emotional approval of objects and concepts.

ЧЕРНЫЙ

Folk	W. Eur.	Lit.	Zhukovsky
кудри брови соболь вороны	black: horse arms eyes schwarz: Täter Mantel Mund schwärzlich: Gewimmel	кров (ночи) ЭМ: 1 птица (ночи) ЭМ: 175 покрывало ВМ: 8 верх АиР 17: 4 тучи Р 1: 3	(1a) black: ворон Л 15: 9 / гроб Св 9: 9 ночь Г 58: 4 рясы Б 13: 2 / конь РР 18: 4 (schwarz) (1b) dark, mysterious: тень Г 46: 3 мгла Г 57: 7; 74: 11 лес Г 49: 8; 69: 8 щель К 7: 3 (schwarz) пучина К 20: 1 (schwarz)

Comments

(1a) *Chernyi* is used in the conventional sense.

(1b) The epithet acquires overtones of mystery and foreboding, and is regularly employed in ballad settings where it is applied to all the physical locations of the action. (Cf. 18th-c. usage: *chernyi* + *serdtse, sovest'* to mean evil.)

ЧУЖОЙ

Folk	W. Eur.	Lit.	Zhukovsky
сторона	fremd: Boden	/	(1a) foreign: край Л 13:8 / город Г 37:2 страна L 1:5 / (1b) alien, strange: брег ИЖ 3:5 / страна В 10:7; 29:3
			Comments (1a) C*huzhoi* is used in the conventional sense; cf. 18th-c. usage: *chuzhoi* + *strana, storona, storonka*. (1b) The epithet is used as the antonym of *rodnoi* and implies spiritual dissimilarity as well as the poet's hostility towards the object.

ГРОБОВОЙ

Folk	W. Eur.	Lit.	Zhukovsky
доска	sepulchral: sound	доска М 3: 11	(2) sepulchral: келья Л 15: 3; 17: 3 / прах Л 16: 4 / покров Б 10: 3 / саван Б 18: 1 (winding) одежда А 10: 3 / (1b) deathly, gloomy: голос Ва 19: 4 / цвет Б 29: 3 (dead) тень Г 28: 8
			Comments (2) *Grobovoi* is used frequently and occurs primarily in 'Gothic' descriptions of ballad settings. (1b) The epithet acquires overtones of mystery and melancholy, and is employed as a synonym for *mrachnyi*.

ЗЛАТОЙ/ЗОЛОТОЙ

Folk	W. Eur.	Lit.	Zhukovsky
цепочка крест перстень венец узды	golden (Ger.) Stern Becher Pokal gülden Gewand Sporen	бокал ЭМ: 50	(2) containing, made of, covered in, gold: перстень Св 1: 10 венец Св 2: 10 крест В 12: 1 струны ГГ 4: 5 (in der Saiten Gold) цепь З 26: 3 (silver) кубок К 2: 4; 25: 1 / (1a) golden (of colour), yellow: струя Э 5: 8 волны ЭП 11: 3 (golden) (1b) happy, blessed: юность Г 13: 2 весна Г 15: 9 сновиденья Ка 12: 6 /
			Comments (2) and (1a) *Zlatoi/zolotoi* is used frequently, supplied when no epithet is present in the foreign source, or used to replace the original epithet. (1b) Zhukovsky develops 18th-c. figurative usage (*zlatoi* + *vek*, *vesna*, *dni*); this development is restricted to the form *zlatoi* only. The epithet acquires overtones of spirituality (*zlatoi* + *yunost'*, *snoviden'ya*).

НЕБЕСНЫЙ

Folk	W. Eur.	Lit.	Zhukovsky
царь	heavenly: light vision himmlisch: Licht	господь ГГ 8: 3	(2) heavenly: царь Л 4: 7 царь Г 4: 9; 14: 5 свод В 1: 12 облако В 2: 10 (1b) spiritually exalted: награда Л 7: 2 (Seligkeit) жизнь К 26: 1 (Himmelsgewalt) рай L 11: 1; 11: 3 (Seligkeit)
			Comments (2) *Nebesnyi* is used in the conventional sense. (1b) The epithet is used to modify sacred concepts in religious contexts only (cf. Lomonosov—*nebesnyi* + *dver'*, *sineva*, *tsvet*); it is not applied to secular concepts as in Murav'ev: *nebesnyi* + *dolina*, *pevets*, *krasota*.

ПУСТЫННЫЙ

Folk	W. Eur.	Lit.	Zhukovsky
/	bleak: mountain desolate: place dreary: place	/	(2) desert: сова Л 11:9 / ветер Г 70:7 (1b) empty, deserted: отдаление В 63: 4 вершина З 11:4 (eiry) скала З 24:4; 42:3 / брег Т 13:2 / место По 27:2 / часовня РР 3:2 /
			Comments (2) *Pustynnyi* is used in the conventional sense. (1b) The epithet acquires overtones of vagueness and mystery, and is frequently employed in the description of ballad settings.

RANGE OF SYNONYMS

Zhukovsky's literary ballads	страшный ужасный	святой священный	тихий	одинокий уединенный	пустой пустынный
English literary ballads	awful distressful fearful frightful ghastly hideous	holy blessed divine sacred	calm silent still	alone lone lonely lonesome solitary	bleak desolate dreary
German literary ballads	furchtbar grasslich grausig schrecklich	heilig hochgelobt selig	ruhig still	—	—

FREQUENCY CHART

	epithet	total uses
(1a)	сладкий	21
	черный	28
(1b)	святой	61
	страшный	47
	тихий	46
	бледный	34
	темный	33
	ужасный	33
	легкий	27
	светлый	22
	веселый	21
	милый	20
	тайный	19
	унылый	19
(2)	златой/ золотой	30

SELECT BIBLIOGRAPHY

ABRAMS, M. H., *The Mirror and the Lamp: Romantic Theory and the Critical Tradition*. New York, 1958.

ADDISON, STEELE, *et al.*, *The Spectator in Four Volumes*. Edited by G. Smith. London, 1958.

ALEKSEEV, M. P., 'K literaturnoi istorii odnogo iz romansov v *Don Kikhote*', in *Servantes. Stat'i i materialy*. L., 1948, 96–123.

Arzamas i Arzamasskie protokoly. Edited by M. S. Borovkova-Maikova, L., 1933.

AZADOVSKY, M. K., 'Istochniki skazok Pushkina', in *Vremennik Pushkinskoi komissii*, I. M.-L., 1936, 134–63.

BALASHOV, D. M., *Istoriya razvitiya zhanra russkoi ballady*. Petrozavodsk, 1966.

—— 'Knyaz' Dmitrii i ego nevesta Domna', in *Russkii fol'klor*, IV. M.-L., 1959, 80–99.

BATYUSHKOV, K. N., *Opyty v stikhakh i proze*. SPb., 1817.

—— *Polnoe sobranie stikhotvorenii. Biblioteka poeta, Bol'shaya seriya*, 2-oe izd. M.-L., 1964.

—— *Sochineniya*. SPb., 1885–7.

BAUER, H. F., *Les Ballades de Victor Hugo: Leurs origines françaises et etrangères*. Paris, 1936.

BAYLEY, J. O., *Pushkin: A Comparative Commentary*. Cambridge, 1971.

BELINSKY, V. G., *Polnoe sobranie sochinenii v XIII tomakh*. M., 1953–9.

BERKOV, P. N., 'Iz istorii russkoi parodii XVIII–XX vv.', *Voprosy sovetskoi literatury*, V. M.-L., 1957, 220–66.

—— 'K istorii teksta *Gromvala*, G. P. Kameneva', *Izvestiya AN SSSR, Otd. obshchestvennykh nauk*, No. 1 (1934), 63–84.

BESTUZHEV, A. A., *Sochineniya v dvukh tomakh*. M., 1958.

BLOK, A. A., *Sobranie sochinenii v vos'mi tomakh*. M.-L., 1960–3.

BOBROV, E. A., 'Iz istorii russkoi literatury XVIII i XIX stoleyii', *Izvestiya Otd. russkogo yazyka i slovesnosti*, XI, No. 4 (1906), 320–39.

BOGACH, G. F. *Pushkin i moldavskii fol'klor*. Kishinev, 1963.

BRATTON, J. S., 'Studies in the Literary and Sub-Literary Ballad in the Nineteenth Century'. Unpublished D.Phil. thesis, Oxford University, 1969.

Briefe von und an Gottfried August Bürger. Edited by A. Strodtmann. Berlin, 1874.

BRUNOT, F., *La Pensée et la langue*. Paris, 1922.

BULAKHOVSKY, L. A., *Russkii literaturnyi yazyk pervoi poloviny XIX veka*, II. Kiev, 1957.

BÜRGER, G. A., *Werke und Briefe*. Leipzig, 1958.

—— See also *Briefe von und an Gottfried August Bürger*.

BUSLAEV, F. I., *Istoricheskaya grammatika russkogo yazyka*. M., 1863.

—— *O prepodavanii otechestvennogo yazyka*. L., 1941.

BYCHKOV, I., *Bumagi V. A. Zhukovskogo, postupivshie v imperatorskuyu Publichnuyu biblioteku v 1884 g*. SPb., 1887.

CHERNYSHEVSKY, N. G., *Polnoe sobranie sochinenii v pyatnadtsati tomakh*. M., 1939–53.

CLEMENT, N. H., *Romanticism in France*. New York, 1939.

CROSS, A. G., *N. M. Karamzin*. Carbondale, Ill., 1971.

DANILOV, Kirsha, *Drevnie rossiiskie stikhotvoreniya sobrannye Kirsheyu Danilovym*. Edited by A. P. Evgen'eva and B. N. Putilov. M.-L., 1958.

DANILOV, V., 'Istochnik stikhotvoreniya Pushkina *Gusar*', *Russkii filologicheskii vestnik*, LXIV, No. 3–4 (1910), 243–52.

DAVIE, Donald, *Articulate Energy: An Inquiry into the Syntax of English Poetry*. London, 1955.

DERZHAVIN, G. R., *Stikhotvoreniya. Biblioteka poeta, Bol'shaya seriya*, 2-oe izd. L., 1957.

DMITRIEV, A. I., *Poemy drevnykh bardov*. SPb., 1788.

DMITRIEV, I. I., *Polnoe sobranie stikhotvorenii*, *Biblioteka poeta, Bol'shaya seriya*, 2-oe izd. L., 1967.

—— See also Karamzin–Dmitriev.

DMITRIEV, M. A., *Melochi iz zapasa moei pamyati*. M., 1869.

DOLGOVA, N. M., 'K voprosu ob istochnikakh ballady A. S. Pushkina *Zhenikh*', *Uchenye zapiski Gor'kovskogo gosudarstvennogo universiteta*, XLVIII (1958), 27–36.

EHRHARD, Marcelle, *V. A. Joukovski et le préromantisme russe*. Paris, 1938.

EICHSTÄDT, Hildegard, *Žukovskij als Übersetzer*. Munich, 1970.

EIKHENBAUM, B. M., *Lermontov. Opyt istoriko-literaturnoi otsenki*. L., 1924.

—— *Melodika russkogo liricheskogo stikha*. SPb., 1922.

—— *Skvoz' literaturu*. L., 1924.

—— *Stat'i o Lermontove*. M.-L., 1961.

EMERSON, O. F., *The Earliest English Translations of Bürger's 'Lenore'*. Cleveland, Ohio, 1915.

ENTWISTLE, W. J., *European Balladry*. Oxford, 1951.

ERLICH, V., *Russian Formalism*. The Hague, 1965.

ETKIND, E. G., 'Materiya stikha'. Unpublished manuscript. L., 1969.

—— *Poeziya i perevod*. M.-L., 1963.

—— *Razgovor o stikhakh*. M., 1970.

—— 'Stikhotvornyi perevod kak problema sopostavleniya stilistiki'. Unpublished thesis. LGPI im. Gertsena, L., 1965.

EVGEN'EVA, A. P., *Ocherki po yazyku russkoi ustnoi poezii v zapisyakh XVII–XX vv.* M.-L., 1963.

FEDOROV, A. V., 'Slovoupotreblenie i ego osobennosti v stile elegii i ballad V. A. Zhukovskogo', *Uchenye zapiski LGPI im. Gertsena*, CCLVII (1965), 141–52.

FEVCHUK, L. P., *Lichnye veshchi A. S. Pushkina*, L. 1970.

FITZGERALD, R. P., 'The Style of Ossian', *Studies in Romanticism*, VI, No. 1 (1966), 22–33.

FRIEDMAN, A. B., *The Ballad Revival*. Chicago, Ill., 1961.

FURST, L. R., *Romanticism in Perspective: A Comparative Study of the Romantic Movements in England, France and Germany*. London, 1969.

GAEVSKY, V. P., 'Pushkin v litsee i litseiskie ego stikhotvoreniya', *Sovremennik*, XCVII, No. 7 (1863).

GALICH, A. I., *Opyt nauki izyashchnogo*. SPb., 1825.

GARKAVI, A. M., 'Zametki o M. Yu. Lermontove: Lermontov i Zhukovsky. (Iz istorii russkoi ballady)', *Uchenye zapiski Kaliningradskogo pedagogicheskogo instituta*, VI (1959), 274–85.

GERASIMOVA, L. V., 'Epitety v proizvedeniyakh Karamzina', in *XVIII vek*, VIII. L., 1969, 290–8.

GEROULD, G. H., *The Ballad of Tradition*. Oxford, 1932.

GERSHENZON, M. O., 'Sny Pushkina', in *Pushkin. Sbornik I*. Edited by N. K. Piksanov. M.-L., 1924, 77–96.

GILLIES, A., *Herder*. Oxford, 1945.

GINZBURG, L. Ya., *O lirike*. M.-L., 1964.

GORLIN, M., 'Les Ballades d'Adam Mickiewicz et Puškin', *Revue des Études slaves*, XIX (1939), 227–41.

GORODETSKY, B. P., *Lirika Pushkina*. M.-L., 1962.

GRAY, R., *The Poems of Goethe*. Cambridge, 1966.

GRECH, N. I., *Opyt kratkoi istorii russkoi literatury*. SPb., 1822.

—— *Zapiski o moei zhizni*. M.-L., 1930.

GREGG, R. A., 'Tatyana's Two Dreams: The Unwanted Spouse and the Demon Lover', *SEER* XLVIII, No. 113 (1970), 492–505.

GRIBOEDOV, A. S., *Polnoe sobranie sochinenii*. SPb., 1911.

GRONICKA, André von. *The Russian Image of Goethe: Goethe in Russian Literature of the First Half of the Nineteenth Century*. Philadelphia, Pa., 1968.

GUKOVSKY, G. A., *Ocherki po istorii russkoi literatury i obshchestvennoi mysli XVIII veka*. L., 1938.

—— 'Pushkin i poetika russkogo romantizma (Problema natsional'no-istoricheskogo kolorita v romanticheskoi poezii), *Izvestiya AN SSSR, Otd. literatury i yazyka*, No. 2 (1940), 56–92.

—— *Pushkin i russkie romantiki*. M., 1965.

—— *Russkaya literatura XVIII veka*. M., 1939.

—— *Russkaya poeziya XVIII veka*. L., 1927.

HERDER, J. G., *Von Deutscher Art und Kunst*. Edited by E. Purdie. Oxford, 1924.

HODGART, M. J. C., *The Ballads*. New York, 1962.

IEZUITOVA, R. V., 'Iz istorii russkoi ballady 1790-kh—pervoi poloviny 1820-kh godov'. Unpublished Candidate's Thesis, Institut russkoi literatury, L., 1966.

Ippokrena. M., 1799–1801.

ISAČENKO, A. V., *Grammaticheskii stroi russkogo yazyka v sopostavlenii s slovatskim*, I. Bratislava, 1965.

ISTOMIN, V., 'Glavneishie osobennosti yazyka i sloga proizvedenii V. A. Zhukovskogo (1783–1852)', *Russkii filologicheskii vestnik*, No. 3 (1893), 1–48.

Istoriya russkoi literatury, I–X. M.-L., 1941–56.

Istoriya russkoi poezii, I–II. L., 1968–9.

KARAMZIN, N. M., *Polnoe sobranie stikhotvorenii, Biblioteka poeta, Bol'shaya seriya*, 2-oe izd. M.-L., 1966.

KARAMZIN–DMITRIEV, *Izbrannye stikhotvoreniya, Biblioteka poeta, Bol'shaya seriya*. L., 1953.

KATENIN, P. A., *Izbrannye proizvedeniya, Biblioteka poeta, Bol'shaya seriya*, 2-oe izd. M.-L., 1965.

—— See also *Pis'ma P. A. Katenina*.

KAYSER, W., *Geschichte der deutschen Ballade*. Berlin, 1936.

KIND, F., *Lenardo's Schwärmereyen*. Leipzig, 1797.

KOBILINSKI-ELLIS, L., *Das goldene Zeitalter der russischen Poesie: W. A. Joukowski, seine Persönlichkeit, sein Leben und sein Werk*. Paderborn, 1933.

KOSTKA, E., *Schiller in Russian Literature*. Philadelphia, Pa., 1965.

KOSTROV, E. I., *Ossian, syn fingalov, bard tret'ego veka: gall'skie stikhotvoreniya*. M., 1792.

KOZLOV, I. I., *Polnoe sobranie stikhotvorenii, Biblioteka poeta, Bol'shaya seriya*. L., 1960.

KROEBER, K., *Romantic Narrative Art*. Madison, Wisc., 1966.

KUKULEVICH, A. M., and LOTMAN, L. M., 'Iz tvorcheskoi istorii ballady Pushkina *Zhenikh*', in *Vremmenik Pushkinskoi kommissii*, VI. M.-L., 1941, 72–91.

KYUKHEL'BEKER, V. K., *Izbrannye proizvedeniya v dvukh tomakh, Biblioteka poeta, Bol'shaya seriya*, 2-oe izd. M.-L., 1967.

LARTSEV, V., 'Ballada v sovremmenoi poezii', *Zvezda vostoka* (Tashkent), 9 September 1963, 123–33.

LERMONTOV, M. Yu., *Sochineniya v shesti tomakh*. M.-L., 1954–7.

LERNER, N. O., *Rasskazy o Pushkine*. L., 1929.

LEVIN, Yu. D., 'Angliiskaya poeziya i literatura russkogo sentimentalizma', in *Ot klassitsizma k romantizmu*. Edited by M. P. Alekseev. L., 1970, 195–297.

—— 'Karamzin, Batyushkov, Zhukovsky—redaktory sochinenii M. N. Murav'eva', in *Problemy sovremmenoi filologii. Sbornik statei k 70-letiyu akademika V. V. Vinogradova*. M., 1965, 182–91.

—— 'O russkom poeticheskom perevode v epokhy romantizma', in *Rannie romanticheskie veyaniya. Sbornik statei*. Edited by M. P. Alekseev. L., 1972, 222–84.

—— 'Ob istoricheskoi evolyutsii printsipov perevoda', in *Mezhdunarodnye svyazi russkoi literatury. Sbornik statei*. Edited by M. P. Alekseev. M.-L., 1963, 5–63.

—— *Ocherk stilistiki russkogo literaturnogo yazyka kontsa XVIII—nachala XIX v. Leksika*. M., 1964.

Levkovich, Ya. L., 'Perevody Pushkina iz Mitskevicha', in *Pushkin. Materialy i issledovaniya*, VII. L., 1974, 151–66.

Lewis, Matthew G., *Tales of Wonder*. Dublin, 1801.

Lomonosov, M. V., *Polnoe sobranie sochinenii*. M.-L., 1950–9.

Lotman, Yu. M., 'Neizvestnye stikhotvoreniya A. Meshchevskogo', *Uchenye zapiski TGU*, CIV (1961), 277–80.

—— 'Problema narodnosti i puti razvitiya literatury preddekabristskogo perioda', in *O russkom realizme XIX veka i voprosy narodnosti literatury*. M.-L., 1960, 8–51.

Lupanova, I. P., *Russkaya narodnaya skazka v tvorchestve pisatelei pervoi poloviny XIX veka*. Petrozavodsk, 1959.

Lyubitel' slovesnosti, SPb., 1806.

Makogonenko, G. P., *Ot Fonvizina do Pushkina. Iz istorii russkogo realizma*. M., 1969.

Maksimov, D. E., *Poeziya Lermontova*. M.-L., 1964.

Maslov, V. I., *Ossian v Rossii (Bibliografiya)*. L., 1928.

Mastera russkogo stikhotvornogo perevoda, Biblioteka poeta, Bol'shaya seriya, 2-oe izd. L., 1968.

Matlaw, R. E., 'The Dream in *Yevgeniy Onegin*, with a Note on *Gore ot uma*', *SEER* XXXVII, No. 89 (1959), 487–504.

Mendel'son, N. M., 'Narodnye motivy v poezii Lermontova', in *Venok M. Yu. Lermontovu. Yubileinyi sbornik*. M.-P., 1914, 163–95.

Merzlyakov, A. F., *Stikhotvoreniya. Biblioteka poeta, Bol'shaya seriya*. L., 1958.

Mikloshich, F., 'Izobrazitel'nye sredstva slavyanskogo eposa', *Drevnosti. Trudy Slavyanskoi kommissii MAO*, I. M., 1895.

Mikushevich, V. B., 'K voprosu o romanticheskom perevode', in *Aktual'nye problemy teorii khudozhestvennogo perevoda. Materialy vsesoyuznogo simpoziuma*, I. M., 1967, 69–79.

Miles, Josephine, *Eras and Modes in English Poetry*. Berkeley and Los Angeles, Calif., 1957.

—— *Renaissance, Eighteenth-Century, and Modern Language in English Poetry: A Tabular View*. Berkeley and Los Angeles, Calif., 1960.

Mnemozina. M., 1824–5.

Mnimaya poeziya. Materialy po istorii poeticheskoi parodii XVIII i XIX vv. Edited by Yu. Tynyanov. M.-L., 1931.

Mordovchenko, N. I., *Russkaya kritika pervoi chetverti XIX v.* M.-L,. 1959.

Morozov, A. A., 'Parodiya kak literaturnyi zhanr (K teorii parodii)', *Russkaya literatura*, No. 1 (1960), 48–77.

Moskovskii telegraf. M., 1825–34.

Moskovskii zhurnal. M., 1791–2.

Murav'ev, M. N., *Stikhotvoreniya, Biblioteka poeta, Bol'shaya seriya*, 2-oe izd. L., 1967.

Narodnye ballady. Biblioteka poeta, Bol'shaya seriya, 2-oe izd. Edited by D. M. Balashov. M.-L., 1963.

Nazarova, L. N., 'K istorii sozdaniya poemy Pushkina *Ruslan i Lyudmila*', in *Pushkin. Issledovaniya i materialy*, I. M.-L., 1956, 216–21.

Nebel, H. M., *N. M. Karamzin. A Russian Sentimentalist*. The Hague, 1967.

Neiman, B. V., 'Pushkin i Lermontov. Iz nablyudenii nad stilem', in *Pushkin. Sbornik statei*. Edited by A. Egolin. M., 1941, 315–48.

Nemirovskaya, K. A., '*Pesn' o veshchem Olege* i letopisnoe skazanie', *Uchenye zapiski LGPI im. Gertsena*, LXXXVI (1949), 13–56.

Neumann, F. W., *Geschichte der russischen Ballade*. Königsberg and Berlin, 1937.

Neustroev, A. N., *Istoricheskie rozyskaniya o russkikh povremennykh izdaniyakh*. SPb., 1874.

Nevskii zritel'. SPb., 1820–1.

Nowottny, W., *The Language Poets Use*. London, 1962.

Ober, K. H. and W. U., 'Žukovskij's Early Translations of the Ballads of Robert Southey', *SEEJ* IX (1965), 181–90.

—— 'Žukovskij's First Translation of Gray's *Elegy*', *SEEJ X* (1966), 167–72.

Ostaf'evskii arkhiv knyazei Vyazemskikh. SPb., 1899.

Ostolopov, N. F., *Slovar' dervnei i novoi poezii*. SPb., 1821.

Otchet imperatorskoi Publichnoi biblioteky za 1887 god. SPb., 1890.

Otechestvennye zapiski. SPb., 1839–84.

Pamyati V. A. Zhukovskogo. Kiev, 1883.

Passage, C. E., 'The Influence of Schiller in Russia, 1800–1840', *Am SEER* V, No. 12–13 (1946), 111–37.

Pautynskaya, V. A., 'Ob ispol'zovanii termina "epitet" ', *Uchenye zapiski 1-go MGPIIYa*, X (1956), 107–24.

Percy, Thomas, *Reliques of Ancient English Poetry*. London, 1765.

Pervov, P. D., 'Epitety v russkikh bylinakh', *Filologicheskie zapiski*, I–VI (1901); I (1902).

PETUSHKOV, V. P., 'Imena prilagatel'nye v poezii V. A. Zhukovskogo: Opyt stilisticheskogo analiza'. Unpublished thesis, LGPI im. Gerstena, L., 1951.

PIKSANOV, N. K., *Oblastnye kul'turnye gnezda*. M.-L., 1928.

Pis'ma P. A. Katenina k N. I. Bakhtinu. SPb., 1911.

PLETNEV, P. A., *O zhizni i sochineniyakh V. A. Zhukovskogo*. SPb., 1853.

Poeticheskaya frazeologiya Pushkina. Edited by V. D. Levin. M., 1969.

Poety nachala XIX veka, Biblioteka poeta, Malaya seriya, 3-e izd. L., 1961.

Poety-Radishchevtsy, Biblioteka poeta, Bol'shaya seriya. L., 1935.

Poety 1790–1810-kh godov, Biblioteka poeta, Bol'shaya seriya, 2-oe izd. L., 1971.

Poety XVIII veka, Biblioteka poeta, Malaya seriya, 3-e izd. L., 1958.

POLEVOI, N. A., *Ocherki russkoi literatury*. SPb., 1839.

Polyarnaya zvezda. SPb., 1823–5.

POSPELOV, G. N., *Teoriya literatury*. M., 1940.

POTEBNYA, A. A., *Iz zapisok po teorii slovesnosti*. Khar'kov, 1905.

Priyatnoe i poleznoe preprovozhdenie vremeni. M., 1794–8.

Problemy romantizma: Sbornik statei. Edited by U. R. Fokht. M., 1967.

PUKHOV, V., 'V. A. Zhukovsky—sostavitel' i izdatel' sbornikov stikhotvorenii russkikh poetov', *Russkaya literatura*, No. 3 (1959), 186–8.

PUSHKIN, A. S., *Polnoe sobranie sochinenii*. M.-L., 1937–59.

Pushkin, rodonachal'nik novoi russkoi literatury. Sbornik nauchno-issledovatel'skikh rabot. Edited by D. D. Blagoi and V. Ya. Kirpotin. M.-L., 1941.

PUTILOV, B. N., *Slavyanskaya istoricheskaya ballada*. M.-L., 1965.

REINER, E., 'La Place de l'adjectif épithète en français': théories traditionnelles et essai de solution', *Wiener romanistische Arbeiten*, VII. Vienna, 1968.

REIZOV, B. G., 'V. A. Zhukovsky, perevodchik Val'tera Skotta: *Ivanov vecher*', in *Russko-evropeiskie literaturnye svyazi: Sbornik statei k 70-letiyu so dnya rozhdeniya akademika M. P. Alekseeva*. Edited by P. N. Berkov *et al.* M.-L., 1966, 439–46.

REZANOV, V. I., *Iz razyskanii o sochineniyakh V. A. Zhukovskogo*, I. SPb., 1906.

ROBERTSON, J. G., *A History of German Literature*. London, 1962.

ROBERTSON, M. E. I., *L'Épithète dans les œuvres lyriques de Victor Hugo publiées avant l'exil*. Paris, 1927.

Rossiiskii muzeum. M., 1815.

ROTHE, Hans, *N. M. Karamzins europäische Reise: Der Beginn des russischen Romans. Philologische Untersuchungen*. Berlin and Zürich, 1968.

ROZANOV, I. N., *Lermontov—master stikha*. M., 1942.

Rusanova, N. B., 'Epitety Derzhavina', in *XVIII vek*, VIII, L., 1969, 92–102.

Russian Folk Literature. Edited by D. P. Costello and I. P. Foote. Oxford, 1967.

Russkaya ballada, Biblioteka poeta, Bol'shaya seriya. Edited by V. I. Chernyshev. L., 1936.

Russkaya literaturnaya parodiya. Edited by B. Bogak, N. Kravtsov, and A. Morozov. M.-L., 1930.

Russkaya poeziya. Edited by S. A. Vengerov. SPb., 1893–7.

Russkaya starina. SPb., 1870–1917.

Russkaya stikhotvornaya parodiya, Biblioteka poeta, Bol'shaya seriya. L., 1960.

Russkie pisateli o perevode XVIII–XX vv. Edited by Yu. D. Levin and A. V. Fedorov. L., 1960.

Russkii al'manakh. SPb., 1832–3.

Russkii arkhiv. M., 1863–1917.

Russkii romantizm: Sbornik statei. Edited by A. I. Beletsky. L., 1927.

Russkoe narodnoe poeticheskoe tvorchestvo. Edited by N. I. Kravtsov. M., 1971.

Ryleev, K. F., *Polnoe sobranie stikhotvorenii, Biblioteka poeta, Bol'shaya seriya*, 2-oe izd. L., 1971.

Samarin, M. P., 'Iz marginalii k *Evgeniyu Oneginu*', *Naukovi zapiski naukovo-doslidchoi katedri istorii ukrains'koi kul'turi*, No. 6 (1927), 307–14.

Sankt-Peterburgskii vestnik. SPb., 1778–81.

Schenk, H. G., *The Mind of the European Romantics*. London, 1966.

Schiller, Friedrich, *Sämtliche Gedichte*. Münich, 1965.

Schlegel, K. W. F., *Lectures on the History of Literature*. Translated by J. G. Lockhart. Edinburgh, 1818.

Scott, Sir Walter, *Minstrelsy of the Scottish Border*. Edited by T. Henderson. London, 1931.

Seidlitz, C. J. von. *Wassily Andrejewitsch Joukoffsky. Ein russisches Dichterleben*. Mittau, 1870. (See also Zeidlits.)

Semenko, I. M., *Poety pushkinskoi pory*. M., 1970.

Serchevsky, E. N., *A. S. Griboedov i ego sochineniya*. SPb., 1858.

Serman, I. Z. *Konstantin Batyushkov*. New York, 1974.

—— 'O poetike Lomonosova (Epitet i metafora)', in *Literaturnoe tvorchestvo M. B. Lomonosova. Issledovaniya i materialy*. M.-L., 1962, 101–32.

—— 'Poeziya K. N. Batyushkova', *Uchenye zapiski LGU*, III (1939), 229–83.

Severnye tsvety. SPb., 1825–32.

Shakhovskoi, A. A., *Komedii, stikhotvoreniya, Biblioteka poeta, Bol'shaya seriya*, 2-oe izd., L., 1961.

SHALYGIN, A. G., *Teoriya slovesnosti*. SPb., 1916.

SHCHERBATSKY, V. M., *Zanyatiya po stilistike v starshikh klassakh srednei shkoly*. M., 1951.

Shekspir i russkaya kul'tura. Edited by M. P. Alekseev. M.-L., 1965.

SHEVYREV, S. P., *O znachenii Zhukovskogo v russkoi zhizni i poezii*. M., 1853.

SHKLOVSKY, V. B., *Chulkov i Levshin*. L., 1933.

SIDNEY, Sir Philip, *The Complete Works of Sir Philip Sidney*. Edited by A. Feuillerat. Cambridge, 1912–26.

Slovo, VIII. M., 1918.

SMYRNIW, W., 'The Treatment of the Ballad by Shevchenko and his Contemporaries in Relation to Western Balladry', *Canadian Slavonic Papers*, XII, No. 2 (1970), 142–74.

SOKOLOV, A. N., *Ocherki po istorii russkoi poemy XVIII i pervoi poloviny XIX veka*. M., 1955.

SOMOV, O. M. *O romanticheskoi poezii: Opyt v 3 stat'yakh*. SPb., 1823.

SOUČKOVÁ, Milada, *The Czech Romantics*. The Hague, 1958.

SOUTHEY, Robert, *Poems of Robert Southey*. Edited by M. H. Fitzgerald. London, 1909.

SPERANSKY, M. N., *Russkaya ustnaya slovesnost'*. M., 1917.

STEPANOV, N. L., *Lirika Pushkina: Ocherki i etyudy*. M., 1959.

STRUVE, Peter, 'Walter Scott and Russia', *SEER* XI, No. 32 (1933), 397–410.

SUMAROKOV, A. P., *Izbrannye proizvedeniya, Biblioteka poeta, Bol'shaya seriya*, 2-oe izd. L., 1957.

—— *Stikhotvoreniya, Biblioteka poeta, Bol'shaya seriya*. L., 1935.

SUMTSOV, N. F., 'Issledovanie o poezii A. S. Pushkina', in *Khar'kovskii universitetskii sbornik v pamyat' A. S. Pushkina*. Khar'kov, 1900.

Syn otechestva. SPb., 1812–52.

Teleskop. M., 1831–6.

TIKHONRAVOV, N. S., *Sochineniya*. M., 1898.

TIMOFEEV, L. I., *Teoriya literatury*. M., 1948.

TOMASHEVSKY, B. V., *Pushkin*. M.-L., 1956; 1961.

—— *Stikh i yazyk. Filologicheskie ocherki*. M.-L., 1959.

—— *Teoriya literatury: Poetika*. M.-L., 1931.

TROTSKY, L. D., 'Ot dvoryanina k raznochintsu: V. A. Zhukovsky', *Sochineniya*, XX, M.-L., 1926, 3–9.

TRUBITSYN, N. N., *O narodnoi poezii v obshchestvennom i literaturnom obikhode pervoi treti XIX v*. SPb., 1912.

Trudy Obshchestva lyubitelei rossiiskoi slovesnosti. M., 1812–26.

TSYAVLOVSKY, M. A., *Stat'i o Pushkine* M., 1962.

TUDOROVSKAYA, E. A., 'Stanovlenie zhanra narodnoi ballady v tvorchestve A. S. Pushkina', in *Russkii fol'klor*, VII, M.-L., 1962, 67–83.

TURGENEV, A. I., *Khronika russkogo. Dnevniki (1825–1826 gg.)*. M.-L. 1964.

TVOROGOV, O. V., 'Leksika *Pesni o veshchem Olege* A. S. Pushkina', *Uchenye zapiski LGPI im. Gertsena*, CLXIX (1959), 229–53.

TYNYANOV, Yu., *Arkhaisty i novatory*. L., 1929.

—— *Problema stikhotvornogo yazyka*. L., 1924.

UHLAND, Ludwig, *Gesammelte Werke*. Leipzig, n.d.

ULLMAN, Stephen, *Language and Style*. Oxford, 1964.

—— *Semantics: An Introduction to the Science of Meaning*. Oxford, 1962.

URSINUS, A. F., *Balladen und Lieder altenglischer und altschottischer Dichtart*. Berlin, 1777.

VAN TIEGHAM, Paul, *Le Romantisme dans la littérature européenne*. Paris, 1948.

Velikorusskie narodnye pesni. Edited by A. I. Sobolevsky. SPb., 1895–1902.

VESELOVSKY, A. N., *Istoricheskaya poetika*. L., 1940.

—— *V. A. Zhukovsky. Poeziya chuvstva i serdechnogo voobrazheniya*. SPb., 1904; 2-oe izd. 1918.

Vestnik Evropy. M., 1802–30.

VIGEL', F. F., *Zapiski*. M., 1891–3.

VINOGRADOV, V. V., *Stil' Pushkina*. M., 1941.

—— *Yazyk Pushkina*. M.-L., 1935.

VOLKOV, R. M., 'Narodnye istoki tvorchestva A. S. Pushkina', *Uchenye zapiski Chernovitskogo gosudarstvennogo universiteta*, XLIV, No. 13 (1960), 3–46.

—— 'Russkaya ballada pervoi chetverti XIX stoletiya i ee nemetskie paralleli (Ballady P. A. Katenina)', *Uchenye zapiski Chernovitskogo universiteta*, XXXVII (1957), 3–48.

VOLM, M. H., *W. A. Zhukowski als Übersetzer*. Ann Arbor, Mich., 1945–50.

VOL'PE, TS. S., *V. A. Zhukovsky v portretakh i illyustratsiyakh*. L., 1935.

WEINTRAUB, WIKTOR, *The Poetry of Adam Mickiewicz*. The Hague, 1954.

WORDSWORTH and COLERIDGE, *Lyrical Ballads*. Edited by R. L. Brett and A. R. Jones. London, 1963.

YAKUBOVICH, D. P., 'Lermontov i Val'ter Skott', *Izvestiya AN SSSR, Otd. obshchestvennykh nauk*, No. 3 (1935), 243–72.

YASHCHENKO, A. L., '*Faust* Gete. Rannie otkliki v Rossii (V. A. Zhukovsky i A. S. Pushkin)', *Uchenye zapiski Gor'kovskogo universiteta*, LXV (1964), 189–204.

ZAGARIN, P., *V. A. Zhukovsky i ego proizvedeniya*. M., 1883.

ZAGOSKIN, M. N., *Polnoe sobranie sochinenii*. P., n.d.

ZAMOTIN, I. I., *Romantizm dvadtsatykh godov XIX stoletiya v russkoi literature*. SPb.-M., 1911–13.

ZEIDLITS, K. K. (*sic*), *Zhizn' i poeziya V. A. Zhukovskogo, 1783–1852*. SPb., 1883. (See also Seidlitz.)

ZELENETSKY, A., *Epitety literaturnoi russkoi rechi*. M., 1913.

ZHIRMUNSKY, V. M., 'K voprosu ob epitete', in *Pamyati P. N. Sakulina. Sbornik statei*. M., 1931.

—— *Valerii Bryusov i nasledie Pushkina: Opyt sravnitel'no-stilisticheskogo issledovaniya*. P., 1922.

ZHUKOVSKY, V. A., 'Neizdannyi konspekt po istorii russkoi literatury.' Edited by L. B. Modzalevsky in *TONRL* I, M.-L., 1948, 283–315.

—— *Polnoe sobranie sochinenii*. 12-oe izd. SPb., 1902.

—— *Sobranie sochinenii*. M.-L., 1959–60.

—— *Sochineniya*. 7-oe izd. SPb., 1878.

—— *Sochineniya*. M., 1954.

—— *Stikhotvoreniya*. 5-oe izd. SPb., 1849–57.

—— *Stikhotvoreniya, Biblioteka poeta, Bol'shaya seriya*. L., 1936.

—— *Stikhotvoreniya i poemy, Biblioteka poeta, Malaya seriya*. L., 1958.

—— (ed.), *Sobranie russkikh stikhotvorenii*. M., 1810–11.

(*V. A.*) *Zhukovsky. Ego zhizn' i sochineniya. Sbornik istoriko-literaturnykh statei*. Edited by V. I. Pokrovsky. M., 1912.

MANUSCRIPTS

Gosudarstvennaya biblioteka im. V. I. Lenina, Moscow. Fond 104.

Gosudarstvennaya Publichnaya biblioteka im. M. E. Saltykova-Shchedrina, Leningrad. Fond 286.

Institut russkoi literatury (Pushkinskii dom), AN SSSR Leningrad. Fond 244, 475, and others.

Tsentral'nyi gosudarstvennyi arkhiv literatury i iskusstva, Moscow. Fond 198.

INDEX